Imperial Germany bears a double legacy of militarism. It was, in the eyes of many, the archetypal militarist state. It was also the setting in which the modern idea of militarism developed. Drawing on material from the highly-charged intellectual and political debates of the time, Nicholas Stargardt traces this development from its inception in the 1860s until the outbreak of the first world war. In the process the very terms of discussion changed. 'Militarism' originally expressed an older enlightenment critique of the absolutist state, but by the 1900s wars had come to occupy centre-stage. Issues like the arms race and the military–industrial complex displaced more traditional concerns about authoritarian rule, and militarism gradually acquired its modern meaning. This book is part of a wider discovery by historians of the way political identities and ideas intermeshed, contributing to the rise of civil society and new types of politics in modern Europe. The political history of the main protagonist of anti-militarism, German Social Democracy, is cast in a new light, as Stargardt reveals the lasting influence of older radical traditions and reappraises the role played by its espousal of Marxism.

The German idea of militarism

The German idea of militarism
Radical and socialist critics, 1866–1914

Nicholas Stargardt

*Royal Holloway and Bedford New College,
University of London*

CAMBRIDGE
UNIVERSITY PRESS

Published by the Press Syndicate of the University of Cambridge
The Pitt Building, Trumpington Street, Cambridge, CB2 1RP
40 West 20th Street, New York, NY 10011-4211, USA
10 Stamford Road, Oakleigh, Melbourne 3166, Australia

© Cambridge University Press 1994

First published 1994

Printed in Great Britain at the University Press, Cambridge

A catalogue record for this book is available from the British Library

Library of Congress cataloguing in publication data

Stargardt, Nicholas.
The German idea of militarism: radical and socialist critics, 1866–1914 /
Nicholas Stargardt.
    p. cm.
Includes bibliographical references.
ISBN 0 521 42010 5
1. Militarism – Germany – History. 2. Socialism – Germany – History – 19th
century. 3. Germany – History – 1866–1871. 4. Germany – History –
1871–1918. 5. Germany – Politics and government – 1871–1918. 6.
Sozialdemokratische Partei Deutschlands – History. I. Title.
DD103.S73   1994
943–dc20   93-8243   CIP

ISBN 0 521 42010 5 hardback
ISBN 0 521 46692 x paperback

To my parents

Contents

Illustrations

Acknowledgements

When Heinrich Heine was stopped at the Prussian border in November 1843, he scoffed at the customs officers who searched his bags for contraband lace and banned books. 'My head', he rejoiced, 'is a twittering nest of books good enough to be confiscated.' In this book I have attempted to recapture part of the subversive tradition to which Heine so eagerly subscribed and bring it into the mainstream of writing about German history and the history of political thought. I have been helped by more people than I can possibly thank personally here.

This book grew out of a doctoral dissertation, and I am extremely grateful to Gareth Stedman Jones, who acted as my supervisor, shared freely his sense of how to link intellectual and political history and encouraged me to reopen closed questions. To John Dunn I owe a great debt, amongst other things, for persistently pressing with his uniquely enthusiastic scepticism those deceptively simple questions which are so very difficult to answer. With their great insight into wider European comparisons Emma Rothschild and Jay Winter advised me wisely and supported me generously. And I am grateful to my PhD examiners, David Blackbourn and Neil Harding, who made many helpful suggestions about how I might turn the thesis into a book.

Among the many other colleagues and friends who helped I would particularly like to thank: John Barber, Volker Berghahn, Larry Epstein, Richard Evans, Ernest Gellner, Adrian Gregory, Geoffrey Hawthorn, Steve Hayhurst, Istvan Hont, Michael John, Gerd Krumeich, Götz Langkau, Jonathan Lawrence, Lin Chun, Catherine Merridale, Wolfgang Mommsen, Saras Narsey, Geoff Pugh, Bob Rowthorn, Hans-Christoph Schröder, Michael Sonenscher, Erika Swales and Piet Wielsma.

The Provost and Fellows of King's College, Cambridge I would like to thank for supporting my research and making me feel such a welcome member of their community. My postgraduate research was supported by the British Academy, the German Historical Institute, London, and the German Academic Exchange Service. The librarians and archivists of Cambridge University Library, the British Library, the German Historical

Institute, the library of the London School of Economics, the Public Records Office at Kew, the Archiv der sozialen Demokratie in Bonn-Bad Godesberg, the International Institute of Social History, Amsterdam, the Institut für die Geschichte der Arbeiterbewegung in Berlin, the Brandenburgisches Landeshauptsarchiv in Potsdam and the Württembergische Landesbibliothek in Stuttgart have all let me use their collections.

Richard Fisher, my editor at the Press, and my copy-editor, Hilary Gaskin, charmed and cajoled me and despatched the manuscript with near-alarming efficiency. Finally, I can hardly thank my parents properly for their encouragement, suggestions, and tales of the Social Democratic culture which was destroyed in 1933; instead, I dedicate this work to them. Unfortunately, whatever vagaries of fact and interpretation which remain are mine.

Abbreviations

AdSD	Archiv der sozialen Demokratie, Bonn-Bad Godesberg
IISH	International Institute of Social History, Amsterdam
ILP	Independent Labour Party
NZ	*Die neue Zeit*, Berlin
PRO	Public Records Office, Kew
SFIO	Section Française de l'Internationale Ouvrier
SPD	Sozialdemokratische Partei Deutschlands
Sten. Ber. RT	*Stenographische Berichte des deutschen Reichtags*
ZPA	Zentral Parteiarchiv, Institut für die Geschichte der Arbeiterbewegung, Berlin

Introduction

Since the industrial revolution armies have often been compared to machines, the commanders and disciplined masses of men to their cogs and moving parts. The military mind tends to derive pleasure from this tidy and efficient simile, the critic of militarism a horror that rational and sentient beings could become so unquestioning, unthinking and submissive. This book explores the formation of this second point of view. A particular incident often draws together and expresses a multiplicity of ideas better than any theoretical tract. The incident which caught my attention occurred in the autumn of 1906. The German Empire was at its zenith. The Prussian army was widely heralded as the most efficient, best led and best trained in the world. At the time, the town of Köpenick – one of the oldest settlements around Berlin – had still to be swallowed up entirely by greater Berlin and, as we shall see, at least retained its administrative independence. On this particular autumn day, a Prussian infantry captain alighted from a train at Köpenick at the head of two squads of soldiers he had commandeered from the Berlin garrison.

After clattering across the square from the station, the captain posted a fusilier at each of the town hall's three entrances and made his way to the first floor office of the administration's secretary. There the military man informed the civilian that he was under arrest and should make himself ready for the trip to Berlin. A sentry was stationed on either side of him. With five grenadier guards still behind him, the captain entered the mayor's office. Himself a lieutenant in the reserve, the mayor leapt to his feet on seeing epaulettes and a royal Prussian blue uniform. As the captain later recounted, 'When he attempted to argue and persuade, I placed two grenadiers in front of him and handed him his hat.'[1]

The police inspector was discovered fast asleep in his office. When the captain shook him awake and reprimanded him for dereliction of duty, the man backed away in fright and was only prevented from escaping from the building by the sentries. A rather cowed inspector now begged for permission to leave so that he could bathe. Nothing more was seen of him. Meanwhile, crowds were gathering outside, a meeting of city councillors was being held in the chamber, and finally the mayor's wife arrived to be by her husband's side in his time of trouble. Gallantly offering them both coffee, the captain allowed the lady to accompany her husband to Berlin. By a lucky chance, the sergeant [*Oberwachmeister*] of the District of Teltow also turned up, immediately sprang to attention and placed himself at the disposal of the captain, who entrusted him with organising two railway carriages for the return trip to Berlin. The acting mayor also reported for orders, while the captain was making out a receipt for the town treasury's cash balance of 4000 marks; he carefully locked away bills for some 2,000,000 marks in the safe, pocketed the cash and dismissed the acting mayor.

The captain made his own way back to Berlin, where he settled himself in a café from which he could watch the sergeant punctually leading his escort and prisoners to the Neue Wache Barracks. The captain attracted no attention in the café; by now he had transformed himself into an anonymous civilian. The uniform made the man.

Köpenick did not end there. The hero of this episode turned out to be a 57-year-old shoemaker and ex-convict, Wilhelm Voigt. He confessed to his 'subversive' act and stood trial before a packed and spell-bound court. The exploits of the 'Captain of Köpenick' caused a furore. Having served a total of 27 years' hard labour,[2] Voigt had managed to commandeer two squads of soldiers, take over a town hall and arrest the municipal authorities, all on the strength of wearing a captain's uniform and the knowledge of military commands he had gleaned from his own one year's service as a soldier and from military books in the prison libraries. As an ex-convict Voigt had been expelled from one town after another by the police authorities. All he had wanted at the Köpenick Rathaus was a passport – which under a 'catch-22' regulation about residence requirements he had previously been refused – so that he could leave Germany; and in this he failed. Halfway through his occupation of the building he realised he had come to the wrong office.[3]

Predictably, French journalists saw the entire episode as one more palpable proof that German society had been drilled into complete and blind subservience to the military machine. In Britain, the *Times* remarked archly that such things were only possible in Germany. To contemporaries the entire incident somehow expressed the quintessence of Prussian militarism. Soldiers had unhesitatingly obeyed the commands of an officer, though he apparently came from another unit. The civic authorities had not questioned the right of an army officer to march in and usurp their jurisdiction, without written orders. The co-operation of senior figures in the municipal administration and the civil service had been assured by their own pride in belonging to the reserve officer corps. Less privileged civilians had simply done their national service and learned to obey the hard way. Such reactions were entirely predictable. Public opinion in France had been obsessed with German militarism since the defeat in the war of 1870. The Prussian annexation of Alsace and Lorraine and the crassness of declaring the new German Empire in the Hall of Mirrors at Versailles, not to mention the indemnity France had to pay, all contributed to a veritable sense of national inferiority in the Third Republic.[4] The German military was both reviled and anxiously imitated. In 1898, Admiral Tirpitz had initiated the naval race between Germany and Britain; the predictable result had been to drive the mutually hostile but also mutually anti-German governments of France and Britain together. By the time of Köpenick the *entente cordiale* which would take them into the first world war on the same side was already two years old. British caricaturists had already begun to study the strutting Prussian officer in place of their more familiar French and Russian butts. Theirs was the picture Köpenick assumed to the outside world. It is also the image reproduced by many subsequent historical accounts of German militarism.

What was not part of this somewhat predictable and external image of militaristic Germans was the laughter. In Germany itself – and especially Berlin – people laughed and laughed. And laughter turned out to be subversive too. The Social Democratic press treasured up every detail as part of their indictment of German militarism. For the rest of October, *Vorwärts*, the daily of the German Social Democratic Party, gleefully recounted Voigt's adventures and the commentaries of the foreign press on this misadventure of German militarism.[5] In any case, October 1906 was an inauspicious date for the Prussian army. It was the centenary of Napoleon's routing of the Prussian forces at Jena, a defeat which – as radicals fondly remembered – had led to the era of Prussian reform. Köpenick unleashed a cascade of laughter that drowned out decades of threats and bluster from the Kaiser and high-ranking military personnel.[6] An ageing Junker, Oldenburg-Januschau, might tell the Reichstag in 1910 that one Prussian lieutenant with ten men ought to clear their chamber, but the 'Captain' had already done it.[7] Colonel Reuther might do a real Köpenick in 1913 when he imposed a state of siege on the little Alsatian town of Saverne (in German Zabern), but he had to arrest a large number of people and lock them up in cellars – for laughing.[8] Köpenick was, in Franz Mehring's mocking words, a 'second Jena'.[9]

Nor was the German public allowed to forget its significance. In 1932, on the eve of the Nazi seizure of power, Carl Zuckmayer wrote a brilliant comedy around the incident; after the war it entered the permanent theatrical repertoire of both East and West Germany. As a German radical Zuckmayer remembered to include the public response in his play.[10] But

1 'Shoemaker Voigt from Tilsit, the victor of Köpenick', from
Simplicissimus, 1906

the same year that Zuckmayer's play was first performed Franz von Papen detailed a lieutenant and twelve men to oust the Social Democratic government of Prussia, who duly vacated their offices muttering threats about future judicial proceedings.[11] Scenes of historical farce, it seems, may presage grave historical tragedies.

Hitherto the history of militarism has focused on hard structures. Historians are generally agreed that the German Empire was an authoritarian state whose constitution was a 'sham'. Ministers, like the army, were responsible to the Kaiser, not the Reichstag, whose parliamentary powers were restricted to blocking, rather than introducing, legislation and whose members were excluded from holding office. Furthermore, its power over the purse had already been curtailed by Bismarck; army and naval budgets only came up for approval every seven and five years. The Bundesrat, the Federal Council of the states, might draft and introduce legislation but Prussia, with its own system of government based on the highly anti-egalitarian three-class franchise, carried half the votes within its deliberations. Even at the Kaiser's dining table the Imperial Chancellor as a mere civilian gave place to the military entourage, while the Minister for Finance felt he had really made it on his promotion from sergeant to lieutenant. After Bismarck military attachés constantly rivalled the Foreign Office abroad and at home a key military figure like Admiral Tirpitz was able to dominate Chancellor Bülow and prescribe essential policies from the Naval Office for fifteen years.[12]

But militarism is not only about institutions and power. It is also about culture and ideas. 'Militarism' was a relatively late addition to the modern political vocabulary. And it was added by those Colonel Reuther interned for laughing rather than by the colonel himself. Militarism had more to do with the mockery and indictment than the object which was being mocked and indicted. The concept originated in German civil society, not in the peculiarities of the German state. From the outset a derogatory epithet, militarism became a common slogan in the 1860s, invoked by a diverse array of critics of Bismarck's Prussia and Napoleon III's France.[13] Their object was indeed the 'garrison state' they saw being reconstructed around them. But in still absolutist Russia such criticism was simply not possible. The civic space did not yet exist. It is noteworthy that it was domestic civil protesters rather than foreign observers who first designated these Bonapartist and Bismarckian regimes the epitome of militarism. Opposition to the unification of Germany by force of Prussian arms was the one issue which bound together a motley collection of opposition groups in the late 1860s. There were radical republicans, South German particularists, Catholics and labour associations. Each meant something rather different by militarism but for a brief and significant moment of German history the neologism provided them with a common slogan of opposition. Protest against militarism thus offers some measure of the emergence of civil society out of reformed absolutism. This book concentrates on the changing motifs depicted as militarism between the 1860s and 1914.

How much does it matter what the origins of militarism are? After all, each generation has its own images to furnish the content of the term: for some, Jack London's iron heel crushing a human face; for others, the cynical waging of war to serve *Realpolitik* or imperialist gain; to yet others the failure to define the purposes for which wars were being fought at all. Few critics of militarism have abjured all violence. Anti-militarism and absolute pacifism – or pacificism as it was called before 1918 – are not the same thing at all.[14] Most anti-militarists have had some measure of legitimate violence against which they can calibrate the scale of militarism. But just what this scale is and how it should be constructed is hardly a matter of consensus. What indeed could be less consensual than the forcible imposition of the political will of one group of people upon another? If ever Carl Schmitt's claim that the primary dichotomy of political theory was the partisan distinction between friend and foe applied, then surely it ought to apply here.[15]

Modern political theory also offers less overtly partisan definitions of militarism, even if they still carry their particular brands of politics about on their backs. If these theories and the historical scholarship with which each is associated have built up a persuasive and coherent account of militarism, then perhaps the intellectual origins of the concept should interest no one except intellectual historians. To set our expectations about this question of origins in order we might do well to approach them crabwise by moving sideways from the present. Four general definitions of militarism are currently in widespread use, each embedded in a different tradition of political theory:

1   A process of reciprocal armament which creates its own destabilising and irrational dynamic, leading towards economic ruin and/or war
2   A state which subordinates civil authority to the military in one or more arm of government
3   State coercion on behalf of capitalist class interests against subordinate classes within the nation and/or against other nations
4   The failure to subordinate military to political goals in the waging of war

These four definitions correspond broadly to pacifist, liberal, Marxist and realist approaches respectively. Consonant with their own pre-existing concerns, each of these four theories also presents a different solution to militarism. Pacifists, Liberals and Marxists all predicted a world without war; realists did not. Pacifists saw the solution to war in disarmament and frequently demanded it on ethical grounds. Liberals and Marxists generally also accepted disarmament as an 'end goal' but set it up as the culminating moment in a longer process. For the Liberal tradition, militarism was essentially a hangover from absolutist times, which modern industry, trade and representative government ought to sweep aside. In the 1880s Herbert Spencer transformed this polarity between enlightened and pre-enlightenment forces into a sociological dichotomy between 'industrial' and 'military societies'. In it he equated the forces of peace and progress with industrialisation in a highly determinist and positivist fashion, whilst taking the 'primitive' savagery of Fiji islanders as characteristic of 'military society'.[16]

The determinism if not the details of this sociological approach converged with that worked out by Marxists after the deaths of Marx and Engels; except they postponed the triumph of peace and progress until after class conflicts within industrial capitalism had been transcended. This vantage point at least permitted them to explain – as Spencer and perhaps even Richard Cobden could not have done – how it was that 'civilised' industrial states could prepare for and wage the greatest wars of all. But their solution also turned out – at least in the experience of this century – to be chimerical. The 'socialist' or 'post-capitalist' regimes of the old Eastern Europe spent an enormous if still unquantified amount of their national income on armament.

The failure of all these programmes to transcend war ought to be so much grist to the mill of American realists. After all the realist tradition never claimed that war could be ended. But by reducing war to a matter of political expediency realists also leave out of the equation precisely the questions of subordination and violence which transform human beings into blind instruments and which ever since Kant spoke about the 'Kingdom of ends', of treating all human beings as ends in themselves, have been so central to the debate.

All four definitions date back to at least the nineteenth century and all were used in Imperial Germany. They also reappear in the interpretations of historians writing about Imperial Germany. This intermingling of subject matter, interpretative frameworks and modern political theory is potentially highly confusing. It places a premium on avoiding muddling overlaps. It is therefore worth considering these four positions in a little more detail.

The first definition takes the arms race as its referent; the theme of systemic irrationality has been stressed by contemporary peace researchers such as Dieter Senghaas.[17] Behind it stand arguments about the inherently destabilising domestic and international repercussions of reciprocal armament. Through overtaxing populations or diverting state expenditure from civil and cultural projects to the arms race governments create the basis for transforming even liberal democratic regimes into anti-liberal 'garrison states'. In its domestic themes this account merges with either liberal or Marxist versions at this point. But in its primary focus on international rivalries, the pacifist story foretells common economic ruin or a preventive war launched by one of the players who was on the point of being forced out of the game. One of the first statements of this position was Kant's insistence that external peace was a necessary precondition for the domestic liberty of a republic.[18] From the 1850s on, many of the same arguments in favour of international disarmament were promoted by the Peace Society.[19] Often disarmament was linked to other great causes, such as anti-slavery and especially free trade as in the writings of the organiser of the first Peace Congresses, Richard Cobden. Not surprisingly, since military spending was the principal item on any state's budget until the post-1945 period at least, disarmament was almost always linked to low taxes. By the 1890s and 1900s, Kant's slightly wry plea for 'perpetual peace' had been inscribed on the banners of social democratic sporting and recreational organisations as an ethical endeavour. The first congress of the Second International, which met in Paris to celebrate the centenary of the French revolution, denounced the arms race as a cause of war.[20]

Like the pacifists – and unlike Marxists and liberals – realists also concentrate on military action as a purely external activity, war. For the realist tradition, warfare is a normal, indeed the central, role of government. This assertion rests upon a geopolitical framework in which the main function of the state is to safeguard itself from threats from other states.[21] As Otto Hintze insisted, 'All state organisation was originally military organisation.'[22] War becomes pathological and illegitimate when it is waged without reason, without policy. Conversely, the measure of legitimate violence is set by Clausewitz's dictum about war being the pursuit of policy by other means.[23] A war without aims or whose aims are dictated by strategic rather than political concerns would count as militarism. This realist tradition is frequently denoted as 'reason of state', and its adherents have been predictably well entrenched under regimes which considered themselves to be the primary powers of their day: in the eighteenth century people spoke of '*raison d'état*', in the late nineteenth of '*Staatsräson*' and in the post-1945 US Department of State simply of 'realism'. In its German manifestation, *Staatsräson* was one of the unifying principles of the Prussian historical school, whose leading exponents have included Otto Hintze at the turn of the century, Friedrich Meinecke in the inter-war years, Gerhard Ritter in the post-war period, down to Michael

Stürmer and Andreas Hillgruber in the present.[24] For them realism is *Realpolitik* and its heroes would include Frederick II of Prussia and Bismarck. But like the revisionist German Foreign Office of the 1920s, they would generally concede that the later Imperial period and especially the conduct of the first world war provided evidence of militarism, or – in Ritter's words – an 'over-rating of the military aspect of things'.[25]

But it is noteworthy that this tradition did not acknowledge the actual term 'militarism' at all until after Germany's defeat in the first world war. Until 1914 the word belonged entirely to the radicals and oppositionalists. After the outbreak of the war, sections of the Wilhelmine establishment attempted to take over the concept and set it alongside patriotism and national defence as a true teutonic virtue. After the defeat of 1918, it was only the proto-Nazi extreme Right which persisted in claiming that the manly, military virtues represented the positive content of militar*ism*.[26] Conservative nationalists continued to eschew the term, even if like Meinecke and Ritter they still preferred to minimise its negative content. At a more historical level, their approach certainly does make sense of the construction of eighteenth-century absolutism, especially in Prussia, where the state was primarily geared to war and expansion. But it does not do justice to the complex administrative structures or the intervention in society and economy which characterised the nation state which Bismarck constructed and in which the term 'militarism' was actually coined.

In marked contrast, liberal political theorists have focused on domestic political arrangements from the outset. Their prime interest lay in safeguarding civil society from the state, rather than safeguarding the state from other states, and this led them to concentrate on the domestic role of the army. From their perspective, the casual admission that the military aspect of things might have been 'over-rated' hardly begins to touch the question of a society in which Köpenick could occur. This tradition of military criticism has its origins in classical republicanism and its early modern reappraisal. The key to the relation between the citizen and his state for this tradition was at least as much the right to bear arms as the right to vote. It was a duty of citizenship to be prepared to die for the polity which guaranteed individual freedom, just as an army composed of citizens was the only domestic guarantee of that collective freedom against despots and their standing armies. Both the French and American revolutionaries immortalised this principle.

This juxtaposition between absolutism coupled with hired mercenaries and the free citizens' militia of the republic is one of the few elements of humanist political theory to survive the twists and turns of three hundred years of debate as successive generations struggled to take account of representative government, commercial society and finally capitalism. It is one of the unbroken threads connecting Machiavelli through the English, Dutch, French and finally German enlightenment critics to radical and socialist writers of the late nineteenth century. It winds through the writings of Harrington, Spinoza, Montesquieu, Rousseau, Kant, Fichte, and even Hegel to such Wilhelmine critics as the Left Liberal historian Ludwig Quidde, the founders of German Social Democracy Wilhelm Liebknecht and August Bebel, and the so-called 'pope' of orthodox Marxism Karl Kautsky.[27] It is also a tradition whose ideal was tarnished by the reality of war fought by that modern proxy of the armed citizenry, national service armies. After the Great War, only the Communist Left continued to advocate the citizens' militia. Even on the eve of the first world War other anti-militarists had turned decisively away from the militia and towards international disarmament. For this long-enduring and fundamental democratic principle, 1914 marks the end of civic humanism and the enlightenment.

But a less radical version of liberal anti-militarism survived the state-building efforts of the late nineteenth century and the disillusionment of the first world war. In this version it mattered relatively little whether the army was a permanent professional or a part-time citizen force so long as it could be held responsible to a civilian government and respected the independence of civil society. This was the position of most Prussian 'Young' Liberals at the time of the constitutional conflict between Bismarck and the Prussian Chamber.[28] From this point the balance between military and civil authority becomes an issue of jurisdiction, legal norms and sanctions. This is the central issue behind Köpenick. It is also a subject which has continued to exercise its fascination over historians trying to unravel the roots of Nazism.

As the full horror of the holocaust was absorbed in the aftermath of the second world war, many from the side of the Western allies found themselves asking: 'If the German nation was collectively guilty of Nazism, what abnormal historical development could lead to such uniquely awful consequences?' In the immediate aftermath of the war, while the British occupying authorities were writing memoranda about how to water down 'evil teutonic blood' and 'educate the Germans for self-government', even liberal-minded British historians were drawn towards psychological and semi-racist explanations. The Germans simply had a warped national character. The sorts of militaristic and authoritarian motifs of Imperial Germany described so brilliantly by Heinrich Mann in *Der Untertan* or Elizabeth von Arnim in *The Caravaners* were joined to other threads. The Great Elector, Frederick the Great, Bismarck and Wilhelm II became the central figures in a tapestry depicting external conquest and domestic intolerance whose closing sequences revealed the

Götterdämerung of 1945.[29] The telos of the Prussian historical school was preserved but in demonic guise.

Following the post-war division of Germany this essentially Whig reading of German history was pursued under two very different auspices. In East Germany, where history writing and above all German history writing came under the jurisdiction of the Central Committee of the Socialist Unity Party, the tale of the pre-1945 militaristic German governments continued to be writ very large; and incidentally produced some good basic research.[30] But in place of the liberal dichotomy between the authoritarian state and the prematurely stifled civil society East German historians set out their version of a Marxist theory of militarism. In it repression and conquest served the ends of finance capital. Continued class rule at home, and abroad the quest for colonies and the inter-imperialist rivalries which allegedly resulted in the first world war, now held pride of place. The putatively liberal bourgeoisie was dismissed as a weak, vacillating and finally anachronistic force. Only Social Democracy – and eventually only the faction around Rosa Luxemburg and Karl Liebknecht, which went on to found the Communist Party in 1918 – was accredited with really opposing German militarism at home.[31] The 'base-superstructure' Marxism so central to this account and even its own history of the radical Left have been comprehensively discredited.[32]

Meanwhile in West Germany the Whig interpretation of the peculiarly disappointing German past and the nation's collective responsibility for Hitler was brought into the mainstream by a generation of historians who were deeply committed to the democratic values of the Federal Republic. Inspired by the work of Eckart Kehr and Fritz Fischer and armed with the functionalist sociological categories of American Weberians, Hans-Ulrich Wehler, Volker Berghahn and what might be called the 'Bielefeld school' of socio-political historians challenged the conservative consensus which had been preserved within the guild of German historians during the Adenauer years.[33] From the late 1960s on, Wehler and his colleagues established a telos for the illiberal Prussian past similar to that already laid down by Taylor, Barraclough and the East Germans. But whereas Taylor and Barraclough had generally agreed with the Prussian historical school that the accent ought to be placed on geopolitical externalities – read by the one side as aggression and the other as defence – Wehler insisted that the militarism of Imperial Germany stemmed entirely from domestic considerations. The *Kaiserreich* assumed the now familiar form of a semi-absolutist regime protecting the entrenched interests of the landowning Junkers, and challenged by the 'modernising' forces of urbanisation and the industrial revolution. Potential challengers, like the industrial bour-geoisie, had been bought off and 'feudalised' through the honours system, most ominously by admission to the reserve office corps of which the Köpenick *Bürgermeister* had been such a proud member.

With their truly Habermasian attention to the twin goals of 'overcoming the past' and developing a liberal 'public sphere' as issues of national importance, Wehler's ideas have also been very publicly criticised from extremely divergent points of view during the last decade. The so-called 'historians' debate' attracted prime coverage in newspapers like the *Süddeutsche Zeitung* and the *Frankfurter Allgemeine*, not to mention weeklies such as *Die Zeit*, on a scale unimaginable in Britain.[34] Three key elements of the Wehlerite interpretation did not – in my opinion – survive the interrogation. First, there was static rigidity imposed by functional explanations which bypass actors' understanding and intentions and proceed directly to the balance sheet of consequences: whether the end result 'stabilised' or 'destabilised' the system hardly offered a subtle or sophisticated measure of political behaviour.[35] Second, the assumption that illiberal routes to industrialised 'modernity' were 'peculiar' derived from the conviction that a 'normal' and repeatable route existed somewhere else. This assumption depended on a rather murkily idealist reading of French and British history and a disregard for the question of how most continental civil societies emerged out of reformed absolutism.[36] Third, there is the issue of the telos itself. Among liberal academic circles acceptance of the *Sonderweg* (Germany's special path) served as both an atonement for the 'mistaken' past and a guarantee of the present liberal democratic state at which German history had finally 'arrived'.[37] Three years after reunification, such an assurance would be comforting if not entirely convincing. But in any case all those who hope for a future must also hope that history has not yet ended. A teleology in which the past is pressed into a single line of continuity which has to lead up to the present and stop there carries its own built-in obsolescence. The least of Hegel's accomplishments was when he was tempted into dignifying the Prussian state as the ultimate goal of world history.[38]

The generations who could have accepted personal guilt for the Third Reich are passing. Their experiences and memories are also being overtaken and reshaped by new issues which follow from the reunification of the country, among them new racist and xenophobic movements which have consciously traded on echoes of the Nazi past. In the new Germany, it is not clear how the historiographic debate will turn. There is no new model on offer. But that is not a good reason for clinging to the old one. It is also not at all clear that the best way of understanding German militarism is by stacking up such large blocks in order to fashion over-arching interpretations of the past. During the last decade a more cautious and sceptical generation of historians has tended to deconstruct or even detonate the blocks themselves. Semiotics, post-structuralism, deconstructionism and post-modernism have all found their way into history writing.[39] The wider effect of these initiatives has been to interest other historians in how social identities were constructed and contested: nations and classes have both come under scrutiny and the commonsense generalities of a decade ago have begun at best to be carefully qualified, at worst to fragment irretrievably.[40] Scholars working on subjects as diverse as British and Russian history have been attempting to relate intellectual ideas and political strategies in order to explain the formation of their working classes.[41] Whilst I would not wish to conflate the study of ideas about militarism with the study of wider social *mentalités*, I do think some aspects of this new approach are very useful.

From the point of view of political theory it is striking that not one of the four meanings with which militarism has been endowed was as new as the word itself. Only Marxism is partially exempt from this generalisation, and even in this case Marx and Engels neither coined the term nor paid it much attention at first.[42] Two things emerge clearly. First, no strong and convincing theory of militarism is to be had. It does not have a tightly drawn referent, or an obvious solution. Not only is there no consensus over these questions, but none of the competing answers to them is particularly persuasive either. Second, militarism is a term of critical appraisal. It never was nor could be an objective category of analysis, except by lopping off all its wider meanings in order to make it synonymous with a single issue, like the arms race. But to do this would be historically inaccurate. It would also be redundant because all that would have been achieved would be to muddy the waters further by mixing militarism up with a term which already served its own purpose. Militarism continues to command such a central position by dint of its role in political rhetoric rather than political theory. Its theoretical claims have to be painstakingly assembled out of other concepts. But to invoke militarism itself is to draw a line. It is not surprising that it was resistance to militarism that justified British and American participation in two world wars, not to mention all the little wars since, down to the Falklands and the Gulf. 'Militarism' describes not just a pathological state of affairs; it is also the liberal's call to arms. Since we cannot get much sense out of militarism by subjecting it to theoretical interrogation, we have little choice but to go back to its origins and discover how it came to possess the various and mutually contradictory meanings it does.

Putting the history of the idea of militarism and the writing of German history side by side reveals a strange parallel. All the parties to the historians' debate were repeating arguments made at the time. Wehler's static structures of state power manipulating society from above read like the liberal pacifist Ludwig Quidde's tract on *Militarism in the Empire Today*, which a delighted Wehler duly rediscovered and published.[43] Equally self-consciously, his critics from the right, like Michael Stürmer and Andreas Hillgruber, descend from Otto Hintze. On the left, Geoffrey Eley was probably unaware of the parallels between his analyses and those Karl Kautsky penned at the time.[44] Such similarities are far too good to be true. What contemporary commentators wrote is not just so much additional information and interpretation for a data set. They stood in a totally different relation to the regime they described from either foreign observers or subsequent generations. The former were part of that society in a way in which the latter two types never could be. The very fact that such diverse and highly polemical accounts of the role of the German army were published inside Imperial Germany is testimony to how far civil society had emerged beyond the tutelage of army or state by the late nineteenth century. For the radical Right, Eley showed how much of the nationalist intolerance came from populist social movements of the *Mittelstand*, rather than simply from manipulation from above.[45] But the very autonomy of such a civil society itself depended on that whole complex of civil law, judicial independence and relatively disinterested administrative competence that went to make up the *Rechtsstaat* of which the National Liberals were so proud.[46] The frequent cases of *lèse-majesté* brought against the authors of anti-militarist articles illustrate just where the limits of that autonomy were drawn.[47]

The rise of civil society therefore provides a better starting point for the investigation of militarism than does the authoritarian state itself. Two things need to be uncovered in this pursuit: what was meant by militarism; and what purposes it served. Taken together the answers to these two questions should tell us how the meaning was contested, expanded and changed as well as why it was sustained at all. It might, after all, have been discarded and forgotten instead of entering the mainstream of political rhetoric. Because militarism is a rhetorical rather than a rigorous theoretical concept, it is intimately connected to the intentions, programmes, strategies and propaganda of political actors. The changed meanings of militarism should therefore also provide us with insight into just how, when and possibly why its protagonists altered their objectives. But at the same time the two questions – the what and the how of thinking about militarism – also need to be treated separately. In order to recover what people meant by it who were instrumental in keeping the subject in the public arena we have to suspend our disbelief and use the methods of intellectual history to reconstruct what they said and wrote. Investigating how and why they invoked militarism at all, let alone why they changed their minds about its meaning and significance over time, is at least as much a matter of political history, of revealing the dramatic irony beneath the script.

Since militarism was coined in Germany and France in the 1860s it is easy to see when such a study should begin. This book focuses on the German tradition, partly because of the difficulties of reconstructing even that story. But partly, too, because even in their domestic debates French anti-militarists regarded Germany as the archetypal militarist monarchy from the 1870s on; and the impact of two world wars has done so much to proselytise that perspective. My story ends in 1914, because the first world war changed all the alignments of German politics and also – to foreshadow one of my own conclusions – because I think all of the modern images of what militarism represented were already in place before the war itself broke out. The subject has many ironies and this is one of them.

One of the most difficult tasks in writing this book has been to keep a careful balance between the political and intellectual sides of the problem. It is difficult to show how they influenced and permeated one another without trampling over the rather different methods and criteria used by political and intellectual historians. In order to do justice to these different concerns I have tried to separate the different strands without violating their historical context. I have therefore set – and with one notable exception generally respected – the turn of the century as a simple if rather crude chronological dividing line between the two parts of the book.[48] Within each part I have taken a thematic approach, which has allowed me to unravel the way political and intellectual issues were entwined in each strand. In the first part, I explore how an anti-militarist tradition was formed in Imperial Germany, concentrating on the 1890s, a decade during which, as historians generally agree, mass politics emerged. It was also a period in which Social Democracy became the only major political force to carry the anti-militarist banner. The first two chapters focus on the construction of the Social Democratic anti-militarist programme out of three separate traditions of criticism. The positive referents of these three traditions were democracy, tax reform and national defence. The third chapter rounds off the section by exploring the attempts by the *doyen* of party orthodoxy, Karl Kautsky, to develop a political theory about militarism.

Part II discusses how the original programme buckled under new strategic challenges. Each of its three main components became separated and detached from the others, as the party tried to respond to new pressures and circumstances. The next three chapters trace the fate of each of these planks of the anti-militarist platform in turn. In chapter 4, it is democratic critique; in chapter 5, fiscal reform and the development of ideas about armament and economic development; in chapter 6, the conflict between national defence and the prevention of war. The 1900s were the heyday of what Kipling called the 'jingo'; in Germany they were described more aurally as '*Hurrahpatrioten*'. Their shrill cacophony as much as the real machinations of the great powers – not least Wilhelm II and his government – pushed and prodded the SPD into pacifist resistance. The original identification of militarism with despotic government became increasingly overlaid by references to the arms race and the likelihood of world war. Events did not prove them wrong. But, as is well known, when war was actually declared in August 1914, the SPD abandoned its opposition and voted in favour of a war, which it more than any other party in Germany had foretold and attempted to forestall. Paradoxical as it may seem in the face of such overwhelming political failure, the ideas about militarism which were generated during this period are still with us.

Part I

The anti-militarist tradition, 1866–1900

1 Democracy and cheap government

When the word 'militarism' entered general usage in the 1860s, it acquired a wide currency in two countries at the same time, France and Germany. In the late 1860s the France of Louis Napoleon and Bismarck's Prussia were regarded as the dominant continental powers; each had defeated Austria in the previous decade. They were both engaged in rearmament and it was obvious to some observers that Bismarck's alleged policy of uniting Germany under the Prussian eagle could only be taken the further step of including the Southern German states if France was militarily defeated. But only avid readers of international news like Marx and Engels equated militarism with the impending war on the continent.[1]

Most political actors concerned themselves mainly with the domestic ramifications of rearmament and the rapid state building under way. Both in France and Germany the 1848 revolutions had failed to achieve their democratic and republican ambitions. They had ended in a prolonged period of repression, censorship and – for many of the revolutionaries – exile. Only in the early 1860s were conditions relaxed and freer associational life tolerated. Domestic oppositions could now voice their alarm that central authority had grown so rapidly. To protest against this strengthening of the domestic power of the state in both France and Prussia critics invented a new epithet, militarism. This parallel development in the two countries gave the idea of militarism an international currency, and secured it a similar meaning when it first entered French and German political lexica in 1869 and 1870.[2] But both the international balance of power and domestic politics in the two countries changed dramatically after Prussia defeated France in the war of 1870–1.

1871 marked a turning point in French ideas about militarism. It lost the purely domestic connotations of a 'garrison state' straddling civil society that it had carried in the 1860s. Two national traumas left the Third Republic internally weak and divided: the military defeat with the attendant loss of Alsace and Lorraine, and the Paris Commune, whose suppression was followed by a terrible vengeance exacted upon the communards. The Left was torn in the 1880s between supporting General

Boulanger as a populist who would wreck the corrupt 'bourgeois republic' and opposing him as a new Bonaparte in waiting who would destroy republican government and start a new war with Germany. At the turn of the century, the Dreyfus affair raised equally difficult choices, between letting monarchists and clerics destabilise the republic and joining a radical coalition government which included General Gallifet, the butcher of the Commune. The thread of military inferiority to Germany ran through these crises. So too did the image of the new German Empire as a model of the sort of militarism the French Left was trying to prevent revisiting at home. Jaurès shocked the German delegates to the Amsterdam Congress of the International in 1904 by telling them that they lived in an imperial and feudal regime while the French lived in a republic and that the SPD would remain powerless even if it won a majority in the Reichstag.[3]

In Germany too anti-militarist politics changed fundamentally after 1871, in a sense revealing the mirror opposite of what happened in France. Between Prussia's victory over Austria in 1866 and its war with France in 1870 there was a feverish four-year period of anti-militarist activity. A wide range of political groupings refused to accept the expulsion of Austria from the German confederation, or Prussian tutelage over the new North German Federation. Saxons and South Germans, Liberals and Catholics, not to mention the labour associations, all sounded the tocsin about the Prussian danger. All flung the militarist epithet at the Prussian regime. The war with France and German unification closed this chapter. Gradually, in the course of the next two decades, most Liberal and Catholic politicians in Germany made their peace with the Empire and ceased to criticise militarism and even to use the term. Within Germany militarism might have dropped out of the political vocabulary altogether but for sections of the relatively small South German People's Party and the new, indeed the first, mass political party, German Social Democracy. This development in itself makes the tradition of anti-militarist critique within Imperial Germany interesting. How much, one wonders, did the rapid electoral rise of the SPD depend on its anti-militarist rhetoric? Moreover their account of German militarism is interesting in its own right, for these critics knew their society and polity well and ran all the personal and political risks of sustaining their attack from within.

What did the word 'militarism' signify when it was first coined? How did it gradually come to be a Social Democratic monopoly? In the process, how did the SPD alter the meanings it had inherited from the national and federal movements of the 1860s? The first question involves the relation between the neologism of the 1860s and older enlightenment and Liberal thought on the military question. To answer the second question, how Social Democracy came to monopolise the term, we must consider why other movements abandoned their outright opposition to the government and the way Social Democracy preserved its hostility to the 1871 settlement.

The idea of militarism

From its inception there has been no consensus about what militarism actually meant. Each of the political groups which had bandied about the militarist idea even in the 1860s and 1870s implied something different. What they had in common was a horror of the Prussian army. What that army actually represented remained debatable. At least four distinct political movements were involved in this debate: Prussian Liberals; South German and greater German Liberals; Catholics; labour associations and Social Democrats. Each in turn had different shadings. At the beginning of Bismarck's conflict with the Prussian Diet Prussian Liberals were dominated by the conservative 'Old' Liberal grandees, who were critical of only minor aspects of the Moltke-Roon army expansion. They both broadly supported the quest for an efficient standing army and accepted royal prerogative over it. They had been only too glad of its defence against the 'red spectre' in 1848.[4] Not till the Liberal Party in the Prussian Chamber entered direct confrontation over Bismarck's unconstitutional levying of taxes did it swing further to the left. Then the debate spilled out into the press and public meetings. As it became more public, so too the voices of radical liberals and democrats could be heard more clearly, demanding constitutional change: either an army in some fashion accountable to parliament, or the wholesale replacement of the old absolutist standing army with a citizens' militia. With the militia demand the term militarism entered the fringes of debate. What few Prussian Liberals opposed was Bismarck's 'little German' solution to the national question, the crafting of war into the new *Realpolitik*, or the exclusion of Austria from the German Federation.[5] This was not the case outside Prussia.

The real anti-Prussian and anti-militarist pressure mounted after the war of 1866, especially in the Southern states which still remained outside the new North German Federation and in states like Saxony which were included in the Federation but had sided with Austria in the conflict. This frenetic agitation against things Prussian came to an end in its turn when the critics were themselves engulfed in the nationalist euphoria which accompanied and followed the Franco-Prussian war of 1870. As one German historian has argued persuasively, it was during this four year period, even more than in the constitutional conflict within Prussia, that agitators and pamphleteers put the idea of 'militarism' into popular circulation. All of the groups involved worked it in with a number of older and newer terms in a loosely interchangeable way. 'Absolutism', the 'military state' and 'military domination', 'caesarism' and 'corporatism', all concepts in use since at least the enlightenment, ranged alongside newer categories like military economy, military system, and militarism itself. There does not seem to have been much effort to differentiate them.[6]

South Germans regarded Prussia from the outside and had least trouble linking the garrison state with the ordinary lives of its citizens via the conveyor belts of police-minded rules and regulations, military service and 'blind obedience' to superior officers. Not surprisingly, they were most concerned to forestall their own inclusion in this 'ruthless' system. Their alternative was to project the model of the existing *Südbund*, the federation of the South German states, on to the international plane either as the kernel of a European federal state or, more modestly, a resurrected German Federation.[7]

Radical democrats delivered a more nuanced critique. Eduard Löwenthal, for example, had claimed in 1870 that heavy new tax burdens led to mass poverty and hunger, so reducing labour productivity. Like the good Left Liberal he was, Löwenthal idealised industry in *laissez-faire* terms. For him armament and state intervention could only stimulate banking and stock-exchange swindles. In the eyes of a Liberal free trader such behaviour was as pathological to the economy as the standing army was to the state. His twin remedies were free trade and 'European political union'.[8]

The labour movement was almost as deeply divided as Liberalism as a whole. The Social Democratic Workers' Party which Wilhelm Liebknecht and August Bebel founded in Eisenach in 1869 came out of the workers' associations movement, in turn an offshoot of radicalism. It was only the threat of war between Austria and Prussia which had forced the associations to accept an explicitly political role for the first time. Once the war was lost – from their largely Saxon and entirely 'greater German' point of view – they had to choose between working with or against the new reality. Lassalle and his rival General German Workers' Association chose to accept the *fait accompli*, and indeed offered to join forces with Bismarck in return for universal suffrage and state co-operatives.[9] The 'Eisenachers' – as they would be called – followed the opposite course and stepped up their anti-Prussian campaign.[10] Like the radicals, they stressed the iniquities of indirect taxation, warned that a standing army spelled absolutism and called for the introduction of representative government, a people's militia and a progressive tax system.[11] As early as 1867, Wilhelm Liebknecht had indicted the army for 'depriving agriculture and industry of its best workers [and] loading down the people with an ever greater tax burden.'[12]

Friedrich Engels exemplified the confusion within the German labour movement. He opposed the expulsion of Austria from German affairs but by the time of the Franco-Prussian war was willing to accept the new Reich as a viable framework within which to build a national labour movement.[13] In 1865, however, he published an important tract on the *Prussian Military Question and the German Workers' Party* in which he argued in favour of carrying universal conscription through in Prussia at least as far as the government was preparing to. 'The more workers who are trained in the use of weapons,' Engels wrote, 'the better. Universal conscription is the necessary and natural corollary of universal suffrage; it puts the voters in the position of being able to enforce their decisions gun in hand against any attempt at a coup d'état.'[14] This was the first time that the working class was depicted in the military role allocated to the citizenry in democratic enlightenment thinking, and it was a formulation to which both Engels personally and the German Social Democratic party remained loyal well into the 1890s.[15]

The question remains about the novelty of 'militarism'. Was it simply a neologism to describe well-established points of criticism, or were its features different from previous attacks on the military? As I suggested earlier, most of the features linked to the idea of militarism at this stage were not new but were an accretion from older debates. The dichotomy between militias and standing armies as representative of a choice between democracy and despotism went back in an unbroken line to the Italian humanists. The critics of the 1860s could look back to the radicals of 1848, who had tried so unsuccessfully to put militias into the field. Intellectually, they could turn to the pre-1848 writings of Carl von Rotteck, and from him to the pre-Napoleonic writings of Kant and Fichte, and so on back to Machiavelli.[16] The line of continuity is evident in the slogans and metaphors as well as the central ideas. It was Rousseau who first drew attention to the Swiss militia as the model for a democratic state.[17] It was Kant who revived the Abbé St Pierre's slogan of 'perpetual peace' in 1795, though not it must be said with the same degree of enthusiastic optimism.[18] Two years earlier and enthused by the Jacobins' revolutionary war, Fichte anathematised the military as a 'state within the state'.[19] All three images stuck. Certainly until 1871 and possibly until later this line of democratic critique was the predominant one.

The second traditional line of criticism was the resources argument. Even if he was not the first to put it forward, Montesquieu made the case so eloquently that later writers were very fond of quoting him. He argued that the allocation of social resources, both tax revenues and people, needed to maintain the military forces of absolutist monarchs imposed crippling burdens on the population, thereby discrediting the old adage 'Si vis pacem, para bellum.'[20] Here too Kant followed his line of argument. So in 1847 did Richard Cobden, explicitly claiming Montesquieu's ideas as an inspiration for founding the Peace Society.[21] Not surprisingly, some German Liberals – most influential among them the advocate of protection for 'infant industries', Friedrich List – extended to industry the pacific role which mercantilists had already linked to trade. From this point of view, the division of labour and industrial technology led to a productive and co-operative domestic social order in which the marauding military activities and values of the old absolutist state had no place.[22] The attack on the tax burden was continued well beyond the 1860s, by radicals in France and Britain as well as Germany.[23]

What is striking here is that the emphasis upon the pacific tendencies of trade and industry has mercantilist origins. The very question could not have been put at the time of Machiavelli. There first had to be an intellectual framework in which to think about 'commercial society' and its needs. During the 1860s and 1870s there was relatively little innovation on this line of thought. Even Marx and Engels, so rigorous in their criticism of political economy in other areas, did not attempt to get beneath this formulation of the problem of trade, taxes and armament.[24] It would be left to the next generation of Marxists to restate the economic side of the problem in a fundamental sense.

The third and newest string to the anti-militarist bow was national defence. The numbers and *élan* of the *levée en masse* which the French managed to raise during the revolutionary wars impressed most continental observers, especially those defeated in them. Gneisenau and Scharnhorst both lauded the principles of a *Volk in Waffen* – a people in arms – and the principle of universal conscription, without the French practice of purchasing 'substitutes', was enshrined in the Prussian Army Law of 1814. Clausewitz, after serving with the Russian army, was fascinated by the powers of popular resistance and was the first to analyse the military role of the militia.[25] But as a political argument in favour of the full-scale militia system, the idea of maximising military capability only really entered radical discourse during the 1850s and 1860s. This realignment of militias with ideas of *Realpolitik* is evidenced by the transition from the enlightenment idealism of Rotteck's writings to the more restrained 'realism' of a Rüstow in the 1850s and 1860s.[26] This was not the end of radical democratic ideas about militias and the state. But it did mark the acceptance by the liberal nationalist movement in Germany that 'perpetual peace' was a long way off and that even the republican nation state would have to provide efficient and effective defence. Freedom could now be equated with a readiness for war, the popular *élan* of the armed people contrasted with the professionalism of standing armies. If the new generation of pamphleteers was too ill read in the military classics to be aware of Clausewitz's endorsement, they still felt more at home with Prussian Reformers like Scharnhorst and Gneisenau than with Montesquieu and Rousseau. Both the point of intellectual vantage and the choice of historic heroes were transmitted by German radicals to the labour movement.[27]

These were the most important motifs of anti-militarism but they were not the only ones. The step of accepting responsibility for national defence held further possibilities. In 1864, H. B. Oppenheim suggested for the first time that there might be a positive link between military efficiency and industrial society. Ostensibly attacking Bismarck for trying to use war as means of manufacturing domestic consent, Oppenheim went on to assert that 'industrialism' provides the best soldiers.[28] By the turn of the century, Social Democrats would condemn the Prussian parade ground in one breath and in the next assert that the industrial proletariat – especially the skilled Social Democratic workers – made the best soldiers. Oppenheim had effectively if unwittingly established the ground-rules for much of the future debate. By the turn of the century both critics of militarism and military strategists and planners accepted Oppenheim's criteria. Ideas of military efficiency were reconstructed according to the norms of industrial efficiency from this point on. Extreme nationalists had as much right as Social Democrats and Left Liberals to criticise the Junker in uniform as the monocled relic of a previous age. To the Left he was a threat to Germany's democratic future. To the radical Right, he stood in the way of the full realisation of Germany's military potential. In the 1860s, these developments still lay in the future. Oppenheim had not yet decisively won the battle for Liberal opinion.

'Militarism' already meant a range of rather different things, depending on the radicalism of its critics, but in all cases it was a pathological term, referring to that set – or more and more frequently sub-set – of military practices which was deemed beyond remedy. Probably all that the coining of the new word itself tells us is a little about the need for a simple common slogan in political controversy. The anti-Prussian opposition of 1866–70 wanted to draw a sharp ideological line across the political sands, a line which lent their rather motley and 'particularist' alternatives to the Prusso-German solution greater coherence than they really possessed.

These 'modern' contributions to the military question during the 1860s had done little more than hedge the older enlightenment tradition with new constraints. That radical anti-militarists felt the pressure to endorse military needs gives a clear indication of the broader drift towards accepting Bismarckian 'blood and iron' politics in Liberalism as a whole. Between the declaration of the Second Empire in 1871 and its collapse in the November revolution of 1918, the political scope for talking about militarism in Germany was to narrow further. First the National Liberals in the 1870s, then the Catholic Centre in the 1890s and finally the Left Liberals in the early 1900's all abandoned so inflammatory a term, even when they had already restricted its application to an ever smaller range of pathological phenomena. Only Social Democracy continued to invoke the term to demonstrate its opposition to the very constitution of the state.

The parting of ways

German unification affected all political movements. National Liberals immediately embarked joyously on a partnership of state-building with Bismarck. Their support in turn helped Bismarck to persuade the new Reich electorate that German unification was a truly national concern. He barred only a minority of culturally or politically undesirable 'enemies of the Reich' – Guelphs, Poles, Jews, Catholics and Socialists – from membership of this ideal community.[29] As the political movements of the Catholic Centre and Social Democratic parties grew in strength, so they too clamoured for recognition as part of the nation. Catholics and socialists may have imagined their nation in quite different terms to Bismarck, but they came to accept his geography and the desirability of defending it. In the elaborate marriage of Prussian dynastic institutions and German Liberal traditions, the military occupied a uniquely important symbolic place. The ideological objective was not just to show that Hohenzollern steel had succeeded where Liberal colloquies had failed. That was indisputable. The point was rather to destroy the very basis of a Liberal opposition by convincing Germans that the Empire had implemented the domestic political details of the Liberal programme. Universal suffrage, associational and political life, a relatively free press, all guaranteed by a state governed by that centrepiece of Liberalism, a civil code; these were a great deal.[30] But the metaphor remained a mixed one. German history was taught as Hohenzollern history. Popular subscriptions were raised all over Germany in the ensuing decades to erect towers to Bismarck. Sedan Day on 2 September became an even more important national celebration than the Kaiser's birthday. Imperial Germany shared with Britain in the 1880s and 1890s the ideological distinction of transforming a traditional monarchy into a popular one. High points of this working on the public mind were the opening of the Kiel canal in 1893, the big navy, and the consecration of the *Völkerschlachtdenkmal* in Leipzig in 1913 to mark the centenary of Prussia's victory over Napoleon in the 'Battle of the Nations'.[31] This Wilhelmine commemoration could hardly have been in greater contrast to the festivities of 50 years before when radicals had led the way, calling on Leipzig's fund of type-setters and printers.[32]

The army played a central role here as the much vaunted 'school of Germandom'. When Berlin was being rebuilt as a major commercial and political capital, the huge Siegesallee dwarfed in scale if not elegance the Frederician Unter den Linden. To complete the reconciliation and obfuscation of rival political traditions, imperial publicists and educators applied the language of the radical *Volkswehr* to that nub of the constitutional crisis of the 1860s, the Prussian army. Heinrich von Treitschke went so far as to embrace the term 'militarism' as an accolade to the Prusso-German Reich.[33] But this did not catch on until after 1914. Instead, in shaping an official ideology, the Right seized the ideological clothes of the revolutionaries of 1848. The Prussian army – with its increasingly universal conscription, relatively short service system and local regiments – became 'the people in arms'.[34]

The army was still a subject of criticism, but the familiar questions of the 1860s – the lack of constitutional safe-guards, the fact that the army and government of the Imperial Chancellor remained answerable only to the German Emperor just as in the older Prussian tradition – were tempered by the experience of 1871 and, in any case, had now to be tackled along with newer social questions. One might criticise the conditions in which conscripts served their three – and later two – years, or ridicule the exclusively aristocratic atmosphere of the officers' corps and yet implicitly accept that Germany was now a nation state. Opposition parties might share a common hostility to regressive indirect taxation and deplore the fact that army and navy swallowed up the lion's share of the budget, but nonetheless differ fundamentally among themselves over whether the army was a legitimate national institution. These issues were to provide the stamping ground on which Wilhelmine parties would decide for or against retaining the word 'militarism' in their rhetorical armouries. Recourse to the militarist epithet continued to signify deep and principled hostility. The images it raised were altogether too searing for it to serve as an instrument with which to administer mild reproof.

It is true that by the end of the century only a scattering of Left Liberals and the phalanx of the Social Democratic Party consistently rejected the Bismarckian solution. But the attenuation of Catholic opposition did not follow an even path. In the 1870s Catholics were identified as the number one 'enemy of the empire'; the so-called *Kulturkampf* was an attempt to carry through Liberalism's secularising and anti-clerical programme. For this Bismarck and the National Liberals could count on the support of Left Liberals and the sympathy, if not the votes, of Social Democrats. As in contemporary Italy this conflict between Catholicism and the state had polarising effects. Not surprisingly, the heyday of Catholic opposition was in the 1870s rather than the 1860s.

Catholic writers readily equated such state intervention with Prussian militarism. The Jesuit Georg Michael Pachtler revised radical images by aligning the Prussian state and industry even more sharply than Oppenheim had – and casting both in an entirely negative light. His anti-militarist ideal was a rural patrimonial society which, he claimed, expenditure on arms was destroying. Young men were being lost to the labour force, so undermining the family as an economic unit.[35] But at the level of political policy, Pachtler's stance was an extreme one even within the Centre Party. He would settle for nothing short of the restoration of traditional society as he saw it and a curtailment of the new agency of the state. Philipp Wasserburg, the political leader of the Centre Party in Hesse, on the other hand, demanded only full parliamentary controls over the budget.[36] By 1874 this had become established Centre policy.

For too long historians concerned themselves with the failure of a Liberal-Social Democratic coalition to form in late nineteenth-century Germany.[37] But in fact Liberals had already distanced themselves from the labour movement in the 1860s.[38] The 1874 debate on budgetary powers saw the position of the National Liberals crystallise. While Bismarck demanded an *Aeternat*, or the right to levy taxes for military budgets in perpetuum without Reichstag approval, and Left Liberals and the Centre called for annual budgets, it was the National Liberals who forced a compromise solution: seven yearly budgets, the *Septennat*. From now on, the National Liberals were to be the government party *par excellence*. The self-images of the establishment rested on the realities of the Conservative–National Liberal coalition in the Reichstag, the famous Bismarckian cartel of 'rye and iron'.[39] Having made their choice National Liberals would lose their left wing in the 1880s. Unable to tie their new enthusiasm for overseas empire to a strongly rooted sense of social identity and a mass constituency, the National Liberals would end the century as patricians trapped on a populist stage. They preferred to retreat from the perils of mass politics by restricting the franchise in Hanse cities like Bremen and Lübeck, or in Saxony.[40]

National Liberals proved the most ardent supporters of the naval programme of the 1900s. They believed that colonial markets would benefit German industry and that imperialism provided a viable ideological alternative to socialism; through social imperialism the working class could be won over to the 'nationalist standpoint'.[41] There was nothing peculiarly German about these ideas. Joseph Chamberlain was actively canvassing them in Britain. But the turn from free trade to protection and empire did drive a further wedge between Liberals and Social Democrats.

Only the extreme revisionist Right of the SPD would endorse the new Liberal imperialism in the 1900s; most of the party remained loyal to the old free-trading Liberalism of a bygone era.[42] But in any case, by the turn of the century the National Liberals had been a party of government and Social Democracy a party of pure opposition for almost 30 years.

It is more pertinent to ask why the Wilhelmine opposition of the 1880s – the Catholic Centre Party, the Left Liberal Progressives and the Social Democrats – did not forge a Gladstonian coalition.[43] Why this opposition was not more united has also been debated. The two most successful mass parties in the 1880s and 1890s, the Catholic Centre and the Social Democrats, were both maligned as 'enemies of the empire'. But common persecution did not overcome mutual suspicion and hostility. It is in fact their failure to form some kind of alliance rather than the failure of a 'grand coalition' between Liberals and Social Democrats which condemned anti-militarism to political impotence. Yet even in the late 1880s and early 1890s, the Centre still preached anti-militarism and voted down the military budget; and this in the teeth of pressure not just from the government but also the Vatican to vote in favour. But the prospects of a more durable anti-militarist bloc proved ephemeral.

In the 1890s the vicissitudes of mass politics ensured that these parties would go different ways. With the unbanning of Social Democracy and Bismarck's resignation in 1890, the two parties began to compete on the same terms. Both built up large party organisations: by 1914, there were 865,000 members of the Centre compared with one million Social Democrats; when Max Weber came to develop his theory of the professionalisation of politics, he looked to the Social Democrat Friedrich Ebert and the Catholic Matthias Erzberger as his examples of party functionaries who rose to positions of national leadership.[44] But the immediate consequences of this freeing up of political competition was that the two movements found themselves in competition for the same electorate. Until 1890 most Catholic workers had voted along confessional lines. By the 1903 elections, the SPD was making headway not just in culturally exceptional areas like Munich and Alsace-Lorraine, or in places where the confessions were mixed like Dortmund, but in areas that were industrial and Catholic, like Düsseldorf, Cologne, Essen and Krefeld. Only regions like the Saarland which were entirely Catholic and heavy industrial would remain strongholds of the Centre.[45] Even in Württemberg, the Social Democratic Free Trade Unions had far outstripped their Catholic counterparts by 1909.[46]

Faced with such a breakdown of confessional loyalties, the Centre Party had to find a new *raison d'être* through which it could differentiate itself from its rival. Social Democracy preached the liberal virtues of free trade, consumer co-operatives and atheistic secularism to urban workers and artisans. An alternative vehicle of mass politics was being established at the same time by those unlikely populists, agrarian conservatives. In order to find a mass following for their policies of agricultural protection, in 1893 they launched the Farmers' League. It drew on anti-semitic, anti-free trade and anti-socialist rhetoric to legitimate and link large landed and peasant interests as representatives of the German *Volk*.[47] The Centre Party both imitated and innovated. It strove to enlist not only peasant support but also a diverse urban constituency, consisting of artisans, small businessmen and white-collar workers, by pillorying Jewish department stores and Social Democratic co-operatives. This new and extremely heterogenous constituency was given the symbolic social identity of the *Mittelstand*, projecting an imaginary unity back from politics which hardly existed in its adherents' daily lives. In 1896, Conservatives and the Centre joined forces to obtain legal restrictions on consumer co-operatives and thenceforward worked together on '*Mittelstand* defence'.[48]

The next step involved building bridges between the old adversaries of the *Kulturkampf*, the National Liberals and the Centre. Co-operation between the two parties on the all party Reichstag committee which drafted the civil code was a vital turning point. For the Liberals the civil code formed the coping stone of the German *Rechtsstaat*, their traditional goal of a state governed by the rule of law. For the Centre it marked the end of the *Kulturkampf*. Their civil rights were assured and their acceptance as political partners opened up tantalising prospects. By 1898, the Centre was more than ready to join the 'rallying of conservative forces', or *Sammlung*, which the government was preparing to launch the naval laws and to rebuild the anti-Social Democratic coalition.[49] By this juncture it was too late to expect an anti-militarist alliance between the Centre and SPD. Soon the Centre was regarded as more conservative than the National Liberals themselves.

There was another factor apart from mass politics which played a major part in this realignment of the parties at the beginning of the 1890s – generational change. The old Centre and Left Liberal leaders, like Windhorst and Richter, either died or stepped down at about the time that Bismarck resigned and the young Kaiser embarked on his 'new course'. The new men of the Centre, like the lawyer Ernst Lieber, were both less aristocratic and more anxious to be accepted within the Empire. The battles of the 1860s and 1870s were not theirs to go on refighting. They were only too willing to be co-opted into an anti-socialist coalition, in much the same way as Catholics in the so-called 'educated and propertied bourgeoisie' hoped for admission to the reserve officer corps. Social Democrats, by contrast, continued to be barred from many of the professions, including universities.[50] The party leadership too remained in the hands of veterans of the 1860s and 1870s. Only with the deaths of Paul Singer in 1910 and August Bebel in 1913 did the generational change work its way through to the top of the SPD; and when this did happen it may have been all the more disturbing for having been so delayed.

A final causal factor was the threat of repression. The last occasion when the Centre and SPD joined forces to vote down a military budget was in 1892. Both then and when the conservative *Sammlung* was formed in 1898, the government used the threat of a military coup to help to isolate the SPD and pull the Centre into line.[51] But in abandoning anti-militarism in favour of protective tariffs and great power politics, the Centre was probably swayed most by its new *Mittelstandspolitik*. Whether the pressure in Berlin was the allure of office or the fear of coercion, it was here that policy changed first. The national leadership led the way enthusiastically, even if local notables were sometimes more reluctant to drop their traditional hostility to 'militarism', especially in the South where older anti-Prussian particularisms lingered long.[52]

After the Centre defected, only the Social Democrats and sections of Left Liberalism continued to raise the slogan of militarism on a regular basis. The Left Liberals found themselves increasingly divided on the issue, especially on North–South lines. It was the South German People's Party which was the most principled and consistent. In the more democratic Southern states it would be possible, in the 1900s, to rebuild anti-clerical coalitions between National Liberals, Left Liberals and Social Democrats, that 'grand bloc' which proved so chimerical at the national level.[53] For decades a Bavarian aristocrat led the SPD in his state, something unthinkable for a Prussian Junker. But within the Reichstag the Left Liberal South German People's Party was an insignificant grouping. It might sponsor the historian and pacifist Ludwig Quidde to write the most trenchant non-socialist critique of Wilhelmine militarism (see chapter 3 below). Even in its Southern stronghold of Württemberg, however, the party was accused of having become the tail of the SPD. The lines of division within Liberalism as a whole were refracted in Left Liberal politics. By the turn of the century, North German, especially Prussian, Left Liberals increasingly supported colonial and naval policies. And those sections which were more sympathetic to free trade were also more hostile to Social Democracy. Not until 1910 would there be serious attempts to build bridges at the national level.

The effective isolation of Social Democracy was complete. Between it and the other major parties of Imperial Germany lay an ideological gulf. It was also a matter of manners, social status and social boycotts. The SPD might be legal, but its parliamentary tactics of uncompromising opposition, with frequent recourse to the filibuster, outraged Centre and National Liberal deputies alike.

The Social Democratic programme

To have survived twelve years of prohibition and persecution, in which thousands of party workers and leaders had been sent into internal or foreign exile, been imprisoned, lost their livelihood, seen their family lives destroyed, and yet to have gone on to organise a highly dedicated clandestine party was a major achievement.[54] As soon as the anti-socialist laws lapsed in September 1890 Social Democracy had to organise itself afresh. A legal, open party seeking a mass membership was an altogether different undertaking from securing mass support at elections.[55] Party leaders continued to rely on elections as an index of the movement's popularity, but they also had to overhaul the party organisation. Soon they would also have to face the constraints of the new politics being worked out by their rivals on social policy and the military question.

It is a striking illustration of Social Democratic faith in rationality that the party began its reorganisation by renaming itself and adopting a new programme. This was neither accidental nor opportunistic. For ten years a group of young journalists, led by the exiled editor of the underground daily, Eduard Bernstein, and Karl Kautsky, the editor of a new theoretical journal called *Die Neue Zeit*, had disseminated what they understood to be Marxism.[56] In their endeavours they were helped by the ageing Friedrich Engels, who gave them much advice and penned a number of highly successful popularisations of his and Marx's ideas. More importantly, perhaps, the rising leader of Social Democracy, August Bebel, joined forces with them. A self-employed wood turner by trade, he entered labour politics in the 1860s through the liberal workers' educational movement. Self-taught, intelligent and highly effective, he had helped to found the Social Democratic Workers' Party in 1869 with that veteran of the 1848 revolutions, Wilhelm Liebknecht. With his careful yet unbending sense of the socialist mission Bebel rose to become the party's supreme strategist and charismatic leader from the end of the 1880s until his death in 1913.[57] At the head of the largest socialist movement in the world, Bebel inevitably became the most famous and respected figure in the Second International.[58] It was this group which drafted the new programme which was adopted at the party's Erfurt congress in 1891.

As the founding moment of what came to be known as orthodox Marxism, the Erfurt programme has been a much discussed document. It became the model for so many other Social Democratic parties in the 1890s and 1900s; its chief theoretical architect, Karl Kautsky, was lauded as the 'pope' of Marxism. The first part of the programme set out the historical 'laws' which justified socialist politics: capitalist development, crisis, the growth of the proletariat, its immiseration and the possibility of organising production rationally under social ownership. The second part of the programme established a series of basic demands which amounted to a liberal democracy with a number of labour laws. Historians have long debated the misfit between these two parts. A number have tried to read the distinction between the SPD's revolutionary theory and reformist practice during the 1900s back into the programme itself. From this point of view the revolutionary aspirations of the party are espoused in the first theoretical part, while its mundane reformist practice comes to light in the second.[59]

What this interpretation overlooks is that in the context of Imperial Germany radical and democratic ideas were considered seditious and revolutionary. Indeed, the government felt more threatened by such a direct challenge to monarchy and the existing state than by any predictions about the course of capitalist development. During the 1880s when the Prussian secret police did its utmost to prevent the distribution of Bernstein's paper, *Der Sozialdemokrat*, with its radical democratic politics, the Prussian censor found nothing culpable in the 'scientific' subject-matter of *Die neue Zeit*. Likewise in the 1890s and 1900s, it was attacks on the army and the Kaiser rather than abstract justifications of the socialist revolution which would land Social Democratic leaders in gaol for *lèse-majesté* or even high treason.[60] As one historian has suggested, Social Democracy was most revolutionary as long as it clung to its radical liberal politics, which its Marxism in fact helped to displace.[61] Within this radical politics the SPD's espousal of the people's militia occupied an important place, second only in the party programme to demands for full parliamentary and local democracy.[62]

As one might expect from a party which originated in the anti-Prussian movement of the late 1860s, Social Democracy preserved the other main theses of that radical anti-militarism. Alongside the democratic militia came the attack on the fiscal–military state. In place of indirect taxation to pay for arms, the programme stipulated the introduction of graduated direct taxes on income, property and land. Taken together these two paragraphs carried most of the weight of Social Democratic anti-militarism. The ideas are much the same as in the Gotha programme of 1875, as well as repeating the gist of Wilhelm Liebknecht's resolution to the German Workers' Association at its Nuremberg Congress on 7 September 1868.[63] But the context had changed. The particular mix of ideas and policies was new; so by necessity was the way Social Democracy set about establishing its political identity. Finally, militias were supposed to be strategically more effective than standing armies in matters of defence. The point of this claim was to drive a wedge between the military policy of the government and the ideological high ground of national defence. In so doing, Social Democracy inevitably committed itself increasingly explicitly to defending the nation from external attack.

Already in the 1890s, there was a tension between the abstract and essentially idealist formulations of the Social Democratic programme and the needs of mass propaganda. Social Democratic leaders, Bebel in particular, tried to compensate for this by filling in the practical detail of socialist policies. Whether it was insurance provision or the military budget, he spent a great deal of time drafting model alternatives to government legislation. He took great pains to explain how militias would be costed and organised, with the result that between the mid-1890s and 1911 a socialist utopian literature on the army began to circulate in both the French and German parties. In order to overcome the division between soldier and civilian various civil substitutes to the parade ground were proposed, such as gymnastic preparation at school, shortening the period of basic training to six months and lengthening service in the reserves. The prominent position accorded to gymnasts in Social Democratic rallies and May Day celebrations had a role to play here too.[64]

The reward of all this labour was propagandistic rather than real. It put the party in a position to be able to refute accusations of utopianism or impracticality. At the same time the ideal of the 'socialist state of the future' could be held up as a justification for self-sacrifice and activism. As Bebel well understood, even to win reforms in Imperial Germany it might be necessary to threaten revolution. Party theorists described existing military practices and power within the state as a 'militarist system'. With it they contrasted an ideal system, putatively practicable, consistent and comprehensive. Without such a utopian alternative in mind it is doubtful whether the party could have explained how militarism formed such a totality or why German society should break with it so completely.

The three main elements of this critique were held together by the form in which they were presented. They were repeated endlessly in Reichstag speeches, and were then reprinted in the Social Democratic press, or even released as separate brochures. In the campaign against Caprivi's army bill during the winter of 1892–3, *Vorwärts* reported over 750 public meetings.[65] Major theorists and leaders in the party produced a brochure and pamphlet literature on the militia justifying it on historical grounds. Bernstein in his multi-edition history of *The English Revolution* had long since traced the militia idea back to Harrington's *Oceania*, and claimed him as an ancestor of modern socialism.[66] On a less theoretical plane, Social Democratic journalists were assiduous and prolific in uncovering military abuses. That the journalists often faced fines or imprisonment for digging out the army's dirty secrets gave added weight to their revelations. It is here that the programmatic demands and theoretical assertions of the leaders were worked into the texture of daily life and cemented into the social democratic identity. The moral conviction invested in the party's programme and ideology were inextricably tied to bitter anger and bitter laughter. In this chapter I shall consider two of the major themes, democracy and taxation, in turn. The third theme, national defence, is treated in the next chapter, because it is bound up with a separate set of questions about nationalism and foreign policy.

Soldiers versus civilians

It was well known that Wilhelmine generals, the Kaiser and more than one chancellor toyed with the idea of carrying through a *Staatsstreich*, military repression in order to revoke the constitution.[67] It is important to distinguish between the political reality of such moves – most of which were leaked to the press, often indeed to Social Democratic papers – and the publicity material they afforded to the SPD. Repression had already been tried selectively under the anti-socialist laws, and their failure left two further options open. One was to carry out much harsher measures, which would have entailed full-scale military and police action, suspending civil rights, and revoking the democratic suffrage of the Reichstag if not abolishing it altogether. This was what Bismarck wanted to do when he fell from power in 1890.[68] His successor Caprivi contemplated it in 1892–3, when the Reichstag rejected his expansionist military budget.[69] The first Naval Law of 1897–8 was accompanied by a controversial and ultimately abortive Subversion Bill.[70] And in the mid-1890s, the Chief of Staff, Count Waldersee, had a number of conversations with Bismarck, Wilhelm II and the Chancellor in which he argued strongly in favour of a pre-emptive strike against the SPD. The matter was urgent, Waldersee claimed, because the army was in danger of becoming so infiltrated by Social Democratic members that it would cease to be a reliable instrument of power.[71] In the event, none of these threats was actually implemented. In 1893 and 1898, the Reichstag approved the army and navy bills demanded of it. But it also rejected the Subversion Bill together with some equally controversial legislation against strikers. Day to day government remained in civil rather than military hands, even if the army itself remained beyond ministerial control.

Neither the talk of repression nor its widespread publicity seem to have bothered Wilhelm II or many of his advisors. In so far as they served any rational political objective, the Emperor's Potsdam addresses to Guards' entrants warning them that they might have to 'shoot and cut down your own relatives and brothers' in order to crush the 'internal enemy' warned the SPD not to think too seriously about political power.[72] This sort of language became a proxy for real violence within elite circles. It instigated and legitimated a rhetorical extremism which the radical Right picked up and amplified later. But it also stopped at the legal limits – most of the time.

Social Democracy certainly responded within strictly legal guidelines. Editors who attacked the army, or military policy in general, often landed in prison or paying heavy fines for *lèse-majesté* or insulting the entire officer corps.[73] The attendant court cases provided the SPD with further material for propaganda, and the technique of turning the dock into a moral and political prosecution became a revered socialist tradition. Bebel's and Wilhelm Liebknecht's high treason trial in 1872 became an inspirational model. Karl Liebknecht's trial and subsequent imprisonment for publishing his book *Militarism and Anti-Militarism* in 1907, or Rosa Luxemburg's arraignment in 1914 for speaking out against maltreatment in the army, also commanded national attention.[74] These legal risks gave Social Democratic anti-militarism its particular heroic and agitational aura. Party leaders used their parliamentary immunity to denounce the system in its entirety, though even August Bebel took legal advice on risky passages.[75] Lacking such guarantees, the Social Democratic and Left Liberal press adapted its style to its subject-matter and became adept at sticking strictly to the details of individual scandals or choosing just the right quotations to condemn the authorities in their own words. In place of editorial comment, the press could always quote its leaders' speeches from the court and Reichstag records with impunity, so that paradoxically the very presence of censorship tended to heighten the national standing of a small group of parliamentary spokesmen and so contributed to the oft-noted centralisation of power within the party.

In October 1892, the *Fränkische Tagespost* revealed details of military and civil contingency plans. Six years later, the central party daily *Vorwärts* published a letter from the Prussian Minister of the Interior reprimanding the Erfurt police for not using their weapons in a number of local disturbances. Rumours of the high level discussions of a *Staatsstreich* circulated across the entire German press in the 1890s, fuelled partly by intrigues in ruling circles. The Kaiser's own speeches were cited so frequently that finally, in 1907, Wilhelm Schröder published an entire volume of Wilhelm's inflammatory utterances, which has proved as invaluable to historians as no doubt it was to SPD agitators at the time.[76]

One of the normal Social Democratic ripostes to sabre-rattling was to point out that too many soldiers were already supporters of the party for

2 'The rabble; the crowd; the people [Der Pöbel; die Menge; das Volk]', from *Simplicissimus*, 1897

the government to use the army against the labour movement. Quite how much truth lay behind this assertion is obscured by the vested interests at stake. The General Staff submitted a memorandum of 28 January 1897 asserting that 'from a military point of view' it was impermissible to allow Social Democratic influence in the army to grow further without taking counter-measures. Waldersee recommended and Kautsky presciently feared that the way to deal with the labour movement would be to reintroduce 'small well-paid, professional armies to be deployed in the first place against internal enemies'.[77] But Kautsky at least was perceptive enough to realise that the strategic imperatives of Germany's international position made such a solution illusory.[78] What lay behind this thesis of the internal rupture of the military machine was a crude sociological determinism.

Both Friedrich Engels and Prussian conservatives like Massow equated the demographic growth of the industrial working class with an automatic 'reddening' of the army.[79] To an extent, the army was able to slow down the assertion of this alleged logic by recruiting more heavily from rural areas, especially from the Junker estates East of the Elbe where the landlord still held sway as administrator, judge and military commander. According to Bernhardi in his popular book *Germany and the Next War*, published in 1911, when only 42.5% of the population lived in the country-side, rural areas still provided some 64% of recruits. By comparison, 22% came from small towns and a mere 13% from large cities and medium sized towns put together.[80] A recent study of the early months of the war demonstrates the same skewed social composition among German casualties.[81] In the 1890s, such sociological determinism was if anything even more fashionable in labour circles than in the officer corps. Bebel even drew upon it as a rhetorical threat in the Reichstag to press the government to initiate genuine reform.[82] But, whereas the SPD turned to this argument to justify restricting its activities to civil society,[83] the military authorities introduced a whole series of anti-socialist measures into the army.

These measures took two forms, persecution and indoctrination. Police had to report on socialists among the local intake of each year's recruits; the army blacklisted Social Democrats, barred their appointment to the non-commissioned officers' corps, and banned socialist literature and newspapers. The second set of measures were 'educational'. Army chaplains and officers regularly harangued their troops about the evils of atheistic socialism and extolled the nation, the Hohenzollern dynasty and religion. Both sides of this effort were highly problematic. Social Democrats were privately gleeful that their literature still circulated.[84] Occasional courts martial do not seem to have prevented this. Harsh sentences, like the NCO who was sentenced to a six-year term and a dishonourable discharge for bringing Social Democratic papers to the barracks, simply gave the SPD further publicity material.[85] In a bowdlerised fashion, chaplains and officers may have unintentionally introduced ignorant recruits to forbidden fruit and awakened a curiosity where there was none before. A notice like the one posted on a pub warning that it was 'Out of bounds since frequented by prostitutes, pimps and Social Democrats' may have aroused quite unjustified expectations.[86] Many of the homilies they delivered to their squadrons and companies were so ignorant that one exasperated major-general recommended that officers really ought to read the Social Democratic press if they were to combat its propaganda better.[87] The Imperial Russian army knew better than to try.

What is clearer from the archives is that the rise in Social Democratic support in the 1900s proved too great for the civil authorities to monitor. By 1907, the Prussian War and Interior Ministers had to re-interpret the ordinances of 1894, relaxing the blacklists so that rank-and-file members of the party and trade unions were let through the net and insisting only that prominent leaders and party activists should be monitored.[88] In February 1914, the same distinction was extended to the coveted bourgeois institution of the one year volunteer.[89] In any case, it has been suggested that shortage of competent NCOs may have led many officers to wink at Social Democratic affiliations in any case.[90] Certainly, party leaders of both Left and Right trends liked to boast that Social Democracy provided the best soldiers.[91]

Although the officers' corps also underwent demographic change, so that by 1913 some 70% of its members and 50% of the General Staff were of bourgeois origin, it was able to perpetuate its aristocratic ethos by the way it socialised its entrants, and this included rejecting students from the fraternities who opposed the formally banned but widely continued practice of duelling.[92] On such issues the Centre Party and SPD could still unite in condemning the reactionary backwardness of the officers' corps.[93] Politically too it was very exclusive, and reflected the allegiances of the old Bismarckian cartel. Conservatives and National Liberals were *comme il faut*; Catholics, and still more rarely Left Liberals, might be tolerated as second class citizens, but Jews and Social Democrats were barred entirely until the first world war.[94] Reserve officers were warned by the Kaiser and the Prussian Minister for War that they risked losing their commissions if they canvassed for the SPD even as private citizens in Reichstag elections.[95] It is questionable whether they even knew what figures of fun and loathing SPD cartoonists of *Kladderadatsch* and *Der wahre Jacob* or the Munich Left Liberals on *Simplicissimus* made of the pea-brained, monocled Junkers in uniform and aspiring bourgeois reserve lieutenants.[96]

As far as the lived experience of national service conscripts went, relations with non-commissioned officers (NCOs) were much more important than with commissioned officers. Although Prussia officially abolished flogging in the army as early as 1808, and Bavaria in the wake of the 1848 revolution, illicit as well as sanctioned corporal punishments continued to be meted out in the armed forces on a scale sufficient to evoke a concern that grew with public debate. The repertoire of the German NCO included beatings, sometimes ending in death or disablement, endless physical exercises, binding to trees, and even forcing recruits to eat their own excrement.[97] Because of the risks involved in publicising abuse or seeking redress, conscripts' despair is easier to measure than the scale of maltreatment itself. Between 1876 and 1895, according to one historian, the suicide rate among soldiers in the Prussian army averaged 216 per annum.[98] According to another account, the suicide rate for the whole of the German army during the 1878–1908 period varied between 220 and 240 per annum, some fourteen times the *per capita* civilian level. Though no continuous series exists yet, there appear to have been about three times as many suicides in the German as in the French armies between 1870 and 1908.[99] By 1908, the SPD had its own statistics.[100]

Social Democracy first gained a handle on this issue when a secret decree by the Duke of Saxony, the commander of the 12th Army Corps, found its way into *Vorwärts* in January 1892. The order was devoted to admonishing officers to check the ill-treatment meted out by NCOs and gave an official imprimatur to the Social Democratic charge that examples of torture were not individual excesses but endemic to the Prussian barracks.[101] The party press chanced upon a similar circular to the 2nd Bavarian Army Corps. The SPD sought to maximise public outrage. *Vorwärts* ran a regular column under the sarcastic heading 'More news from the holiday camps'.[102] It also published a number of anonymous contributions from army and navy personnel, but a great deal of its specialist writings on maltreatment in the army was the work of a retired Bavarian Lieutenant called Rudolf Krafft.[103] From 1890 on, the opposition parties raised the issue of the maltreatment of soldiers whenever the Reichstag debated a military budget.[104] Until research is undertaken on workers' own attitudes to military service – along the lines perhaps of studies in France[105] – we will not know how far this Social Democratic propaganda spoke directly to workers' lived experience.

What is easier to trace is the change in political consensus on the subject. The Prussian War Ministry and Chancellor themselves sponsored a Reich reform of military justice. Despite the Emperor's allegedly exclusive authority over the army, they succeeded. The eventual reform of 1897–9 considerably liberalised the Prussian code, although it fell short of the liberal Bavarian one, let alone the Social Democratic demand that the army

3 'Reform of the military code; Prussian menagerie', from
Simplicissimus, 1898

should come directly under civil law.[106] But even so the new code was still
comparable with contemporary British and French practice.[107]

The reform legitimised SPD concern about military justice without
leading to great improvements in practice.[108] As a result, the initiative for
reform remained in civil society, its relevance further sanctioned by stalled
efforts at official remedy.[109] As the Centre Party press noted in 1903, the
SPD reaped a double harvest of propaganda material and young recruits
eager to join the party.[110] Things had still not changed much by 1914:
challenged to substantiate allegations of torture in the army in February
1914, over a thousand *Vorwärts* readers who were willing to testify before
a civil court about bullying and abuse came forward within a week.[111]

The army was obviously not an unqualified success as the much vaunted
'school for educating the nation'. At the same time the entire issue of
maltreatment was new to the radical democratic tradition of anti-
militarism. To seek redress like this acknowledged the national and social
character of military service, a set of issues with which the old liberal critics
of absolutism and standing armies had not had to engage. The soldier had
been transformed from a paid 'mercenary' into a citizen or a 'worker in
uniform'. At a practical level Bebel especially accepted this new reality; he
repeatedly demanded improvements in the pay and conditions of NCOs as
well as for the troops themselves. What he did not yet acknowledge was
that anti-militarist agitation no longer focused solely on the pure
opposition between army and democracy. The image had become far more
kaleidoscopic, social as well as political.

Whatever threats the authorities might make about impending repression, actual incidents of military action against civilians were the
exception rather than the rule. Clashes occurred during the spontaneous
strike by 120,000 miners in the Ruhr in 1889 and several miners were

killed.[112] But other labour protests in the 1890s were too disciplined to give the military authorities an excuse to intervene. Waldersee might mass and parade 16,690 troops in Hamburg during a spate of strikes in 1896, but found no excuse for deploying them.[113] The workers obeyed their stewards and kept perfect order and until 1909 the government itself respected the right to strike and did not intervene actively to protect scab labour.[114] On most occasions, the armed, often brutal and generally elderly and unfleet-footed police force remained in control.[115] There was no German parallel after 1889 to the type of routine military action against strikers in France which reached a crescendo with the Fourmies massacre.[116] As a result, one might surmise that the demonstrative presence of tens of thousands of infantry and cavalry continued to inspire fear rather than the anger that erupted elsewhere after they had gone into action.

It is also interesting that the proposal within the General Staff to form special units to deal with strikes and riots was never followed up. Several of the companies who patrolled the Mansfeld miners' strike of 1909, equipped with live ammunition and fixed bayonets as well as machine guns and supporting cavalry, actually came from the locality. The Kaiser's threat to divide families against themselves had become manifest.[117] Here too German practice lacked the sophistication of the contemporary Austro-Hungarian or Russian regimes, which routinely deployed troops of different cultural or ethnic origin to suppress dissent. This sort of evidence suggests that the German authorities were no more prepared to move from a show of strength to violent conflict than was the labour movement.

The most horrific single occurrence in the 1890s was probably at Fuchsmühl in Bavaria, where 50 soldiers were sent to clear wood-cutters from a forest on 25 October 1895. Two elderly men were bayoneted to death, and seventeen men and women were wounded, four of them seriously. In the public uproar which followed the SPD again allied with the Centre against the ruling National Liberals in Bavaria and through investigative journalism kept the issue alive long enough to force a debate in the *Landtag* a year later. Finally, in June 1896, the Bavarian government attempted to make amends by introducing a new forestry law.[118]

Like the Reich reform of military justice the Fuchsmühl killings wrung a legal concession of substance from the government, rather than proceedings against a few token individuals. In securing this widening of the public sphere, the anti-militarists may have paradoxically been aided by the very structures they denounced as the essence of militarism. The removal of the army from government control, its status through the Kaiser's *Kommandogewalt* as a Fichtean 'state within a state', made it difficult for any civil authority to turn individual soldiers, let alone officers, into scapegoats. Wilhelm II personally did everything he could to prevent such a development.[119] Ministers thus had very little room for manoeuvre when it came to appeasing public opinion. Their very lack of control over the executive meant that they could only respond by liberalising civil law itself.

The famous Saverne incident of 1913 can be seen in terms of the same conflicts within the state. News of an entire Alsatian town being placed under a state of siege on the orders of a colonel who had seen action in the barbaric war against the Herero people in West Africa provoked an public outcry. The Reichstag passed an overwhelming vote of no confidence in the Chancellor, who had had no say in the matter and behind the scenes was trying to stop the military action. The state of siege was lifted, the arrested citizens released, but at the same time the army command and the Emperor closed ranks to protect the officers concerned.[120] Although the *Times* correspondent once again declared sententiously that such things could only happen in Germany, both the action at Saverne and its resolution were less ominous than the British government's handling of the Curragh incident a few months later.

Citizens as tax payers

The second major area of anti-military criticism was finance. Costs could be seen in two ways, the scale of spending on the army and the distribution of the tax burden. These two themes run together like a thread throughout Social Democratic opposition to indirect taxation, but they only achieved real prominence within party policy in the 1890s. Whereas politics in the 1860s was dominated by the large question of the nation state, the politicians of the 1880s and 1890s were preoccupied with social and economic policy. The military question thus changed from being one about the way Germany would be united or what kind of constitution, if any, the future state would have, to forming the centre of a broader and more diffuse debate about government taxation, tariffs and public spending. The old questions remained, but in a new setting. The Centre and Conservatives made their pitch for peasant and lower-middle-class support on the basis of subsidy and protection. So it is not surprising that the SPD saw its opportunity to rally the working class on the promise of free trade, cheap wage goods and progressive taxation. Since the Reichstag was the most democratically elected part of the German polity, and since also the taxes it levied were the most regressive, and since finally the largest part of the Reich budget was allocated to the army and navy, it was inevitable that this collision over social and fiscal policies should centre on the military budget.

Democratic arguments about Germany's constitution no longer oc-cupied the same central position as they had when the Reich was founded.[121] The tax question became correspondingly more important, especially as the list of protective tariffs grew ever longer after 1879.

The 1893 election campaign marked this shift in emphasis. In 1892 the Reichstag rejected Caprivi's first military bill since becoming Chancellor and the parties went to the polls. The prospects of a broad opposition and a weak government were irresistible. Bebel and Liebknecht made two long speeches in the Reichstag debate which were duly reprinted on the *Vorwärts* presses and circulated widely through Germany.[122] According to the Hamburg police, August Bebel devoted most of his election speech there, on 11 June 1893, to the military question. Apart from advocating shorter service and the end to class distinctions – especially the privileges of the 'bourgeois' one year volunteer – Bebel concentrated his fire on the increasing tax burden on the working class.[123] The SPD held some 750 similar meetings during this election campaign. In his contribution to the Reichstag debate, Wilhelm Liebknecht drew attention to the social costs of disproportionate military spending. In Prussia alone, he pointed out, 1,700,000 children had to attend schools where the ratio of pupils to teachers was of the order of 81–150:1. In ringing tones, he declared that in Germany, 'The barracks stands above the school, just as the army stands above civil authority.'[124]

The democratic idealism of Social Democratic rhetoric had not changed. The dire realities of the Reich were still compared with 'free Switzerland', the one country in Liebknecht's view which allocated a bigger budget to education than to the army. Resources, he stressed, ought to be spent on 'culture', education, roads and social welfare payments. With an increasing emphasis on parsimony, Bebel, Wilhelm Liebknecht and Friedrich Engels all stressed that a militia system would simultaneously double the size of the army and reduce its cost by a half or a third.[125] What had changed was the emphasis. Beside the old appeal to the rights of citizenship a new one was being made to the interests of consumers. This was the party which would choose consumer co-operatives and reject pressure from its South German leadership to adopt peasant subsidies. Protecting the urban standard of living became central to SPD policy even if it meant telling peasant audiences that their class was historically 'doomed'. Not only did the party congress vote overwhelmingly against competing with *Mittelstandspolitik* on its own terms, but August Bebel went so far as to write off anti-semitic populism as 'socialism of the fools'.[126] The result of this policy choice was, as we saw, that the party continued to make inroads into the urban electorate of the Centre Party; cheap wage goods appealed to small businessmen as well as workers. But Social Democracy also had to pay the price of effectively cutting itself off from the peasantry. Ideologically, a pro-consumer policy gelled with the traditional free-trade and *laissez-faire* reading of capitalist development of Marx and Kautsky. Bebel and Liebknecht even allowed themselves the rhetorical indulgence of warning that over-taxation would lead from immiseration to revolution.[127]

By the time the government launched its big navy policy in 1897–8, the SPD had built up its organisation sufficiently to address consumers still more effectively. Through its *Handbooks for Social Democratic Voters*, it catalogued the growing list of taxable goods,[128] made great play of the acceptance of the Tirpitz Plan by its main rival for mass support, the Centre Party,[129] and of the fact that only Social Democracy demanded direct progressive taxation.[130] But the first large harvest from this labour was not reaped until the 1903 Reichstag elections, when the massive costs of the naval programme, with the new tariffs and indirect taxes of 1901–2, had really eaten into mass consumption.[131]

The more that fiscal reform became a pressing political issue in the 1900s, the more obvious it became that it could be taken up on its own. This was not foreseen by Social Democratic leaders in the 1890s, who spoke of it as if it were an inseparable part of the 'militarist system'. This was perhaps understandable at a time when indirect taxes and agrarian protection seemed to be increasing exponentially. Social Democratic observers probably could not imagine that a Prussian Junker might give up his fiscal privileges any more than he would surrender his position in the officers' corps, standing at court or pivotal role in the Reichstag. More recent historians have shared this conviction.[132] What the SPD leadership did not – and perhaps could not – know in 1890 or even 1900 was that the pressure for fiscal reform could be accommodated within the structure of the old state. When just this actually happened in 1913, as we shall see, Social Democratic anti-militarism had already entered a strategic crisis.

Conclusion

In the 1890s Imperial Germany developed its fully fledged party system. Rather like post-1945 Italian politics, the shifting coalitions of the dominant parties were constructed around the negative purpose of excluding the major party of the Left from parliamentary influence: in post-war Italy, it was the Communist Party which was excluded; in Wilhelmine Germany it was Social Democracy. As the newly unbanned member of this party system German Social Democracy's leaders were more intent on formulating their programme, establishing themselves successfully on a legal footing and organising as well as attracting a mass following than with worrying about where precisely the constituent strands of its anti-militarism might lead in the future. On the credit side, the SPD had stationed the militia at the centre of its political, social and fiscal critique. The militia had been established as the foil with which to ridicule expensive schnapps and poor education, the maltreatment of conscripts and lack of legal redress, duels between and social deference towards officers, threats to renege on civil as well as political rights and the actual bayonetting of innocent citizens. As Kautsky reminded the readers of *Die neue Zeit* in 1903, their most important practical task was much less the conquest of political power than the conquest of the masses.[133] Party leaders like the shrewd and long-standing SPD secretary Ignaz Auer, or a revered figurehead such as Friedrich Engels, left their audiences in no doubt in the mid-1890s that the SPD would not be the side to provoke a showdown. Rather it would weaken the hold of the regime over its 'workers in uniform' by using all the legal possibilities of mass propaganda now at its disposal to get the Social Democratic message across, 'by exposing again and again, and under all conditions, the abuses within the system, by organising the proletariat and – because we represent a just cause – by bringing all humane and right-thinking people on to our side'.[134]

The rapid growth in Social Democratic membership and in electoral support might have been cited by Auer to vindicate his claim. It is also true that this support was limited in the main to a particular social group, male and manual, largely North German and protestant workers. The party expended a great deal of energy on convincing people that a class affiliation ought to replace older ones – more particularist ones like family, locality and trade, or else more universal ones like religion. Social Democracy's 70 daily papers and host of recreational organisations from cycling clubs and gymnastic associations to choral societies, not to mention social and economic enterprises from insurance to consumer co-operatives, all helped to root the Social Democratic sense of 'proletarian' identity. Party membership may not have conferred much insight into official Marxist theory, but it meant a great deal more than either simply wanting higher wages or voting at election time.[135] But even judging from levels of electoral participation, the Wilhelmine populace took its right to elect a non-sovereign Reichstag as an extremely serious, political act, however symbolic the value to which it may often have been reduced.[136]

The Social Democrats directed a great deal of their propaganda effort against the state rather than social conditions alone. 'Class justice', 'class education', 'class taxation', and in Saxony and Prussia 'class suffrage' all helped to constitute the Wilhelmine 'class state'. The army became the coping stone of this great imperial arch. On this both Conservatives and Social Democrats agreed. But where the former advertised the army as the 'school of the nation', the latter reviled it as the class institution *par excellence*. This was writ both large and small. In the details of its internal structure the army illustrated Social Democratic ideas of a class society: at the top Junker and high bourgeois officers, gilded sons of the bourgeoisie enjoying the privilege of serving as one-year volunteers, and at the bottom skilled, efficient workers in uniform, beaten and harassed by ill-educated and brutal NCOs. The inability of workers and Social Democrats to break through the social barriers of rank in the army reminded readers of the party press of two wider ramifications. First, the system of military ranks had been applied to the state as a whole. Higher civil servants and government ministers had to be members of the reserve officers corps. More immediate to the lived experience of most Social Democratic voters, the policemen, gate-keepers, night-watchmen and postal clerks who shouted at them, ordered them to apply to another office, closed down their political meetings and could depend on receiving a state pension at the end of it all were all too likely to have come from the non-commissioned officers' corps. As in Britain in the first half of the nineteenth century, so in Germany in the second half there operated a system of appointing *Militäranwärter*, junior ranks with an unblemished record of service, to the lower offices of state.[137] In the second place, the Kaiser and his army commanders appeared only too ready and willing to order workers wanting higher wages or democratic rights to be shot down. When class became a meaningful modern identity in Germany it also took over much of the same ground occupied by older identities such as estate and rank.

Personal memories of Social Democracy's recent persecution under Bismarck's anti-socialist laws merged with a burgeoning literature on the party's 'heroic era'. No doubt the proximity of this experience helped to perpetuate a radical democratic opposition to the army and state in the 1890s. But civil society was changing. The very success of Social Democracy in agitating for new norms in civil and military conduct became part of that change. Faced with the erection of public monuments to glorify Bismarck, the Kaiser and the Prussian army, the party issued its own satirical brochure under the suggestive title *Knock Me Down*.[138] In the 1890s, Social Democrats could be forgiven for believing that the growing self-confidence and political effectiveness of public opinion would stimulate humane and democratic tendencies.

The party programme itself was rational and idealist rather than pragmatic or empiricist. Its political origins lie in the radical democratic heritage of the 1848 revolutions. Intellectually, Social Democratic leaders saw themselves as the heirs to the enlightenment. They strove to subject the realities around them to rational criticism and justify their policies in theoretical terms. The aspirations of the party programme were statist on economic and social policy, but anti-statist on political and military issues. The balance between these elements shifted significantly over time. Their critique mapped out what was pathological about the German army and state. The rhetorical violence of the Kaiser and establishment appeared to express despair. Neither force nor redundant and irrationally romantic symbols could, Social Democrats presumed, halt the forces of progress and enlightenment.

What we do not and cannot know until the study of social attitudes to the army and military service is undertaken is how such ideas and programmes were received by the SPD's constituents. Did the idealist and Liberal democratic origins of the Social Democratic programme prevent the party from addressing the actual experiences of German workers? Or did the programme instil a highly motivating sense of right, reason and historical mission? This was what Bebel believed.[139] It was also the point of Engels' claim that 'The German working class movement is the heir of classical German philosophy.'[140] We cannot answer these questions definitively here. Indeed, both propositions may have been true.

2   Social Democracy and the Fatherland

On 4 August 1914 the co-Chairman of the SPD, Hugo Haase, reluctantly announced the party's declaration in favour of war credits to a packed and expectant Reichstag. Reading in his thin dry voice and cheered on by all of Social Democracy's opponents, he stated that his party was

> not deciding for or against the war today but rather over the question of the means to defend the country ... For our people and its future freedom much if not all would be lost in the event of the victory of Russian despotism, stained as it is with the blood of the best of its own people. In repelling this danger it is a matter of protecting the culture and independence of our own country.[1]

Whatever other motives the parliamentary party may have had for voting in support of the government – a vote which both signalled the end of the Second International and gave credibility to Wilhelm II's grandiose declaration that 'I know no parties any more, only Germans' – the SPD's long-standing pledge of national defence and its horror of Russian tsarism were well known. And they were the only motives to which the party was prepared to admit at the time. Exactly why the SPD made this complete *volte face* from intransigent opposition to collaboration has been debated ever since. What historians have not asked is how seriously the party's own pretext of 'national defence' was an operative term in Social Democratic policy before 1914.

This chapter seeks to address this question of national defence and the fatal part it was to play in Social Democratic anti-militarism. In order to unveil the inner content of the pledge to defend the nation one must disaggregate both terms, defence and the nation. Behind the idea of defence lie theories about military strategy and claims about the technical superiority of militias over standing armies. Behind Social Democratic images of the German nation lie enlightenment ideas about freedom and Social Darwinist views about the hierarchy of cultures. Put together, these two elements – the military and the national – form an explosive compound. On their basis Social Democrats extrapolated their sense of what were legitimate foreign policies for Germany, which of its neighbours were to be admired, emulated and courted and which were to be feared, reviled and fought. It is no secret that Russia held pride of place in the latter category and Britain and France among the former. But only by tracing these attitudes back does it become clear how deep their roots were. Neither Russophobia nor a commitment to national defence were new in the mid-1900s, as one famous historian has alleged.[2] On the contrary, both went back to at least the 1880s. Why did Social Democratic leaders hold such views so tenaciously? In the chapter which follows, I have broken this large question down into four constituent areas: military strategy; the German nation; foreign policy; war scares and the International.

Military capacity and defence

One of the great turning points for Radical anti-militarism came in the 1860s, when it attempted to wrest the ideological mantle of national defence and military renown from Bismarck. To achieve this end, radical Liberals claimed that militia armies were superior to standing armies not just in terms of their civic virtues or lower costs, but also on the ground of military strategy. This was an arrogant and desperate claim. The Swiss militia had been soundly defeated by Napoleon. In 1849, the soldiers of the King of Prussia and the Grand Duke of Baden had little difficulty defeating the revolutionary militias. As I suggested in the previous chapter, probably the best way to understand this claim is to see it as an issue forced upon anti-militarists. A world without war was no longer the imaginable utopia it had been for Kant. War was not only all too real but it was also all too apparent that the Liberal goal of national unity would not be achieved without it. Social Democrats inherited this liability and chose to make the same apology for it. Certainly assertions about the strategic superiority of militias loom large as the third strand of the general Social Democratic critique sketched out in the previous chapter.

In adopting this earlier body of militia arguments, Social Democrats were conscious of their historical debts. Men like Wilhelm Liebknecht, Julius Motteler, August Bebel and Wilhelm Blos had taken part in the national movement. Shortly before the first world war Franz Mehring and Karl Radek wrote extensive articles about the militia ideal and showed how even its organisational principles – like short service and military youth training – derived from Radicalism.[3] Social Democrats also tried to anchor their militia to earlier examples of popular warfare. In his *Not a Standing Army but a People in Arms*! Bebel mapped the militia on to the *levée en masse*. He claimed that its popular elan had made new military strategies and tactics possible. His victorious examples were the English civil war; the French revolution; Scharnhorst and Gneisenau in the

Prussian reform era; the Northern states in the American civil war; Gambetta in the Franco-Prussian war. The conclusion was obvious to him 'that in all the serious catastrophes of the great states – England, France, the USA, Prussia – it was the strength of the people in all its elemental force and not the standing army which freed the country'.[4] Bebel was reiterating a claim Wilhelm Liebknecht had made in 1868 – before the corroborative experience of the Franco-Prussian war – that standing armies were incapable of continuing a war after the first defeat.[5] At an abstract level or in a context freer from militaristic education, these historical analogies might have been convincing, though in fact there is a great deal of difference between the revolutionary upsurge of a *levée en masse* in the face of a foreign invasion and the organisation and training of a militia in peacetime.

But by the 1900s Social Democratic leaders spoke less about *levées en masse* and far more about their blueprint for an orderly and efficient militia. Their turn towards the Swiss militia as model appears new in the German context because it meant turning away from the inspiration of the French revolution.[6] Indeed, the vanishing older generation of Socialist leaders like Julius Motteler had to explain patiently to younger men like Karl Kautsky how decisive had been the ideas of the French revolution in drawing them into politics.[7] The same was true of Engels, and most likely of Marx and Wilhelm Liebknecht as well.[8] It is perhaps ironic that by turning to the Swiss militia, party intellectuals had unconsciously revived Rousseau's original inspiration for a democratic army of 130 years before.[9] The main points remained the same as in the earlier Radical and Social Democratic programmes: preparatory training and exercises at school; short service; arming of the entire active adult male population; and a very small professional cadre of officers and non-commissioned officers. In 1887, Engels asserted that any country could introduce this scheme unilaterally because it would double defence capability.[10] In the 1890s, Bebel and Liebknecht made similar claims.

In the abstract this might have been a persuasive programme. But in Imperial Germany this was an extraordinarily difficult act to pull off. After all, the Hohenzollerns and the Prussian army had been the forces to unite Germany, not the Liberals, Radicals or Social Democrats. And since the foundation of the Reich in 1871 there had been two decades of nationalist education at both a political and a cultural level. All Europe looked towards Germany as the model of military organisation. The spectacle of Wilhelm Liebknecht and August Bebel telling the Reichstag solemnly in 1893 that the reports on the autumn manoeuvres of the Swiss militia proved that they were superior to those of the Prussian army probably reduced some of their conservative opponents to helpless laughter.[11] The very insistence of the SPD on its military realism must provide some measure of its desperately limited room for political manoeuvre.

An idealist programme in realist packaging certainly did become the hallmark of Social Democratic anti-militarism. Parade drill, expenditure on elaborate uniforms, long service and incarceration in barracks were denounced first and foremost for being unnecessary and inefficient from the point of view of military defence. Whenever possible one or other authority on military affairs was eagerly seized on to substantiate the claim.[12] Having removed the counter-argument that these unpleasant practices might be necessary for national defence, Social Democrats could get down to the real task, which was still to denounce them in humanitarian and political terms. The only reason for glorious uniforms, separating soldiers from civil society and drilling and beating them into blind obedience was so that they could be used to attack their own population or other people.[13]

This was an increasingly elaborate route to reach the central thesis of seventeenth- and eighteenth-century critics of absolutism. What it graphically illustrates is the extent to which even Social Democrats feared that the state had succeeded in persuading the population of its national character. Consequently, rather than simply attacking the military system head on, the SPD skirmished around its edges. Proposed Social Democratic reforms included pay increases for non-commissioned officers, more stringent educational qualifications for officers, simplified drill and the need for camouflaging uniforms.[14] In no sense were these reforms intrinsic to the militia ideal. But no doubt Bebel and his colleagues hoped to win the battle of credibility and commonsense. The rise of this sort of debate testifies to the difficulties of preserving the political focus on 'militarism' as an essentially domestic constitutional problem. Its course can be charted by the rise in a socialist literature in Germany and France dedicated to the technical organisation of a militia army. The most important contribution of this kind was Bebel's 1898 tract *Not a Standing Army but a People in Arms*, which was followed by a similar literature in France. Gaston Moch's blueprint on how to organise *The Army of a Democracy* became a model which the German party used in its 1903 *Handbook for Social Democratic Voters* and Karl Liebknecht upheld in his *Militarism and Anti-Militarism*.[15] When Jean Jaurès wrote his magnum opus *The New Army* in 1911, he was continuing a tradition started by Bebel and Moch.[16] The application of these ideas was strictly limited in practice, and probably L. D. Trotsky was the only founder of a real army who was profoundly influenced by this literature.[17]

Even the authors of these guides to army organisation did not expect their ideas to be taken seriously, at least not in Germany. Evidence for this

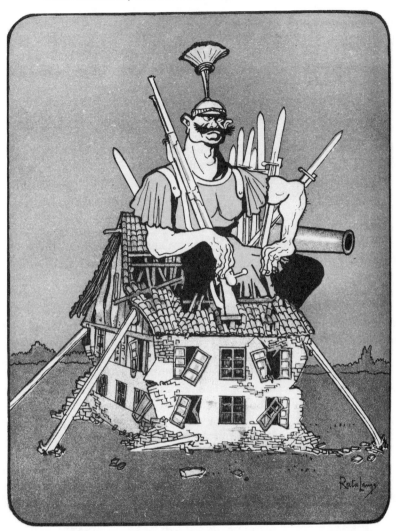

4 'Militarism, protector of the home', from *Der Wahre Jacob*, 1903

state of mind comes from the revisionist debate, in which Bernstein raised a number of technical criticisms of militias. In particular he noted their incompetence in carrying out tactical attacks – a point, one might acknowledge in passing, which was to be borne out fully in the Spanish civil war. The party leadership had nothing new to say in defence of its position. Even when Bernstein and his fellow-revisionist Max Schippel went straight for the traditional centrepiece of the programme, the equation of militias with democracy, the leadership remained startlingly silent on these questions.[18] Karl Kautsky and Rosa Luxemburg attacked Schippel vehemently but they added nothing new or substantial to the discussion.[19] It is not altogether surprising, then, that a few years later Karl Liebknecht took up the revisionists' arguments from the Left. He too argued that militias might be insufficient guarantors of democracy and showed how the supposedly model Swiss militia had been transformed after 1899 into a strike-breaking instrument.[20] The response of the leadership was to fall back on the traditional democratic arguments, and to hope that the inner-party dispute would die down.

Compared with its efforts at 'military science' Social Democracy was much more successful at linking its critique of fiscal policies to nationalist arguments. As Bebel told the voters of Hamburg on 11 June 1893, the increasing tax burden on the working class meant that 'soon the [worker] will no longer be able to develop his physique to a point where he can become a useful, healthy soldier'.[21] Nor were such sentiments entirely rhetorical hyperbole. Two highly conservative gentlemen, Field Marshal Colmar von der Goltz and General Bernhardi, were to express dismay at the physical condition of urban recruits, though one may doubt whether expensive bread and meat were more than aggravating circumstances alongside other factors like relatively low wages, insecure employment and poor housing and sanitation.[22] In 1892, Max Weber, then a young researcher into the condition of East Elbian land labourers, phrased his conclusions in identical terms: 'Today's capitalistic estates exist at the expense of the nutritional level, the nationality and the military strength of the German east.'[23] At this time Weber sympathised with the Pan Germans. This sort of language may have made good electoral copy for the SPD, because it gave a radical twist to the conservative consensus. It also drew the party into the ideological web of assessing social questions from the point of view of Germany's place in the world. Anti-militarism was becoming dangerously close to *raison d'état*.

The nation

If the nub of the problem had been only a formal commitment by Social Democracy to defend the nation, then this might not have had serious political ramifications. All the opponents of the Bismarckian solution to German unity in the 1860s and 1870s had pledged themselves to the same end. Their very rhetorical readiness to defend Germany highlighted their refusal to accept first Prussia and then the Empire either as a territorial definition of the German nation or as a set of national institutions. But this position proved unsustainable. Like other supporters of a 'greater German' solution, the 'Eisenach' wing of the labour movement which Bebel and Wilhelm Liebknecht led had reluctantly had to come to terms with the reality of the Reich.[24] By 1874, Julius Motteler was able to signal the party's capitulation to the little German, or Prussian, solution to the nation state.[25] By 1875 there was no longer any obstacle to unity with the Lassallean wing of the labour movement, which had accepted Bismarck's empire from the outset. Despite its outspoken opposition to the annexation of non-German areas, the SPD gradually gave up its policy of returning them to France, Poland and Denmark and turned instead to campaigning for minority rights for the Danes, Poles and Alsatians within the Reich.[26] So much for the territory of the state; what about its institutions?

A careful study of Bebel's utterances reveals that the Social Democratic leader was able simultaneously to accept the democratic credentials of the Reichstag and to speak of its 'class character'.[27] What he meant by this double-decker formula was that both the territory and the institutions of the German Empire provided the locus for social democratic politics. This acknowledgement justified what Bebel called 'Social Democratic patriotism' in a political fashion: '*Hic Rhodus, hic salta* – stay here and fight with us, here is the ground on which we have to struggle for and create the new age, the new world.'[28] This acceptance of the legitimacy of German unity and Reich institutions – whilst in the same breath rejecting the government, its powers and policies as illegitimate – affected the whole issue of national defence. From 1880 onwards Bebel pledged himself to defend the actual existing Reich and the language he chose to express this commitment was frequently dramatic and personal – and hardly altered over the next three decades.[29]

Quite what was invested in these claims is not immediately obvious. To grasp their intensity one has to turn to the other dimension of the nation state. What did Social Democrats mean by the German nation? Accounts of Social Democratic support for the first world war often tend to emphasise the institutional side of its patriotism, the extent to which it had become 'integrated', negatively or otherwise, into Imperial Germany, or – particularly in the case of the trade unions – the desire to protect the organisational apparatus and personnel which the movement had built up.[30] Without denying these elements some explanatory power, it is nonetheless significant that Social Democratic leaders had declared their willingness to die defending their nation state long before they had any such stake to defend. The nation mattered to them. But what did they mean by it?

Like many a nationalist Bebel rooted his sense of national identity in the distinctiveness of language, culture and tradition.[31] Almost any or no political conclusions could follow from this level of generality. The national agenda of National Liberals, Conservatives and Pan Germans differed widely among themselves – let alone by comparison with the SPD – when it came to specific issues like the internal colonisation of East Prussia or prohibiting the use of foreign languages in public assemblies. But they often shared a similar pride in Prussian traditions, its enlightenment statecraft, romanticism and 'great cultures', and they all denigrated Slavs.

Social Democratic ideas of nationality are most obviously different at first sight. In the way they formulated their pride in Germany in the 1890s and 1900s, Social Democratic publicists strove to create a benign, non-aggressive image of cultural excellence in stark and intentional contrast to the military, colonial and Germanising metaphors of Liberals, imaginative Conservatives and, to some extent, the Centre. Against the sabre, the *pickelhaube* and Krupp cannons, SPD leaders set up their own symbols of Germans' greatness. Germans, especially German workers, were in Social Democratic mythology orderly, industrious, technically expert and exceptionally gifted at organising. It was the volume of German exports rather than the prowess of German arms which the nation ought to celebrate. Bebel and his friends repeatedly brought these examples of German 'civilisation' and 'culture' to the fore whenever they tried to explain what it was their avowed 'proletarian patriotism' sought to defend.[32]

Nationalism and internationalism – the famous dual loyalty of the SPD to the German nation and the international working class – were supposed to be harmonious rather than antagonistic. Time and again, the party's spokesmen emphasised their belief in free trade as, in classically Cobdenite terms, a force for internationalising cultural exchange.[33] Unlike the increasingly protectionist Centre, Conservatives and National Liberals, Social Democrats wanted trade and industry to overcome the separation of the 'great cultured peoples' [*grosse Kulturvölker*]. But unlike radical anti-nationalists (like the anarcho-syndicalists) they did not wish this to occur to the detriment of the cultural level already attained, nor did they believe it could happen quickly. This was obviously a rather progressivist view of culture, even if its political roots still lay in the radical nationalist ideas of the 1848 revolutionaries. It was also the public face of Social Democratic nationalism, the persona it presented at the fraternal exchanges of the Second International, when elaborating Marxist theory or when denouncing official policy in the Reichstag. The International codified this doctrine of universal tolerance when it adopted a vaguely worded resolution on the 'rights of all nations to self-determination' at its 1896 London Congress.[34]

The acid test of any nationalism, Social Democratic included, is its treatment of 'otherness', of those who are barred from inclusion. This is what provides a real measure of its values. The disparity between benign sentiments about one's own community and contempt for those outside it is perhaps most striking among racists and radical nationalists. Both movements became very active on the Right in Germany, France and Britain in the 1890s.[35] Socialists were at the other end of spectrum. But how universal was their tolerance in practice? How far did the spectrum extend? Jean Jaurès and August Bebel – the most influential leaders of the French and German socialist parties – saw no contradiction between nationalism and internationalism, between each championing his own culture and seeking to reach out to other 'civilised countries'.[36] But they were equally confident that theirs were 'great cultures'; in Jaurès' *bon mot*, 'A little internationalism improves the national culture: too much kills it off.'[37] They each saw their own country and party as the exemplar, the nation which would lead the rest of the world into an international political order.[38] But it did not take more than a set-piece debate over party policy within the Second International for the negative side of this national pride to surface.[39] Predictably, these views were reiterated in the domestic *fora* of the two movements – with an accretion of unpleasant clichés about each others' putative national characteristics.

The intellectual materials with which Social Democrats started were not conducive to fostering equal respect for all other cultures and peoples. Perhaps the last thesis of Hegel's to which Marx and Engels clung was his belief that the East represented the infancy of history because it was despotic and static.[40] As ignorant as he was prejudiced and as arrogant as he was ignorant, the young Friedrich Engels denied the very 'historical right' of Slav peoples to form nations at all.[41] In so far as they counted at all, young Hegelian nationalists in Germany reckoned Slav cultures on the 'despotic Asiatic' rather than 'civilised European' side of the scale. As a Marxist tenet these categories went on to influence people who had never read Hegel at all.

'Advanced' and 'backward', 'culture' and 'barbarism', 'stages of development' and 'civilisation' are all terms that recur time and again in Social Democratic references to international relations between the major powers, let alone between the European states and their colonies. The use of these terms involved a merging of two distinct intellectual trends. Until the mid-nineteenth century such terms bore all the marks of the enlightenment and the French revolution. They had predominantly political referents. Crudely, 'advanced' meant a republican government and 'backward' an absolutist one – and the 'movement' which spread such views was broadly 'progressive' because it represented the forces of the new liberal order against the old despotic one.[42] By the 1880s and 1890s, these metaphors had been incorporated within Social Darwinist readings of history. The dichotomy between a state of nature and civil society into which seventeenth- and eighteenth-century thinkers had divided history was no longer fashionable. 'Progress' no longer meant the attainment of constitutional rights alone, but a ladder all peoples would have to ascend towards a 'civilisation', described by its scientific and technical achievements as well as its military and political ones.

The most important intellectual contribution to this reorientation of ideas was undoubtedly the work of the Social Darwinist Ernst Haeckel.[43] As a right-wing nationalist who idealised Bismarck he broke with both the intellectual and political guidance of his mentor Rudolf Virchow in the 1870s. Virchow was not only the father of German pathology but also a prominent Left Liberal Progressive. In the public polemic which followed their breach, Virchow warned Haeckel that the collective determinism of his Darwinist reading of history was crypto-socialist. For his part, Haeckel would have absolutely no truck with Social Democracy, and in 1892 decried the SPD for working towards a 'relapse into barbarism, into the animal-like raw state of the human race'.[44] If Haeckel's natural constituency was as likely to be the radical Right in the era of Wilhelmine imperialism or Weimar Nazism, it should not be forgotten that he profoundly influenced such stalwarts of democratic and Marxist values as Karl Kautsky and Georgi'i Plekhanov.[45] For Kautsky, Darwinist evolution spelled out a line of inevitable cultural ascent to the point where there is 'the cessation of the struggle for existence; this is precisely socialism'.[46]

Second International socialism was not immune to the rise of imperialist and racist ideas in the 1890s. Such ideas had a profound, if more muted, echo. By the 1900s the right wing of the German labour movement cautiously emulated the approval given to colonialism by sections of the French and British movements.[47] The Herero uprising in West Africa in 1906 played a similarly polarising role in Germany to the Boer war in Britain. The government successfully fought a general election on a colonialist and nationalist platform in January 1907.[48] Having suffered its first defeat in twenty years at the polls, the SPD found itself hosting a debate on colonialism when the Second International met for its congress at Stuttgart that summer. Socialists – including German Social Democrats – were divided. Most of the SPD delegates stuck to the traditional position of the centre and centre-left; colonies were a waste of tax-payers' money and the 'savages' ought to be left open to 'civilising influences' of commerce but not colonised.[49] The right wing pressed for a more 'positive' prescription of a 'socialist colonial policy', which could be used as an ideological stepping stone towards embracing real existing imperialism.[50]

Whatever the differences between the two wings of the movement, it is clear they shared certain common assumptions. Colonial peoples were 'savages', Europeans 'civilised'.[51] Even to Marxist radicals it was obvious that colonial liberation would come from the victory of the labour movement in the advanced countries, not from any independent action in backward ones. Colonial peoples were one of the objects of history, the European proletariat its prime subject.

The International might proclaim Marx's and Engels' exhortation 'Proletarians of the world unite', but this did not mean that all proletariats were deemed equal. The equally frequently invoked term 'Russian barbarism' encompassed not just the notion of tsarist despotism but also a more sweeping demonology of the Slavs. This antipathy had its own past in Germany and it was virtually coterminous with the history of the national movement. Tsarist autocracy persisted as the *bête noire* of the German Left from the pre-1848 period until the first world war. Tsarism's counter-revolutionary role in toppling Napoleon and establishing the Holy Alliance, in crushing the Hungarian revolution of 1848 and the Polish insurgents of 1830 and 1863, contributed to shaping an utterly negative Liberal and Social Democratic image of Russian culture as a whole. These fears received a further stimulus by the continual threat of domestic reaction within Germany, of a Kaiser and Junker generals nostalgic for the knout and eager to 'speak Russian' to the Left at home.[52]

Republican France and parliamentary Britain symbolised the future Social Democrats hoped to create. Autocratic Russia enshrined its deepest anxieties about a past which still threatened to return. But the party press, especially in its satirical pages, did not leave the matter there. Russian culture and the Russian people were portrayed in journals like *Der wahre Jacob* not only as brutally oppressed but also as brutish. Lumbering, impoverished, bestial creatures, their feet bound in rags and with thick matted hair shrouding faces unawakened by thought, industry or 'civilisation', adorned the illustrations of the SPD press. Arguably they had a far wider appeal and aroused far stronger and more basic responses than any party analysis of international affairs. Such caricatures also provided a profoundly negative counter-image to the party's own positive picture of orderly and enlightened German culture. 'In the East', Bebel declared to the Reichstag in 1896, 'resides a lack of culture [*Unkultur*] and a piece of barbarism ... True culture finds its home in Central, Southern and Western Europe.'[53]

Quite how Social Democracy's constituents responded to these views or what they themselves believed is uncertain. We know that there were conflicts between Polish and German workers in the Ruhr – and that the local branches of the SPD there remained almost entirely German until

1914.[54] But at an official level the SPD pursued a culturally sensitive assimilationist policy. Jews were welcomed into the party leadership. Until the Reich law on associations forbade it in 1908, the party produced material and held meetings in minority languages. There was no pressure within the party to ape the anti-semitic agitation of the Peasant Leagues; no parallel to the anti-semitic speeches Ben Tillet made to dockers in the East End of London over immigration; nor to the anti-semitism which appeared in sections of the French labour movement during the Dreyfus affair. But until national attitudes are studied more widely in their own right various lines of interpretation remain open, including that ritually denigrating Slavs or colonial peoples as inferior acted as a surrogate for xenophobia much closer to home. One interesting study of Hamburg dockers' pub conversations – as recorded by the secret police from the late 1890s until 1914 – does show that their views of Russia bear an extraordinary similarity to the Russophobic sentiments and arguments propagated by the SPD. In their political discussions the Hamburg clientele also reproduced a range of familiar stereotypes: orderly Germans; hot-blooded Frenchmen; lazy, Catholic and anarchist Italians.[55]

On the basis of such cultural and political hierarchies of nations, it is hard to sustain the impression that the SPD viewed the aspirations and rights of all countries equally. Its leaders made no secret that they feared Russia more than any other European power, and this considerably narrowed the rhetorical ground that separated their benign, humanistic, peaceful patriotism from the marauding, bigoted nationalism of their political opponents. The parties were polarised across the political spectrum but its primary colours were less sharply contrasted than they appeared at first sight.

Foreign policy

Writing about international relations and foreign policy was a specialised affair within Social Democracy. Wilhelmine *Weltpolitik* and the dramatic crises it unleashed ensured that there was no shortage of material to discuss after the turn of the century. Threats of renewed war with France in the 1870s and 1880s had also concentrated socialist minds.[56] But the number of SPD journalists and parliamentarians who felt competent to discuss these issues was small. Those who did immediately entered the party elite. The shortage of able commentators was particularly marked in the 1880s and 1890s. The work fell on the shoulders of a very few; figures like Friedrich Engels, Wilhelm Liebknecht, August Bebel, Karl Kautsky, Franz Mehring, Max Schippel and Rosa Luxemburg. In part, this simply reflected the general lack of educated and skilful publicists in the party.

Most Social Democratic papers did not carry articles on international questions, or if so they often reproduced features from the major mass circulation papers, *Vorwärts*, the *Leipziger Volkszeitung* or the *Sächsische Arbeiterzeitung*. Whether this reluctance to engage in foreign policy discussions reflected editors' views of their readers' interests, or a residual sense of social inferiority – that the domain of secret diplomacy and court protocol was one Social Democrats neither could nor should enter – or a fear that this was political ground on which socialists would always be vulnerable to attack from the nationalist right is difficult to say.

Although Social Democrats produced powerful symbols to stimulate belief in their ideal world – especially through the pageants of May Day and the Congresses of the International – they also prided themselves on being realists. The tensions between these two ambitions run through most of their pronouncements on international relations. Their political and economic analyses of relations between the powers were often incisive and strongly realist. But their measures of assessment expressed their ideals. It is not coincidental that Social Democrats pointed to France and Russia for their comparative metaphors of cultural progress and barbarism and as the key determinants in the Reich's foreign policy. France was the home of the revolution and democracy, Russia of autocracy and reaction.

At the time of the Franco-Prussian war, Bebel and Liebknecht *père* were among the few members of the North German Assembly to maintain their sobriety. They warned in vain that by annexing Alsace and Lorraine Germany would turn France into a hereditary enemy, probably eventually driving it into an alliance with Russia. In any case, they insisted, even in the short term Franco-German antagonism would confer unparalleled influence in European affairs on Russian tsarism. From their more detached vantage point in London, Marx and Engels reached exactly the same conclusions. German policy-makers were preparing an inevitable two-front war for the future.[57] This analysis was startling for its prescience and the tenacity with which the leaders of Social Democracy continued to hold to it. Russian aggrandisement and *revanchisme* in France supplied the lens through which they viewed the kaleidoscope of international affairs.

How these two factors would be valued and assessed was pre-ordained by what Social Democrats thought France and Russia represented. In preparation for their joint celebrations of May Day in 1893, Bebel wrote publicly to the leader of the French Parti Ouvrier, Jules Guesde, affirming that 'The saddest result of that [Franco-Prussian] war was to turn the two most advanced nations of the European continent into deadly enemies.'[58] By annexing Alsace and Lorraine, Bismarck and his successors made themselves morally guilty of preparing the way for a two-front war.[59] 'The Russian empire', on the other hand, as Engels wrote in 1890 for *Die neue*

Zeit, 'constitutes the mainstay, reserve position and reserve army of European reaction, because its mere passive existence is a threat and danger to us'. But Engels thought the threat was far more active than this. Tsarism, he wrote,

limits and upsets our normal development through its constant interference in Western affairs for the purpose of conquering new geographical positions which would secure its domination of Europe and thereby make the victory of the European proletariat impossible.[60]

Both Engels and Bebel historicised their view of Russian expansionism; Alexander III was still pursuing the age-old drive of Peter I and Catherine II towards Constantinople and the Mediterranean.[61] In their reading of history they were only marginally more sympathetic to Russia than Marx had been in his vitriolic and ill-researched 'Revelations of Diplomatic History of the Eighteenth Century'.[62]

When Bebel wrote his most significant article about Germany's foreign policies in 1886, Russia was still formally allied to the Reich. But General Boulanger was at the height of his influence in France, Franco-Russian *rapprochement* was well under way and the newspapers – as well as the correspondence between Bebel and Engels – were full of the prospect of war. Since the Russo-Turkish war of 1877 attention had focused on the Balkans, on tsarist use of Panslavist ideology to champion Balkan independence from the Ottoman Empire, on the burgeoning rivalry between Austria-Hungary and Russia to become the new dominant regional power and on the balancing act Bismarck had played between the two governments at the Congress of Berlin in 1878.[63]

Bebel challenged what he saw as Bismarck's conciliation of Russia. Instead, Bebel prefigured later Wilhelmine policy by advocating that Germany side explicitly with Austria. This, he argued, would serve multiple ends. First, if Russia succeeded in dominating the Balkans the tsarist regime would be so strengthened that it would be able to activate its supposed long-term aim of securing control of the Baltic by over-running Poland and parts of East and West Prussia. In that case, Russia, having already defeated Austria on its own, would ally with France against an isolated Germany. Keeping Russia out of the Balkans was therefore vital in this extraordinarily besieged view of Germany's national security. Secondly, Bebel claimed, the Danube trade was important for the German economy. Bebel even went so far as to argue that the Balkans could provide areas of settlement for Germany's surplus population and better markets for its exports than the colonies it was busy trying to secure in Africa and New Guinea. The correct course of action was then for Germany and Austria together to create an independent federation of [Balkan] states. If Russia were then to declare war, then Germany would oppose it as unanimously as never before. In alliance with Austria and the Balkan states and possibly Turkey, Germany would have the best chances of success in a war against Russia and France, a war which it would otherwise most probably be *forced into under far worse conditions.*[64]

This was a tentative as well as tendentious contribution. Bebel soon dropped the idea of supporting a preventive or preemptive war, but by 1905 it had become an obsession of the General Staff. He did not play with the idea of Balkan colonies again either, especially not after the German Right began to canvass the idea. But he had signalled a general Social Democratic change of heart over the break-up of the Ottoman Empire and Balkan self-determination. Whereas Wilhelm Liebknecht persisted throughout the 1890s in publicising his own – as well as Marx's and Engels' – earlier Turkophile and Slavophobic views, by now even Engels himself was willing to accept the legitimacy of Balkan nationalism.[65] The younger generation around Kautsky and Bernstein pushed hard for this change,[66] and Kautsky in particular remained adamant that all linguistically discrete cultures had claims to nationality.[67] But, in contrast to Kautsky's idealism, Engels continued to insist in the 1890s that national aspirations of Balkan peoples were subject to the constraints of *Realpolitik*, principally containing Russia and preventing world war. When the first Balkan war broke out in 1912, the dominant parties in the Second International hastily reached the same conclusions.[68]

In any case, from the end of the 1880s at the latest, the SPD stopped trying to prescribe an interventionist continental policy for the German Empire. Instead, Engels and Jaurès turned back to the Saint Simonian ideal of a progressive alliance between Britain, France and Germany. 'That', Engels declared in 1891, 'is the true triple alliance.'[69] It was an ideal that liberal socialists like Eduard Bernstein and the editors of the London-based *Nation* kept alive till 1914.[70] In a slightly more realist vein, in 1898 Bebel mourned the missed opportunity of a German–British alliance which might have secured Germany's overseas trade against the threat of a two-front war with France and Russia on the continent.[71] By retreating from the real to the ideal state of international relations, the SPD may well have saved itself from the embarrassment of prescribing a rabidly anti-Russian foreign policy just when ruling circles in Germany were starting to turn towards one.

In its wholly negative evaluation of Russian politics and culture, German Social Democracy found allies in the 'Westernising' wing of the Russian revolutionary movement. The philosopher and 'father of Russian Marxism' Georgi'i Plekhanov fully endorsed the SPD view when he addressed the Zurich Congress of the International on the dangers of war in 1893. Plekhanov was entrusted with justifying the German Social Democrats' fears about a Russian attack. He denounced the radical appeal for a general strike to prevent war demanded by Dutch Social Democrats and French Alamanists, Broussistes and even a section of the Parti Ouvrier.[72] Plekhanov's grounds were exactly the same as those put forward by Wilhelm Liebknecht and Edouard Vaillant in a similar debate in the International two years previously.[73] Even if a general strike could be enforced in Germany and France – which Liebknecht and Vaillant doubted – Plekhanov contended that it certainly could not be in Russia. Without universal enforcement, the result would be an unadulterated disaster: the strike would 'achieve the opposite of what was intended. The [anti-]military strike would disarm the civilised peoples and surrender Western Europe to the Russian cossacks.' For a Russian revolutionary to state this in such a forum inevitably carried greater weight than anything a West European could say.[74] The general strike resolution was defeated and three years later most of its adherents left international Social Democracy to join the anarchists.[75] Even during the Russo-Japanese war of 1904–5, the Geneva-based Bolshevik journal *Vpered* took most of its arguments as to why the defeat of Russia – despite it being the side attacked – was progressive directly from the SPD.[76]

Such perceptions of a Russian threat and cultural backwardness beg the question of what Social Democratic pledges of national defence actually meant. Clearly self-defence was more than just a rhetorical device to head off establishment charges of being anti-patriotic, though no doubt it served that function also. But did Social Democrat leaders possess any general criteria for deciding which situations constituted defence and which an attack? In 1907, Bebel and Kautsky had one of their rare public disputes over precisely this question, Bebel urging his colleague to accept that if he and Wilhelm Liebknecht had been able to assess the war of 1870 correctly at the time, then 'it would be sad if men who have made a virtual profession of politics could not tell whether or not a war was an offensive one.'[77] But he did not say how they would know. After the outbreak of the first world war, exactly how one defined national defence became a fiercely divisive issue, in fact *the* issue around which the most heated polemics between the so-called 'patriotic' and 'internationalist' wings of the labour movement raged.

There is a striking discrepancy between the foci of discussions about national defence before and after 1914. After the outbreak of the war, debate centred on military criteria – who mobilised first or who attacked whom, what Clausewitz would have called tactical and strategic defence. Before 1914 there was far less discussion at all and what there was focused on national rather than military criteria. This was particularly true of

Bebel's favourite example of Social Democratic heroism and sanity, the war of 1870.

Marx and Engels were themselves taken in by Bismarck's falsification of the Ems despatch, much as the SPD leadership would itself be hoodwinked by Bethmann Hollweg's diplomacy in 1914. But in any case Marx and Engels left each other in no doubt that the Franco-Prussian war was 'defensive' simply because they believed it to be a war for Germany's 'national existence'.[78] Bebel and Liebknecht also did not know that the Ems despatch was a fabrication but opposed the war all the same, because, as Bebel put it, what was at stake was the entire Bismarckian policy of the previous period, not – again – the fact that Prussia was the side formally attacked.[79] Bebel's and Liebknecht's particularist hostility to a Prussian dominated 'little Germany' and Marx's and Engels' realist willingness to accept this solution to the national question made such divergent reactions to the war logical extensions of pre-existing policy differences. And although Engels was probably the only socialist leader who had studied Clausewitz seriously, everyone knew his dictum that war was an extension of policy by other means.

In the 1880s and 1890s, Social Democratic foreign policy was essentially conservative and absorbed with containing Russia. Virtually every one of Bebel's numerous assertions that he was personally ready to shoulder a rifle and defend German land contained the clause 'if we are attacked by Russia'. His underlying fears about autocratic aggrandisement and cultural barbarism give this qualifying clause enormous force. As we shall see in chapter 6, the SPD Left only rose to challenge Bebel's assumptions when Russia seemed irretrievably weakened by military defeat and the 1905 revolution.

One way of testing the fit between the putative Russian danger and SPD pledges of national defence is to examine what socialist leaders thought might cause war. The various resolutions passed by the congresses of the Second International about the danger of war all outlined its potential causes. These fall into four categories: dynastic ambitions; the arms race; imperialist rivalries; domestic politics.[80] Of these dynastic ambitions clearly played a major role in the SPD policy of containing Russia. It is not clear how far the other three issues carried over into foreign policy. Bebel predicted that one or other power might launch a preventive war when it could no longer keep up with the arms race.[81] But he reacted to the naval race between Britain and Germany by privately encouraging the British government to accelerate the tempo and force Germany to give up Admiral Tirpitz's dream of *Weltpolitik*. At least in this case he clearly did not fear that the arms race would lead to war.[82] On imperialism, the SPD developed a whole literature to support the contention that capitalist development led to war.[83] And from the time of Napoleon III and Bismarck, French and German socialists were familiar with the idea that anti-democratic regimes waged wars in order to divert their populations from domestic opposition. By the 1890s and 1900s this theory about 'Bonapartist' wars had been put to work to explain the new development of *Weltpolitik* and 'social imperialism'. There is little doubt that these different lines of reasoning were perfectly good ways of thinking about the danger of war. Each of them has provided historians with lines of interpretation about the causes of the first world war.[84]

But the question at stake here is how far they translated into operative political concepts. As more than one historian has pointed out, the concept of imperialism tended to lead to a fatalistic attitude.[85] If war stemmed from rivalry between the great powers, and that rivalry was caused by competition for colonial markets, and the acquisition of new markets was a functional requirement of capitalist development, then it followed that war could not be prevented. It could only be ended when capitalism itself gave way to socialism. This sort of systemic opposition encouraged the view that Social Democrats ought not to have a foreign policy at all.[86] They should simply go on organising the masses, pressing for social reform, and remain true to their unyielding opposition. It was also the line of reasoning most repeated by the Marxist Left before 1914 and during the war. The theory of social imperialism fitted this political strategy even more directly. It neatly assumed a constant primacy of domestic over foreign policy. As such it was only apparent in the SPD's rejection of the naval race and imperialism, not in its assessment of that sphere of foreign policy which it took seriously, great power conflict on the European continent itself.

The idea that a deteriorating position in the arms race could lead to war is a view that went straight back to Kant. Like the dynastic argument, it was also one put forward by the Peace Society. But their conclusion, that the great powers ought to disarm, was one German Social Democrats rejected as utterly implausible in the 1890s. In 1893, Engels recommended disarmament as a propaganda measure, only to be curtly rebuffed by August Bebel.[87] When the first Hague Conference met in 1898 at the instigation of tsar Nicholas II, Kautsky scornfully dismissed disarmament as utopian. He scoffed at the prospect of the sort of multilateral agreement necessary between powers which were irreconcilable colonial rivals. He also pointed out that in any event such governments would still require small standing armies to police and repress their own populations.[88] The sub-text of these brusque dismissals of disarmament in the 1890s may well have been anxieties about appearing sufficiently realistic. It is interesting that when the SPD did take up the pacifist cause from 1911 on, both Bebel and Kautsky became its leading exponents.[89]

By default only one of the four causes of war to which Social Democrats alluded in the 1890s actually operated in their European foreign policy. This one, dynastic ambition, they tied closely to their prediction of Russian aggrandisement and prescription of national defence. As we shall see, in the new century the SPD could reject German *Weltpolitik* and the naval race unconditionally without in the least compromising the party's traditional undertaking to continental security.

War scares and socialist internationalism

Whereas Conservatives like Treitschke or even imperialist Left Liberals such as Weber insisted that war and conquest were natural, politically necessary and – in Treitschke's language – ennobling, Social Democrats turned increasingly towards a pacifist humanism.[90] For them the great age of wars of national liberation was decidedly past. War, they predicted direly, would involve anything from eight to twenty million soldiers, who would face the murderous onslaught of new technology, rifled cannon, machine guns and battleships. Behind the lines, society and economy would be dislocated and thrown into crisis, precipitating mass unemployment and famine at home.[91] Bebel believed from the late 1880s on that the old states and their statecraft could not survive such a conflict.[92] He remained remarkably steadfast in this conviction right up to his death in 1913.[93] This was not the only prophecy available, however. Writing to Paul Lafargue at the height of the Boulanger crisis in 1889, Engels suspected war might lead to

a severe and general suppression of our movement, a strengthening of chauvinism in all countries and finally a weakening, a period of reaction ten times worse than after 1815, as a consequence of the exhaustion of the people bled white [by the war] – and all this against the slender chance that a revolution comes out of this awful war – this horrifies me. Especially because of our movement in Germany, which would be repressed, smashed and forcibly annihilated, whereas peace brings us virtually certain victory.[94]

Against such a background, the early congresses of the Second International quickly agreed to transform the celebration of May Day from a demonstration in favour of the eight-hour day to a worldwide peace rally. Commemorating the twentieth anniversary of the Paris Commune, Wilhelm Liebknecht dubbed the International 'the Peace League of the International proletariat'.[95] To these general pacifist sentiments socialists could bring their own unique organisational skills. The hundreds of thousands of Germans and Frenchmen, not to mention the Belgians, Italians, Austrians, British, Spaniards, Dutch and Poles who turned out for May Day provided a tangible symbol of a wider European identity.[96] The full potential of this political symbol of supra-national co-operation between the 'cultured nations' of Western and Central Europe was only explored in the last few years before the outbreak of the first world war.[97] But already in the 1890s the International projected itself as an image of how European politics could be if Germany and France had socialist instead of militaristic governments. The International *qua* Peace League provided that sense of higher purpose and moral superiority which gave socialists in Germany and France the confidence to vote against military spending and face the propaganda onslaught of their opponents at home. It was the venue where the projected 'triple alliance' of Britain, France and Germany could be tried out.

The contradiction between such grandiloquent anti-war sentiments and asserting the duty of self-defence was not long in coming to the surface. As soon as the Franco-Russian alliance was concluded in 1890, the French right-wing press seized upon SPD statements in favour of national defence as a fresh stick with which to beat the French Left. To leave the matter in no doubt, Engels wrote a long article in the Almanach of the Parti Ouvrier justifying German socialists' right to shoot their French comrades in the event of a Franco-Russian attack on Germany.[98] The ensuing acrimony was like a foretaste of the accusations that flew about after August 1914. It certainly did nothing to increase the impressiveness of the new symbols of international solidarity. Faced with repeated controversies over when exactly May Day should be celebrated, the spectacle of so-called 'anarchists' storming the platform at congresses, and especially repeated debates about the labour movement's inability to prevent war, Bebel was not the only socialist leader to wonder whether, far from adding to the prestige of 'the international working class', International Congresses might only taint its reputation further.[99] There were two solutions to this problem. Both were tried. The first was to throw the disruptive radicals out, and contain the fall-out of future fractiousness by restricting real debate to closed committee sessions.[100] The second step was to draw a sharp line between foreign policy matters and socialist internationalism. Foreign policy – in which operational ideas were hammered out – was preserved as a domain for domestic party discussion. Socialist internationalism provided the rhetorical backdrop for marshalling a movement which believed it would inherit the earth. This demarcation worked quite well until the rise of the nationalist Right and the second Moroccan crisis of 1911 forced the French and German parties to think again and to co-operate far more actively.

As one perceptive French socialist and Oxford don observed about the anti-war debate of the early 1890s,

Either we are strong enough to prevent war from whatever quarter, and so we don't have to consider the question of marching to the frontier. Or we are not (which is highly likely); so, it's not urgent that we reveal our weakness. In that case: 'Mum's the word' in my opinion.[101]

War had become a political liability. The SPD had far more to expect from the fear of war than the actual prospect of one. The Second International acted as an attractive symbol of how the world could be.[102] But the leaders of both French and German socialism were, for the time being, dead set against conceding any supra-national executive powers to the organisation, or agreeing on any anti-militarist measures other than their current domestic practice of voting against the budget.[103] As far as the hard work of building up a mass following and assembling an attractive as well as credible policy were concerned, the leaders of German Social Democracy perhaps rather wisely concentrated on the domestic issues of finance, the high cost of living, barbarous conditions of military service, the danger of military intervention against the labour movement and the undemocratic state.

The tensions between a universal internationalism and a distinct hierarchy of nations necessitated a greater distance from the prospect of an actual war. It was safer to denounce war as an inevitable evil of capitalism, and leave it as a visceral motive for joining the socialist movement. Gruesome descriptions of what war would be like were political weapons. They stirred the most elemental fears. They played on the idea that the international socialist movement was the only peace movement.

Conclusion

The SPD's anti-militarist programme was comprehensive rather than coherent. It consisted of a series of dialectical oppositions, rather than a symphonic structure: in place of standing armies, militias; against regressive indirect taxation, progressive direct taxation; instead of the arms race, social spending; in place of the horror of war, international socialism; instead of colonial rivalry, free trade; and against the threat of Russian barbarism, national defence. These polarities match the facets of Social Democracy's position within Wilhelmine civil society. The fact that its programme endured so long owes more to the SPD's stable position within the Wilhelmine party system – enormously popular, isolated and excluded from power – than it does to the programme's own logical consistency or inherent cogency. This did not augur well for the future. When conditions changed, how long could the old programme be sustained?

Two examples from the period 1912–14 suggest the sorts of unforeseen

5 'Spring flowers', from *Simplicissimus*, 1897

challenges to SPD military policy which would arise. On the domestic front, the SPD had taken from Radical militia enthusiasts the idea that gymnastic training would help to eradicate the difference between soldier and civilian. In the 1890s and 1900s, Social Democratic gymnastics associations flourished and grew very rapidly. But from 1899 on, revisionists like Max Schippel and Eduard David warned that such policies might lead to the militarisation of German society rather than the civilianisation of the German army.[104] In 1911, the Young Germany League was founded in case the normal regimentation and patriotic drills provided at school proved insufficient. By 1913–14, the Prussian War Minister was promoting the scheme of full-scale military exercises from the age of fourteen as a way of winning adolescent loyalties.[105] The SPD had no choice but to jettison its old enthusiasm and come out vigorously against this type of regimentation of German youth.[106]

The second example concerns the navy and *Weltpolitik*. Initially, the SPD had no difficulty rejecting Tirpitz's drive for a big navy and a colonial empire. As we have seen, the party rejected imperialism entirely. Moreover its admiration for British civilisation, democracy and tolerance – which many of the party's leaders had enjoyed as political refugees – led the party to construe Britain as a champion of free trade, oblivious to the fact that it possessed the largest protected colonial markets in the world.[107] So, the SPD found no problem in reiterating its existing policy that the Reich should limit its military policy to territorial self-defence. Social Democratic publications rather smugly quoted the elder Moltke to the effect that Germany could not afford to be both a land and a maritime power and that its destiny lay on the European continent.[108] As with Social Democracy's views of Russian culture, so too its commitment to continental policy was to come home to roost once the naval bubble burst and great power conflict returned to the European arena in 1912. At this point the government returned to its strategic concerns of the 1890s in a deteriorating situation. The General Staff remained engrossed with the problem of a two-front war, and the government with the risk of being overtaken by Russia in the arms race, of whether or not to launch a pre-emptive strike.[109] In this much altered situation the SPD would find that its traditional anti-militarist policies left it dangerously exposed.

3   Karl Kautsky's theory of militarism

At the beginning of the 1890s, Karl Kautsky was at the height of his political influence and intellectual powers. He combined both of these qualities to a rare degree, acting as the intellectual mentor to a generation which included Arturo Labriola, Filippo Turati, Vladimir Ilyich Lenin, Rudolf Hilferding, Rosa Luxemburg and Leon Trotsky. He helped to draft programmes, policy documents and congress resolutions across the continent.

The son of an artist father and an actress and novelist mother, Kautsky came in touch with socialists whilst a student in Vienna in the late 1870s. In 1879 he travelled to Zurich to meet the newly exiled German Social Democratic journalists who worked on Karl Höchberg's newspaper *Der Sozialdemokrat*. There he was greatly impressed by Eduard Bernstein, who became a close collaborator and friend. After meeting Marx and Engels in London in 1881, Kautsky set about establishing his own theoretical journal, which he launched two years later under the title *Die neue Zeit* (the new age). During the second half of the 1880s, he as well as Bernstein lived in London, remaining in constant touch with Engels. Plekhanov, Bebel and the leader of Austrian Social Democracy, Victor Adler, were among their regular visitors and correspondents. It was left largely to Kautsky and Bernstein to draft the new party programme which celebrated Social Democracy's triumphant return to political legality and its formal adoption of Marxism in 1891 at its congress at Erfurt. The Erfurt programme became the model for other Social Democratic Marxist parties in France, Austria, Russia and Italy, not to mention the nascent movements in South Eastern Europe. Kautsky's status as the 'pope' of Marxism, as his Italian comrades humorously and affectionately dubbed him, became consonant with the influence of the SPD as the model party of the Second International.[1]

Kautsky's most famous writings deal with the long-range teleological claims of the Marxist theory of history, the inevitabilities of capitalist crisis and socialist revolution. He wrote prolifically on economics, contemporary politics, early Christianity and evolution, but confessed even as a very experienced politician that he trusted his own judgement least when deciding on immediate questions of political tactics. Not altogether surprisingly, intellectual historians who have studied Kautsky's work have dwelt almost exclusively on his theory of historical change and revolution. In the early 1920s Georg Lukacs and Karl Korsch criticised the positivistic and economically reductionist bases of 'orthodox' Marxism and not entirely correctly ascribed a neglect of political voluntarism to Kautsky. In the late 1960s this attack was revived, especially within the New Left; Kautsky was studied afresh and his reliance on evolutionary Darwinian ideas to map out what one historian aptly referred to as his 'guarantees of history' became a reference point for all that was wrong with orthodox Marxism.[2]

For Kautsky himself, however, the Marxist theory of economic development was only part – if the most important part – of a wider critique of contemporary states and society. He was well aware of historical differences between countries' social and political development. Since the positive demands of the Social Democratic programme were supposed to be predicated upon a critique of present reality rather than merely the desirability of a future utopia, Kautsky could hardly afford to ignore the political structures of Wilhelmine Germany. Almost exclusive focus on his economic and teleological writings has tended to obscure his theoretical treatment of immediate and central political issues. That the SPD's leaders wanted to have such a theoretical imprimatur set on its policies testifies amply to the party's enlightenment values. If they had learned anything from Engels' popularisations of Marxism, it was to pride themselves with starting out with a rational critique of reality. Militarism was not the least item on this agenda. As the previous two chapters indicate, Social Democrats projected a great deal of their sense of identity and moral mission through their preservation and perpetuation of the enlightenment at a time when *völkisch*, racist and generally anti-enlightenment ideas were on the ascendant in Germany.

It has often been assumed that, however badly its proselytisers understood Marx's message, it was more or less inevitable that the socialist movement would turn towards Marxism for its theoretical inspiration. Those who have questioned this assumption have drawn attention to the political conjuncture which helped Marxism to succeed. First, in contrast to the anarchists, Marx and Engels promoted the idea that organised working-class parties were needed, capable of using whatever parliamentary or civic space was permitted to good agitational effect.[3] Secondly and paradoxically, the exclusion of Social Democracy from the state in Bismarckian and Wilhelmine Germany, its persecution by the regime and the social boycott imposed on it by the professional bodies of 'bourgeois

6 Freedom of expression, from *Simplicissimus*, 1907

society' insured that participation in electoral politics could not go beyond agitation.[4] Both of these arguments are ones I find convincing. But why did this well-defined political movement of opposition turn to Marxism? Are we left with a series of historical coincidences; that Engels attacked the ideas of Eugen Dühring before they had too firm a hold in the late 1870s; or that Bebel, Bernstein and Kautsky all made their way to the 'Mecca of socialism' and excellent wine cellar in Regent's Park Road in the 1880s? These may in fact turn out to be the best reasons we have. But it is also striking how few potential intellectual competitors there were in Germany during the 1890s.

The intellectual climate which Kautsky helped to shape in the 1890s was very different from the one in which he grew up. Its hallmarks were aggressive nationalist values and intellectual intolerance.[5] In the 1870s Social Democratic intellectuals had still formed part of the intelligentsia. They were open to the ideas of Rodbertus and Dühring and academic social reformers, the *Kathedersozialisten*, were willing to enter a dialogue with Lassalleanism. This greater freedom of intellectual exchange helps to explain why socialists were themselves so much more eclectic in the 1870s than they would be a decade later. What changed in the interim was the level not of eclecticism but of tolerance.

Students in Berlin during the late 1880s and 1890s, like the future editors of the *Jahrbuch für Sozialpolitik* Max Weber and Werner Sombart or the historian Otto Hintze, found that their most formative experience was attending the nationalist, anti-socialist and romantic lectures of Heinrich von Treitschke. His glorification of war and Prussian statecraft are still well known. Although all of them reacted against Treitschke's teaching to varying degrees (Weber most of all), neither Weber nor Sombart produced their great economic and sociological works until after the turn of the century. Tönnies, the other great establishment intellect of the day, contributed to the rise of anti-modern *völkisch* ideas through his idealisation of the organic medieval community [*Gemeinschaft*]. Contrasting it with the overly individualistic society, or *Gesellschaft*, of capitalist modernity he offered intellectual respectability to the claims of the *Mittelstand*. No one knew yet how to respond to Nietzsche. Some of the radical young intellectuals in the SPD tried to use his ideas to push the party on to a more confrontational course with the government in the early 1890s.[6] But the philosopher's own rejection of the German Empire placed him in the same uneasy position as Richard Wagner. The 'will to power' would only be absorbed into the mainstream of German nationalism around 1910.[7]

Almost by default Karl Kautsky had few challenges to his intellectual ascendancy at the turn of the 1890s. Compared with the other traditions on offer, what he had distilled from the thoughts and writings of Marx and Engels was far more sympathetic to the political ambitions of Social Democracy. If the Social Democratic experience can be generalised, it would suggest that the academic intolerance, political impotence and social boycott to which the organisation was exposed proved highly conducive to formulating systemic theories and political programmes.

Marx, Engels and the Left Liberal tradition

Marx and Engels picked up the idea of militarism in their journalism of the 1860s. They used it casually as a current term to refer to massive increases in armaments and expansion in the scale of conscription then under way in France, Austria and Prussia. At the time they did not trouble further with the issue, and it was only in the late 1870s that Engels wrote about militarism again. His remarks about militarism in the *Anti-Dühring* once more align the term with international rivalry, the arms race and the ever-expanding size of armies. But his real interest now lay in the relation between this transformation of military organisation and class struggles.

In particular, Engels had become convinced that the development of military technology and the rebuilding of European capitals along straight boulevards down which artillery could be easily trained rendered old-style barricades and insurrections out of date. In his search for an alternative, which would return the advantage to the side of the revolutionaries, he hit on the idea of the vanishing army. This thesis correlated the increasingly universal character of military conscription with the increasingly pro-letarian demography of the nation. In Engels' scenario a successful seizure of state power depended upon the disaffection of the army. The morale of the soldiers was in turn determined by the spread of class consciousness among young urban and rural workers.[8] Ever keen on dialectical ironies, he prophesied:

Competition among the individual states forces them, on the one hand, to spend more money each year on the army and navy, artillery, etc., thus increasingly hastening their financial collapse, and, on the other, to resort to universal compulsory military service more and more seriously, thus in the long run making the whole people familiar with the use of arms, and therefore enabling them at a certain point to make their will prevail against the top military command in all its glory. This point will be reached as soon as the mass of the people *has* a will. At this point the armies of the princes become transformed into armies of the people; the machine refuses to work, and militarism collapses by the dialectic of its own development.[9]

Behind this preoccupation with the military constraints on revolutionary politics the reappraisal of the state which Marx and Engels had begun in the 1850s is quite perceptible. In his diagnosis of the *Eighteenth Brumaire of Louis Bonaparte*, Marx had taken stock for the first time of state-building, of the rise of bureaucratic and military institutions. Although Marx in particular was reluctant to give the modern state the credit for its new-found domination over civil society – preferring to seek his explanation in the political division and 'cowardice' of the bourgeoisie – both men began to regard this new 'Bonapartist' state as characteristic of contemporary European capitalism.[10] At first hesitantly, after Prussia defeated Austria in the seven weeks' war, and then with greater assurance, after the Franco-Prussian war and the founding of the German Empire, Engels deployed the Bonapartist model in Germany. Acutely aware of the fact that Germany had not lived through a victorious bourgeois revolution and of the lines of continuity running back to the absolutist and feudal past, Engels depicted Bismarckian 'Bonapartism' as resting on a class compromise between the bourgeoisie and the Junker landlords, rather than the bourgeoisie and the peasants as in the French original. But their common enemy, the allegedly socialist proletariat, remained the same throughout.[11]

These theses have proved to be enormously influential on both Marxist and Liberal historiography of the German Empire.[12] They were also politically influential at the time. The thesis of the automatic 'reddening' of the army proved very popular with the Social Democratic leadership. The Bonapartist model of the Reich came to be accepted by both Left Liberal critics and Social Democrats. But what is not automatically obvious is the role of the military, or militarism, within it. Some historians have suggested that Bonapartism and militarism were interchangeable concepts for Marx and Engels.[13] There seem, however, to be both textual and logical reasons why this could not be the case.

In their texts the two men never defined militarism, did not have recourse to the idea often and did not use it to describe anything more than expanding armies and armament. In other words, they used the term in a more limited fashion than a potential synonym such as army. In the subsequent literature, militarism is associated with a far wider range of political and social behaviour. Logically, it is hard to see quite how Marx and Engels could have developed the idea of militarism into a theory. They had already stressed the centrality of military force by defining state power as consisting 'essentially of bodies of armed men'.[14] This definition did not leave a great deal of room for relativistic distinctions between consensual and coercive sides of the state.

What the Bonapartist model showed to be variable was the relation between state and civil society. But Marx's and Engels' inversion of Hegelian statism was such that they were reluctant to ascribe much independent initiative to the state in any renegotiation of this relationship. To their way of thinking military force alone could not explain an increase in state power.[15] Greater weight would always be given to conflicts within the socially dominant classes which prevented them from establishing direct control over the government. This way of thinking about politics left open the possibility that the army might perform some ideological role of integrating the bourgeoisie into a Bonapartist state. Marx hinted at this in the *Eighteenth Brumaire*, when he wrote contemptuously of all classes in French society bowing before the rifle butt.[16] But the full potential of this idea had to wait until 1910, when Hilferding wrote about the ideology of the imperialist state in his *Finance Capital*.[17]

In the form in which Marx and Engels wrote about it 'militarism' remained a rather vague if critically endowed term to describe armed force as an extension of state policy. In this respect, Marx and Engels had not advanced on Clausewitz. All they had done was to suggest that the military depended on social and financial conditions which could be disrupted. No oppositionist to the Wilhelmine state could afford to leave the matter there.

Open theoretical discussion began in 1893, triggered by the Reichstag's rejection of Caprivi's military bill and the general election which followed. As we saw earlier, only two parties – the South German People's Party and the SPD – made this an issue of political principle in the new freer conditions which obtained after the lapse of the anti-socialist laws. The most eloquent and theoretically inclined spokesman of the South German People's Party was the historian and pacifist, Ludwig Quidde. Like many Southern Liberals he was anti-Prussian and believed in a greater Germany, even though in his case these values had been inculcated during a childhood spent in Bremen.[18] His emphasis on the debilitating psychological effects of militaristic ideas which he claimed had thoroughly permeated civil society was both new and characteristic of the man. Like Weber and a scattering of principled Left Liberal democrats, Quidde particularly criticised the apeing of aristocratic norms by the duelling student fraternities and the bourgeois reserve officers. This 'corruption', in Quidde's phrase, or 'feudalisation of the bourgeoisie', as Weber and after him a whole school of German historians called it, appeared to them as retrograde and archaic.[19] Pointing also to the burgeoning social enthusiasm for veterans' associations [*Kriegervereine*], Quidde suggested that

The most dangerous aspect of its [militarism's] penetration of bourgeois society and of the national mentality [*Volksgeist*] lies in the fact that, together with a national bias, there is widespread acceptance of a specifically militaristic attitude towards war and its justification as well as its role in the development of culture.[20]

In this Treitschkean Germany, he sadly recorded the already isolated position of the republican wing of Left Liberalism, remarking that because of the impact of militarist thinking among the bourgeoisie 'only the fourth estate remains the unbroken champion of all those who value freedom'.[21] Committed to a democratic and neo-Kantian view of politics, Quidde consistently contended that a democratic polity could only be founded upon democratic values.[22] Already in 1893, he recognised the ideological obstacle militaristic beliefs placed in the way of any democratic movement.

On the whole Quidde and Kautsky were happily in agreement as to what constituted the key elements of militarism, the system of military discipline, its extension to the state and civil society and the military sector of the economy.[23] There was nothing particularly new in any of this, and most of Quidde's pamphlet runs very much in a line of continuity with the Liberal tradition of the 1860s. Quidde's contribution was so noteworthy precisely because he was so isolated. It earned him a high reputation in the South German People's Party, whose Württemberg leaders like Conrad Hauss-mann and Friedrich Payer shared his and the SPD's criticism of the officer's corps and maltreatment in the army. But when Quidde went further and satirised the emperor as a modern Caligula, he was made to pay the price. His fellow-historians immediately boycotted him personally and professionally without let-up. In 1896 he was sentenced to a three-month prison term for *lèse-majesté*. Even within the People's Party he would never make it into the leadership or the Reichstag. He became one of those on the isolated left wing after the party merged with the two North German Left Liberal groups to form the Progressive People's Party in 1910. An increasingly energetic member of the small and highly-educated German Peace Society, Quidde remained suspect even within its ranks as a radical democrat, despite the fact that after his spell in prison he abstained from commenting on domestic militarism.[24]

Kautsky on the army and state

Marx and Engels had approached 'militarism' from the realist perspective of great power conflict and the arms race. Quidde had dwelt on the rigours of Prussianism. Karl Kautsky transformed Social Democratic perceptions by setting these same images in the context of capitalist development. Only the Jesuit Pachtler had seriously suggested before that militarism was consonant with capitalism. And he had done so in a backward-looking way, with neither a theory of the trends and dynamic of capitalist development, nor a future utopia in which industry had any place.[25] Kautsky and Bebel popularised Marx's and Engels' view of the Reich as a particular kind of 'Bonapartist' state in which Junkers and big bourgeois allied against the proletariat. Like Engels also, they expected that such an un- and indeed anti-democratic regime would first have to give way to a democratic republic before socialist revolution could be put on the agenda.[26] The struggle against militarism for these writers was as much a struggle for democracy as for socialism. This linking and bridging of the struggle for democracy and socialism is to be found from the very origins of Social Democracy in the radical democratic associations of the 1860s through to the turn of the century. The generation Kautsky trained would take his identification of the state with capitalist development so much to heart that writers like Heinrich Cunow and Rosa Luxemburg would often depict the state in far cruder instrumentalist terms.[27] Compared with them Kautsky *was* statist in his socialism, but also deeply democratic in his concept of the state.

Slightly transposing the *Communist Manifesto*, Kautsky declared that 'the state took on its modern form, that is, became the state of office-holders and soldiers, the tool of the capitalist class'.[28] This statement elides two questions. In what way was the state the tool of the capitalist class? Just how important were the 'soldiers' and the 'office-holders' to Kautsky's theory of the state? Kautsky's thinking proceeded along two separate levels. The first involved generalising about the modern capitalist state *per se*; the second analysing German militarism. One cannot understand the second without the first.

In his generalisations about the state, Kautsky proceeded to link state intervention in the economy with a concept of the state that left it partly independent of the bourgeoisie. His first treated the issue systematically in his long commentary on the Erfurt Programme, his 1892 classic *The Class Struggle*. Free-trading 'Manchesterism' was on the retreat and the advocates of colonialism and protection very much on the offensive. This showed in his account. He stated that even in its infancy this instrumentalist state

could not ... fulfil its mission and satisfy the needs of the pre-capitalist class without either dissolving, or depriving of their independence, those economic institutions which lay at the foundation of the pre-capitalist social system, and taking upon itself their functions ... For instance, the necessity of taking over the whole system of charitable and educational institutions has become so pressing upon the state that it has in most cases surrendered to this necessity.[29]

At the height of their power, he wrote, capitalists were nonetheless most hostile to the interference of the state in their economic activities. Whatever the wishes of the bourgeois, however, 'economic and political development urged the necessity of the extension of the functions of the state'[30] and thereby brought an end to 'Manchesterism'.

Such an extension of state functions occurs, Kautsky continued, not only because 'those that the state assumed from the start become larger, but [because] new ones are born of the capitalist system itself, of which the former generations had no conception and which affect ultimately the whole economic system'. As examples of this process, Kautsky noted that whereas statesmen had previously been concerned essentially with dip-lomacy and law, 'today ... statesmen concern themselves ... [with] finance, colonial affairs, tariff protection and workers' insurance'. He added that the state was forced, partly from its own financial needs, to become directly involved in economic ventures, through 'all manner of state monopolies.' Even 'nationalisation of certain industries' could take place without in the least threatening the survival of capitalism as a whole; on the contrary,

As an exploiter of private labour, the state is superior to any private capitalist. Besides the economic power of the capitalists, it can bring to bear upon the exploited classes the political power which it already wields.[31]

The strategic requirements of the 'military system' also played their part here, leading to the construction of 'arsenals and wharves' and, in conjunction with the needs of commerce, post-offices, railways and the telegraph.[32] There can be no question but that European states, especially the new Germany, were reconstructed in the second half of the nineteenth century in ways that fit Kautsky's details, even if the political motives involved were different and more complex than he allowed.

Kautsky did not argue, however, that the state was simply seizing the initiative. Rather, the increasing centralisation of capital and social division of labour meant that 'separate capitalist undertakings become ... more interdependent upon one another. Along with this grows the dependence of the capitalist class upon the greatest of all their establishments, the state ... '[33] This is clearly a very functionalist view of politics in which the state services the needs of capitalist development. Just how exactly the political agents realised what these needs were is a matter which Kautsky conveniently left veiled in mystery.

What we have then is functional Marxism before functionalism had been theoretically formalised; just as we have a bourgeoisie which is too supine to do more than let the 'soldiers' and 'office-holders' carry out its programme. Kautsky felt justified in concluding that the bourgeoisie was driven to appeal to the state to save it from economic crises with increasing frequency. Thus,

The economic omnipotence of the state, which appeared to the Manchester School as a socialist Utopia, has developed under the very eyes of that school into an inevitable result of the capitalist system of production itself.[34]

In this triumphant conclusion, it is clear that Kautsky here foreshadowed Hilferding's theory of the imperialist state and Bukharin's wartime writing on the imperialist state as the 'New Leviathan'.[35] Moreover, Kautsky was pushing his ideas further along the lines Engels had sketched in the *Anti-Dühring* about the way in which capitalist society, and in this case the state itself, unwittingly prepared all the tools to be put to use in creating socialism.[36]

Having arrived at the point at which the bourgeoisie becomes functionally as well as politically dependent on the state, the stage is set for Kautsky
to explain the general role he ascribed to 'militarism'. Thus far Kautsky
remained remarkably consistent in his theory from the 1880s until the first
world war. It is here, however, that several marked shifts occur in
Kautsky's political argument. The shift occurs at the level of his economic
thought, serving to underline again that his version of Marxism considers
politics very much as a 'superstructure' responding to the dynamism of the
economic 'base'.

In *The Class Struggle*, Kautsky regarded state intervention as the chief
means of alleviating economic crisis. The rationale for this point of view
was provided by his theory of economic crises. As an under-consumptionist, he thought that the main cause of capitalist crisis and ultimately
economic breakdown of the system was a short-fall in demand. Workers
lacked the purchasing power and capitalists sufficiently monstrous
appetites to consume all the commodities being produced. The problem
was, then, to find 'third markets' for the surplus produced. At first,
influenced no doubt by the 'scramble for Africa' and the incursions into
China by the great powers, Kautsky viewed colonialism as the principal
means of staving off capitalist collapse. He even wondered whether new
markets could be found as quickly as relative over-production at home was
increasing.[37] In this scenario, 'militarism' meant the role of military
competition between the great powers in their rivalry for colonies. 'This
situation', he wrote,

is the most powerful cause of the militarism which has turned Europe into a
military camp. There are only two ways out of this intolerable state of things: either
a gigantic war that shall destroy some of the existing European states, or the union
of them all in a federation.[38]

Until now, militarism had appeared only as a minor villain in the sub-plot.
Political and theoretical events conspired to change Kautsky's mind.
Politically, right-wing movements in Germany proselytising populist and
very expansionist forms of nationalism continued to mushroom after the
turn of the century. This became all too evident after the SPD's setback in
the 1907 polls. Kautsky immediately reassessed the role he ascribed to
military expenditure. He now claimed that it served not just as a means to
securing colonial markets but as a safety-valve to syphon off over-
production in its own right.[39] This idea entailed another shift in Kautsky's
economic thought. It meant thinking about the extension of the market as
an intensive process that could occur within the bounds of the domestic
economy as well as in the geographically extensive way colonialism had
appeared to promise. This theoretical shift matched the SPD's response to

Wilhelmine imperialism. The party had concentrated on the fact that colonies, far from being necessary for Germany's development – as even Kautsky's 1891 critique had unquestioningly assumed – were actually a net drain on the national economy.[40]

Far more striking was the reorientation which Kautsky underwent in the period just before the outbreak of the first world war. Fundamental to his change of political position was his acceptance that his earlier under-consumptionist economic theories were deeply flawed. The Austro-Marxists Otto Bauer and Rudolf Hilferding introduced German Marxists to Michael Tugan Baranowsky's refutation of under-consumptionism as the 'law' explaining capitalist crisis. The essence of the case was that the surplus product which neither workers nor capitalists could consume could simply be reinvested.[41] Kautsky's discovery that under-consumptionism was a logically flawed explanation of capitalist crisis in turn undermined the theories he had constructed on its basis. Imperialism could not be understood any longer as the frantic search for 'third markets'. Nor could spending on armaments any longer be depicted as a functionally necessary way of disposing of the surplus product.

Yet the problem could not be ignored. In 1910–14, spending on arms was increasing. The 1911 Moroccan Crisis and the Balkan War of 1912 brought the great powers to the brink of war. Deprived of what he had earlier thought to be such firm economic foundations, Kautsky began to consider the issue politically. Militarism appeared now to him as a political choice, a policy which the German ruling classes had chosen; but which given the right coalition of political opponents could be discarded, as urgent political issues, armaments, colonies and their attendant conflicts could all be reversed without having to await the demise of capitalism. This was the thinking that led Kautsky on the eve of the first world war to argue that 'progressive' elements of capital – those committed to free trade – had every reason to unite with the working class in opposing militarist policies. The wider theoretical issues and political policy involved in these shifts in SPD thinking are discussed in the last two chapters of this book.

Arms expenditure reappeared in Kautsky's picture, no longer as a buffer against crises but as an incubus, swallowing up much productive capacity in its role of protector of the capitalist system. It now had clearly been transformed into one of those 'fetters' to the further development of the 'productive forces' which, according Marx's 1859 'Preface' to *A Contribution to a Critique of Political Economy* and Kautsky's understanding of historical materialism, must result in the destruction of the capitalist mode of production.[42] This was good rhetoric but unsatisfactory theory. For Kautsky had just dismissed his fundamental starting point, the idea that arms expenditure was rooted in the capitalist system.

Kautsky had not given a clear definition of militarism. Rather, 'militarism' is invoked to refer to a number of different things, the army, spending on armaments, aggressively expansionist foreign policies, advocacy of using military force in domestic or international politics. These kaleidoscopic images faithfully reflect the changing priorities of anti-militarist politics in Germany.

Kautsky on German militarism

Bebel once remarked that the army provided the 'ground ... on which the absolutist, military, feudally-organised state power could unite and co-operate with the modern bourgeoisie'.[43] This succinct comment expressed much social democratic thinking and writing about the army and, by extension, militarism. The same perceptions were expounded by Kautsky at rather greater length and in such a way that they read like a classic account of the 'Bonapartist' state in a German context.

Kautsky regarded the Prussian army as the epitome of militarism: whether discussing its function against what Bismarck had called the 'internal' or the 'external enemy', Kautsky was in no doubt that Germany's military preponderance in Europe and its undemocratic constitution made it the most militaristic of European states.[44]

German capitalism has not come to political power through its own resources, but rather through its surrender to Prussian militarism, to which it has sacrificed all its principles, in order to secure the promotion of all its interests. Capitalism has consequently become dependent on militarism and its dependence has grown in proportion to the extent that capitalism has been unnerved and weakened by the growing working class movement.[45]

That this was an analysis of a specifically German context Kautsky made abundantly clear by briefly enumerating the key links in the militarist chains which enthralled society. These consisted of military discipline, the closed officers' corps, the practice of automatically placing retired officers and NCOs in municipal administrations and the civil service, military associations in civil society, and an effective lobbying system which had broken the spine of all bourgeois opposition in the Reichstag to the military budgets.[46] On the constitution of the army, Kautsky accepted Engels' point that rivalry between the great powers of Europe led to mass conscript armies, which increasingly approximated to citizen armies in terms of their recruitment base. At the same time the system of discipline and ranks set them far apart from democratic citizen armies. Blind obedience was achieved by isolating the recruit in barracks, drilling and abusing him until he was reduced to the state of a 'machine without a will of his own, who could be required to shoot at his father and mother ...'[47]

As we saw in chapter 1, this was all good Social Democratic electoral copy as well as political analysis.

Behind the drill sergeants swaggered the officers, drinking and gambling, corrupt and illiterate, an inviolable cast, the bankrupt 'lumpen Junkers' of the thirty years' war, who, having secured their social dominion as a self-perpetuating elite, remained as integral a part of the militarist system as the maltreatment of the recruits under them.[48] It was the officer corps, that relic of absolutism, which held the whole structure together. It was, Kautsky predicted accurately enough, the last bastion against the democratisation of the armed forces and state, and would be the first to attack the working-class movement.[49] The enthusiasm of the military camarilla for persuading Wilhelm II to launch a *Staatsstreich* against the SPD, not to mention the activities of the *Freikorps* and generals in repressing the revolutionary movement in 1919–20, bore and would continue to bear testimony to Kautsky's words.

For him, the purpose of all this drilling and discipline could not be to wage war against the 'external enemy', since, he argued, war between states had come to depend so much on mobilising society's full moral and physical resources that no unpopular wars could be fought in the future. Rather, blind obedience forged the army into an instrument of class power that could be turned loose on the 'internal enemy'.[50] Where Kautsky ended would provide the starting point for Karl Liebknecht to launch a new debate on winning over the army conscripts after the turn of the century.

Conclusion

Kautsky's analysis pushed further than Engels' in his thumbnail sketch of the elements of the militarist system in Germany. Yet, it could be reconciled with Marx's and Engels' ideas on Bonapartism down to the rhetorical insult about the lumpen origins of the power holders. All the same, it is clear that Kautsky was discussing what appeared to him to be a specifically German problem. Kautsky could have meant that he was intent on analysing *all* politics strictly within the context of different national traditions. But this was not the case, as his more general comments on the 'modern' capitalist state showed. At a general level, Kautsky's own attempts to link either military rivalry or military expenditure to the underlying requirements and dynamic of the capitalist economic system were ultimately unconvincing even to their author. In the end, he concluded that there was no direct link and that 'militarism', like imperialism, was more favourable to some capitalists than to others. It was simply a choice of policy.

Kautsky's observations on Prusso-German militarism were something of a bench-mark for the Left. Ludwig Quidde substantially agreed with them. Even when he set out to criticise party orthodoxies on militarism in the 1900s, Karl Liebknecht found himself largely reproducing the same description. Yet, in Kautsky's writings, these insights into the different forms and functions of militarism remained disconnected. As might be expected from the leading Marxist theorist of the day, they were only linked together via his successive economic explanations of the driving pressures of the capitalist system. When he found that he had no place for them in this functional order of things, then militarism became a rather nebulous term. On the one hand, Kautsky had allotted a far greater role to political organisation and administration in his theoretical writings than Marx or Engels had in theirs. On the other hand, he was no more willing than they had been to integrate his analysis into a political theory. At a general level, Kautsky and Engels agreed in regarding the state as functional to capitalism. Those requirements of capitalist social relations which capitalists were themselves incapable of organising *had to be* (in a functional sense) organised by the state. In other words, the dynamism for the changing role of the state came from capitalist development itself. There was no danger of the political 'superstructure' wandering off on its own.[51]

Kautsky and Engels differed on two counts. First, Kautsky accorded greater scope to state intervention in advanced capitalist countries. Although this was a matter of degree, it helped Kautsky to produce an image of a much more directive state which wielded far greater authority over civil society. Second, their views on how the state would have to be reshaped after a socialist revolution diverged. In Kautsky's post-revolutionary world, the civil administration, staffed by the 'intelligentsia', would have to be at hand to plan and control economic and social development under the guidance of a parliamentary democracy.[52] This was a far cry from the admittedly rather confused and confusing remarks of Marx and Engels about the various ways in which the old state form would have to be done away with, whether through a transitory 'dictatorship of the proletariat', a 'smashing' of the old regime and its replacement by a self-governing commune or, on a more philosophical plane, the 'transcendence' and 'dying away' of the state.[53]

What was at stake here were two quite different definitions of the state itself. For Engels, the central and definitional content of state power was 'bodies of armed men', an idea Weber subsequently elaborated into the 'monopoly over the means of violence'. Engels' explanation of the origins of the state as a body standing above civil society and mitigating its conflicts is so similar to Hobbes' – with the substitution of a civil society

rent by class struggles for one being torn apart by individual interests –
that one can hardly doubt either the importance of this coercive role to
Engels' understanding of the state or from whom he derived the concept.

Kautsky, on the other hand, always refers to the civil administration as
'the state'. Soldiers and arms come under the separate and transparently
pathological heading of 'militarism'. This distinction does not produce as
clear an explanation of the origins of modern states as the Hobbes–Engels
theory. But it did perfectly match the SPD's rather paradoxical view of the
state. Just as Kautsky predicted that the civil administration would be
needed in order to run a centrally planned economy, so too the SPD
demanded that the existing state should allocate resources to social
security, education and health care. Just as Kautsky spoke of the existing
army as entirely dispensable, so too the programme he had helped write for
his party demanded the abolition of the standing army and their
replacement with a citizens' militia. When it came to coercion, Kautsky
himself and the SPD as a whole remained wedded to ideas of direct
democracy, of a utopia in which society policed itself. But when it came to
consent – to the universally benign questions of co-ordinating social
welfare and economic production – Kautsky and the SPD argued for
representative democracy and the essential role of delegation and a
bureaucratic division of labour.

Perhaps, because Kautsky already envisaged such completely different
futures for the different arms of the state, he saw no reason to integrate his
analysis of them. To have done so would have complicated his case for
destroying the one whilst preserving and extending the other. Instead, he
shifted the entire military element away from the centre to the peripheries
of state power. This dichotomy between Social Democratic statism on
economic and social matters and its Rousseauian ideal of the armed
citizenry as the manifestation of the general will matched practical
differences in the party's programme and policies.

Unlike his famous contemporaries, Otto Hintze and Max Weber, or
even his younger radical friend Karl Liebknecht, Kautsky simply did not
consider Germany as a paradigmatic case of state formation. Militarism
could therefore, whatever its connections with capitalism, in the last
instance be sloughed off, as the modern body politic emerged from its
antiquated absolutist skin. Parliamentary Britain and Republican France
remained Kautsky's ideal and typical capitalist states. He did not draw any
profound theoretical connections either between the different elements
that he dubbed with the term 'militarism', or between them and the state
as a whole.

Part II

The new militarism, 1900–14

4 Karl Liebknecht and the end of democratic anti-militarism

In retrospect historians have generally pinpointed the Navy Laws and the Conservative *Sammlung* at the end of the 1890s as an important turning point in Imperial Germany. To contemporaries too it was clear that something major was under way. Cassandra-wise, the SPD might decry the big navy; warn of the irreparable damage it would do to Germany's good relations with Britain; denounce the unbearable fiscal burdens it would impose on the poor; lambast the Centre Party and Prussian Left Liberals for abandoning their radical heritage. But even Wilhelmine anti-militarists could not know how grave the consequences would be and how thoroughly their worst premonitions would be fulfilled. They could not know either that their own anti-militarist programme would come under severe pressure. They certainly had no inkling that the three solid pillars of their platform – democracy, tax reform and effective national defence – would buckle and turn outwards, undermining the unity of the party as well as the consistency of its policies.

The next three chapters consider how each of these themes of democratic opposition, tax reform and national defence changed. As the old propaganda programme came under new challenges, there was a corresponding search for new political tactics and strategies. That search in turn prompted the different Social Democratic factions to develop new theories in the hope of winning the argument within the party. These two processes, the new intellectual effort and the unravelling and final collapse of the old essentially domestic and democratic anti-militarist programme, proceeded in tandem. This chapter explores what happened to the democratic critique of the army, concentrating in particular on the thought of its major exponent in the 1900s, Karl Liebknecht.

From the moment the revisionist debate began in the late 1890s it became apparent that a new generation of publicists and theoreticians had arisen in the party. The principal protagonists, Bernstein and Kautsky, were soon overshadowed by younger, better-educated and more fiery advocates – on the revisionist side men like Max Schippel and Richard Calwer, on the side of orthodoxy Marxists like Rosa Luxemburg and

Alexander Parvus-Helphand. The rise of this new generation testified to Social Democracy's success. No longer would Kautsky have to assume pseudonyms to disguise the fact that he had penned an entire issue of *Die neue Zeit* himself for lack of collaborators. Now his patronage and endorsement were keenly sought, not least by his most bitter future critics, V. I. Lenin and L. D. Trotsky.[1]

The new party theorists also brought new and diverse intellectual influences with them. Whereas Kautsky's and Bernstein's generation had been deeply influenced by the Social Darwinist and evolutionary reading of history popularised so effectively by Ernst Haeckel in the 1870s, for the younger generation the neo-Kantian revival of the 1890s often proved a formative experience.[2] This new frame of reference was most marked among the revisionists. It helped to turn them away from economic and evolutionary types of determinism and towards ethical and political voluntarism; socialism became a moral choice society had to make rather than a necessary outcome of general laws of capitalist development. Because this epistemological reorientation so often accompanied arguments in favour of abandoning the party's revolutionary goals, neither Kautsky nor Luxemburg hesitated in rejecting ethical socialism without ever seriously examining its neo-Kantian philosophical premises.[3] In any case, like some of the other young economists in the party – writers like Cunow, and Lensch – Luxemburg concentrated her creative powers on refining Marxist economic and political theory rather than questioning the central role of economic causality within it. Partly because they had previously discounted the importance of political and social values for so long, all members of this group were seriously disoriented by the outbreak of the first world war and the wave of nationalist hysteria in 1914.[4]

There were several intermediate figures in this geography of the Social Democratic intelligentsia. Kurt Eisner, a leading exponent of neo-Kantian revisionism and South German reformism, embraced pacifism in 1909; wartime opposition turned him into a revolutionary and one of the leaders of the ill-fated Bavarian Council Republic in 1919.[5] The intellectual leaders of 'Austro-Marxism', Otto Bauer, Max Adler and Karl Renner, were all inspired by neo-Kantian ideas;[6] so too was another Vienna-trained intellectual, Max Weber, who stood out among his Left Liberal colleagues for advocating an alliance with a reformist Social Democracy and denying that the movement posed any sort of subversive threat.[7]

But the most striking exception to this pre-war rule that intellectuals on the Right were voluntarists and neo-Kantians and on the Left determinists and Marxists was the young Social Democratic attorney, Karl Liebknecht.[8] The only one of Wilhelm Liebknecht's sons to go into politics, Karl enjoyed the distinction of combining neo-Kantianism with a radical orientation. He shared the impatience of revisionists with the frequently fatalistic pronouncements of orthodox Marxists, but his voluntarism was dedicated to fulfilling the old goal of fundamental democratisation via new methods of mass action. Karl Liebknecht would never have had the opportunity to develop his ideas about how to overcome the army as an anti-democratic bulwark had it not been for the rank and file groundswell in Germany which greeted the 1905 Russian revolution. For a limited period this popular upsurge on the Left encouraged discussion about how to immobilise the Prussian army and carry the party programme through. But it was also a moment which passed, overtaken by the nationalism of the radical Right, and all that eventually was left to mark the period was a range of new ideas and heated debates.

The SPD formally anathematised revisionism at its Dresden congress of 1903.[9] The same year saw the most spectacular gains the party had yet made in elections to the Reichstag. Rank and file optimism was running high, boosted no doubt by economic prosperity, a tighter labour market, rising wages and industrial militancy. In such conditions the failure of the party's popular pre-eminence to translate into political influence led to a further increase in grass-roots radicalism. The 1905 revolution in Russia produced an enormous impact throughout Central Europe, stimulating spontaneous political strikes in Germany and a mass movement to reform the notorious three-class franchise in Prussia. Despite Bebel's private anxieties about street politics getting out of hand, the SPD executive responded to this wave of radicalism by calling for mass rallies on 21 January 1906, the anniversary of the 'Bloody Sunday' massacre in St Petersburg.[10] Often these were the first ones held by local party branches.[11]

The radical upsurge sparked two parallel political debates within the party, which involved rank and file activists in the branches as well as organisers and intellectuals. One was about whether and if so in what conditions the party should call for mass political strikes. The other concerned political agitation among working-class army conscripts. Both questions were directly related to the dangers of a military crackdown and revocation of universal male suffrage. In 1905 the SPD decided at its Jena congress only to call for mass strikes in response to such a *Staatsstreich*.[12] Those who canvassed support for an active youth movement and agitation among 'workers in uniform' proclaimed that their whole point was to render such repression impossible in the first place. Both debates died down in 1907. The revolution in Russia turned into Stolypin's counter-revolution, and SPD enthusiasm into horror at the mass hangings.[13] At home the party suffered its first electoral reverse since Bismarck's day. The years 1907–9 also saw an economic downturn and more aggressive and repressive action by employers' organisations.[14] Not till 1910 was a radical suffrage campaign relaunched in Prussia. And then it – and talk of mass political strikes – was accompanied, not by agitation against the dangers of military intervention in domestic politics, but by a mass pacifist campaign against the threat of a world war.[15] Times had changed. Democratic anti-militarism had had its brief heyday during the period 1904–7. Its chief intellectual and political proponent was Karl Liebknecht.

What gave an undercurrent of reality to the extremist rhetoric of Wilhelmine politics was that neither side still really knew whether or not the other intended to abide by the legal status quo, although by 1907 it ought to have been clear that neither seriously intended to breach it. The government had tried to introduce successive subversion bills, and responded to the new SPD mass tactics of the 1905–6 and 1910–14 years by drawing up elaborate plans for military intervention. Some, like the General Staff's 1907 memorandum entitled 'Fighting in Insurgent Towns', we know of only subsequently.[16] But enough of the more detailed variants on this theme fell into Social Democratic hands at the time to provoke acute anxiety and provide good publicity material. There was the order to shoot during disturbances in Saxony, which the *Leipziger Volkszeitung* brought out in 1906,[17] and Heinrich Limbertz, editor of the Essen *Arbeiterzeitung*, was able to quote to the 1910 Party Congress the counter-insurgency dispositions of General Bissing, Commander of the Seventh Army Corps. A state of seige was to be declared as soon as the police could no longer hold demonstrators in check. Artillery and machine guns were to be used in support of the infantry from the local garrison in the event of street rioting and barricades, while the cavalry and other units were to surround the town and cut it off. 'The first measure,' Bissing ordered, 'to be taken at the same time as the state of seige is declared must be the suppression of all seditious newspapers and the immediate arrest of leading journalists, as well as leaders and agitators, irrespective of parliamentary immunity.'[18] *Vorwärts* also lost no time in publishing part of the text and the government was by now seriously embarrassed. The country enjoyed the spectacle of a Prussian Minister of War assuring the Reichstag that these orders had nothing to do with Social Democracy.[19]

The army and police were sent into the Ruhr in great numbers during the 1912 miners' strike – 6,000 police, two regiments and four battalions of infantry and four cavalry squadrons confronting 230,000 miners[20] – but the result of this overwhelming show of force was a standoff rather than violent confrontation. When actual violence broke out, it occurred spontaneously and – significantly – had little to do with either the organised labour movement or the army. In late September and early October 1910 the extremely reactionary police chief of Berlin, Jagow, authorised his men to open fire on spontaneous street demonstrations in the Moabit and

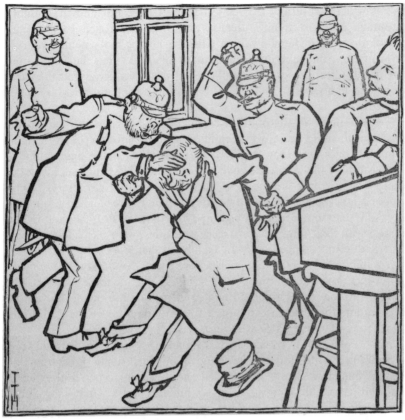

7 Helping police with their enquiries, from *Simplicissimus*, 1914

Wedding districts of the capital. In the street fighting between police and workers that followed, hundreds were wounded and two killed.[21] Tensions were running so high that when an elderly East Prussian Junker, Oldenberg-Januschau, told the Reichstag that a 'lieutenant and ten men' ought to clear the building, workers flocked on to the Berlin streets.[22] The SPD responded to the Mansfeld miners' strike, Moabit and the Saverne affair (see chapter 1) by following its tactics of the 1890s and starting a campaign in the press and parliament.[23] Most of these incidents occurred after the SPD debate on agitation within the army had closed.

The SPD responded entirely differently to the threat of political repression. The discussion about both the army and the mass strike within the party focused on that threat alone. Between 1896 and 1906, National Liberals and Conservatives had already sponsored a series of anti-democratic revisions of the suffrage, most notably in Saxony. Such action at a state level naturally fed fears that the Chancellor and the military entourage at court might attempt to revoke the Reich constitution, provoking a full-scale showdown with the labour movement. From its point of view, the government continued to suspect that the SPD would give in to radical pressure and call mass strikes, even long after the party leadership had made it quite clear that it had no intention of taking the offensive.

A key issue in all the political calculations about whether or not the government would actually take military action revolved around the issue of military discipline. How 'red' was the army? Even in the higher political temperature of the 1900s, the government and the SPD engaged in a lot of shadow boxing over the actual numbers of conscripts and reservists who supported the party. Figures from a third to a half were bandied about with a certain abandon. Bebel claimed, in 1904, that the Prussian and Saxon armies, with their more authoritarian traditions, were particularly Social Democratic in composition.[24] In October 1906, *Vorwärts* asserted that over a million soldiers and reservists were social democrats.[25] There was, however, a clear interest on both sides in exaggerating these statistics. For a sabre-rattling officers' corps there could not be too much infiltration. SPD leaders for their part may well have hoped to scare the authorities away from attempting a *Staatsstreich* at all.[26]

In the 1900s, however, centrist leaders added a new intra-party interest in perpetuating the optimistic teleology of an increasingly proletarian and Social Democratic army.[27] It justified passive complacency in the face of both left- and right-wing anxieties within the party. Right-wing Social Democrats, like Albert Südekum might warn that military discipline induced so strong a 'mass psychosis' among conscripts that even Social Democratic supporters would shoot at workers if so ordered; for him it was clear that all provocative mass actions were suicidal.[28] As an advocate of just such extra-parliamentary politics, Karl Liebknecht drew on the same mass psychosis argument in order to expose the emptiness of the leadership's faith in the army's proletarian demography.[29] As he was to put it in his pamphlet, *Militarism and Anti-militarism*,

There is all the world of difference between voting for Social Democracy, being a Social Democrat and being ready to face all the personal risks involved in anti-militarist activity in the army ... It cannot seriously be suggested that even a third of the army has reached such a position as far as ideas and morale are concerned, nor that military intervention by the Right in the form of violent unconstitutional action – a *coup d'état* – directed against the so-called internal enemy, the labour movement, would be impossible or even difficult.[30]

In spite of this pressure to alter course, the leadership continued to insist on its doctrine of the automatic 'reddening' of the army. At three successive party congresses Liebknecht tried to persuade the party to take its cause to young workers who were about to be called up. In reply Bebel and Richard Fischer warned that this would be dangerous, potentially illegal, and might prompt the very military crackdown it was designed to prevent.[31] Finally in 1906, Bebel was only able to prevent the Congress from adopting Liebknecht's mass anti-militarist agitation by threatening that the entire SPD Executive would resign.[32] But it did have to compromise with the radicals and agree at least to hold meetings advising the young about their legal rights as soldiers. All the evidence is that only the youth section of the SPD implemented this resolution enthusiastically – and the youth movement itself was permitted no national status or much autonomy from the local party *apparat*.[33]

There is no doubt that both central and state governments took even this threat to subvert the army seriously. The relatively liberal Baden Ministry of the Interior swiftly issued a circular ordering the closest possible surveillance over the new army intake, a circular which duly also found its way into the Social Democratic press.[34] When Liebknecht continued to push for more radical agitation, addressed the first national SPD youth congress on the subject of militarism and published an expanded version in 1907, the War Ministry reacted fast. The parliamentary *Fraktion* of the SPD immediately disowned Liebknecht's pamphlet. He was convicted of sedition and served his full sentence of eighteen months.[35] In absentia, he was elected to the Prussian Chamber despite the three-class franchise and when he emerged from prison, Liebknecht found he had become one of the most popular SPD leaders. Alongside Georg Ledebour he would become one of the major figures on the left of the party.[36]

The reasons that led Liebknecht to write about militarism sprang entirely from the impossibility of jolting the party leadership into decisive action. The Bavarian reformist leader of the SPD, Georg von Vollmar, was the first to find a theoretical formula to justify inaction on this front. Militarism, he told the delegates to the 1904 party congress, was no more than a derivative of capitalism; so, it could not be such a threat; nor could anti-militarism be anything but a distraction from the real task, namely organising a mass following so that Social Democracy could end capitalism.[37] For a leading reformist like Vollmar such arguments were little more than ideological window-dressing. But they implicitly appealed to and were repeated by more radical Marxists such as Rosa Luxemburg and Karl Kautsky. To them too, anti-militarism appeared as a side issue compared with the main objective of opposing the capitalist system as a totality.[38]

If he stood any chance of winning the political debate within the party, Karl Liebknecht had to clear two hurdles which separated Marxist intellectuals from his position. First, he had to show that militarism was far more than a mere adjunct to capitalism. Secondly, he needed to back up his assertion that 'There is all the world of difference between voting for Social Democracy, being a Social Democrat and being ready to face all the personal risks involved in anti-militarist activity in the army.' As we shall see, Liebknecht's political persistence and intellectual curiosity led him to take an increasingly critical view of Marxist theory in the process.

Karl Liebknecht's *Militarism*

Karl Liebknecht developed his view of militarism around two new and central ideas. First, he thought militarism existed throughout Europe, in the democracies as well as under absolutism, so that it could be studied in comparative terms, different cases exhibiting varying and selective combinations of the elements present in the general case. Second, he asserted that Prusso-German militarism had attained the status of a paradigm. As one might expect, many of the features of German social and political life that Liebknecht drew attention to were the same as those noted by Engels, Bebel, Quidde and Kautsky before him, but his new comparative perspective cast these features in a very different light.

From the outset, Liebknecht turned away from the 'Bonapartist' model of the German Empire, from the idea of an exceptional regime. He tried to show that militarism was the norm, not the exception. Indeed it was not even unique to capitalism but, as he put it in his 1907 tract, was 'normal and necessary in every class-divided social order, of which the capitalist system is the last'.[39] In effect, Liebknecht was identifying militarism with state coercion itself, 'the forcible subjugation of other nations and of classes within the nation' or in Bismarckian shorthand the 'external and the internal enemy'. Where Engels' and Kautsky's preoccupation with international and economic factors had attenuated the political critique of 1860s radicals, Liebknecht placed the old enlightenment question of the correct constitutional relation between citizen and state back at the centre of the subject. But he had also gone beyond the earlier radical democratic perspective. He found even the radical and Social Democratic ideal of Switzerland wanting, because – as he correctly noted – the Swiss militia could still be used to police strikes and lockouts in the interests of capital. He went to considerable lengths to show the same held for Belgium, France, the United States and Canada as well.[40] Liebknecht was quick to note that in Germany, on the other hand, 'the use of the military in economic struggles is not usual'. This was not because the army was reluctant to intervene but because it did not have to. The police was strong and well armed. The strikers were well disciplined and did not allow themselves to be 'provoked'.[41] In what way did this outwardly less coercive state of affairs make Germany the 'paradigm' of militarism?

Here he returned to familiar ground. Military specialists and critics generally agreed that the key to the army's discipline lay in the professional 'cadres'. Like Quidde and Kautsky, Liebknecht considered so-called 'capitulation' crucial to securing the loyalty of the professional NCOs. It guaranteed them a position in the lower ranks of the civil service once they retired from the army. Any serious breach of discipline – including reading the Social Democratic press – might result in a dishonourable discharge with consequent loss of pension rights and future employment, not to mention a spell in prison.[42] By this penetration of military personnel and codes into the civil side of the state, Liebknecht maintained that the 'whole of public life [had become]... contaminated with militarism'.[43] Again echoing the criticisms of earlier writers, Liebknecht noted the way in which the higher officials of both central and municipal administration were subjected to military discipline. The jurisdiction of the civil courts was constantly usurped by the army. The education system was subordinated to 'the militaristic spirit and the whole militarist conception of life'.[44]

Finally, voluntary associations were so infested with militaristic norms that they 'clasp[ed] the whole of [civil] society in a network of militaristic and semi-militaristic institutions'.[45] Pride of place went to the institution of the reserve officer. Like anti-authoritarian Liberals of the 1890s such as Weber and Quidde, Liebknecht noted how the social pretensions of the reserve officer 'bring the spirit of the military caste into civilian life and immortalise it'.[46] Young men's defence associations, military clubs and ex-soldiers' leagues, as well as overtly political organisations such as the Pan Germans and the Imperial League Against Social Democracy, performed the same role at a mass level. Historians of the radical Right have tended to endorse Liebknecht's picture, emphasising also how the rapid growth of these mass organisations marked one of the principal changes between the early 1890s and the 1900s, between the time when Kautsky and Quidde attacked the Wilhelmine army and Liebknecht did.[47]

Like other Social Democrats, he presented a damning indictment of incarceration in barracks, hard drill, discipline and punishment – both sanctioned and illegal. But whereas August Bebel and Wilhelm Liebknecht had assumed that the very harshness of army discipline produced a radical reaction among the conscripts – dubbing the army itself as one of the best propagandists for Social Democracy – Karl Liebknecht saw the army as a self-enclosed world.[48] Combined with religion, parades and glamorous uniforms military discipline aimed 'to create a special class of proletarians from 20–22 years of age whose thoughts and feelings will be completely opposite to those of proletarians in other, "old" classes'.[49] In a particularly memorable passage, Liebknecht cast his glance over the military system in its entirety, sealing his account with the new terms of mass psychology:

Recruits are drugged, confused, flattered, bribed, pressed, locked, disciplined and beaten. Thus grain upon grain is mixed and kneaded to serve as mortar for the great edifice of the army, stone added to stone, calculated to form a fortress against revolution ... It is of great importance for military discipline that men work together in a mass, within which the independence of the individual is to a great extent abolished ... All the members of this mighty machine are subjected, not only to the hypnotic suggestion of those in command, but also to a special kind of hypnotism, mass hypnotism – which, however, is bound to be without effect on an army made up of educated and dedicated opponents of militarism.[50]

'Mass hypnotism' and 'mass psychosis' had, as we have seen, become familiar terms to Social Democrats when they discussed militarism and its social effects in Germany during the decade before the outbreak of the first world war.[51] Among these terms there is not once a mention of militarism appealing to the intellect, not once the idea that nationalism or the glorification of armed force might be rational. Like many of the enlightenment thinkers of the eighteenth century, Liebknecht reserved Reason for the forces of Progress. In this division between the bright rational future of socialism and the dark irrational forces which were mobilising support for war and civil war, Karl Liebknecht was typical of Social Democratic intellectuals. The SPD restrained its mass propaganda, the liturgy of its secular festivals, to rational appeals.[52] 'Mass psychosis' was relevant to Liebknecht's way of thinking because however much he might try to show that militarism was a 'normal' state of affairs he could only think of pathological reasons why the people connived at being armed against itself.[53] But he had already gone a lot further than his parents' generation towards acknowledging the army's hold over German imaginations.

Mass psychosis also formed the nub of his political argument. The point was not that the psychosis was irreversible, but rather that it was not automatically so. Just as the SPD already countered establishment values and any militaristic ethos in civil society, so Liebknecht argued, unless Social Democracy agitated actively at a mass level against militarist values there was no reason why working-class soldiers should subvert the army command when called upon to fulfil the Kaiser's notorious request to 'shoot your fathers and brothers'. Liebknecht had already warned the orthodox Marxists of the SPD,

True though it is that history is on our side, it is not true that everything happens of its own accord. This kind of quietism and fatalism is a big mistake from the point of view of historical materialism and disastrous as far as agitation is concerned, and can only be countered by agitational activity and by anti-militarist activity in particular.[54]

This description of a state built on servility and admiration for the force of arms fleshed out the Fichtean idiom which Liebknecht *père* had passed down to Liebknecht *fils*: Prusso-German militarism was 'not simply a state within the state, but actually a state above the state'.[55] But how exactly did Liebknecht regard the state? His chronicle of soldiers firing on workers in the democracies of Western Europe is highly indicative. In Germany, these incidents did not occur because everything was weighted against the labour movement. In reaching this conclusion, Liebknecht had, as we have seen, explored the connection between force and consent, between the army and civil institutions. He unhesitatingly placed force at the centre of the state, thereby following Hobbes, Engels and Weber rather than Kautsky.[56] But he also differentiated between those state institutions which manufacture consent and those which secure obedience, between the 'police [and] law courts', which 'work chiefly by means of threats, intimidation and violence', and schools and the church, whose main instruments appeared to him to have been stultification, belief and fear.[57]

The obvious inference was that in Germany militarism not only represented the perennial threat of coercion; it was also built on consent, thereby enmeshing both the state and society in an all encompassing system of power.

Militarism, together with the Catholic Church, is the most highly developed Machiavellianism in the history of the world, and the most Machiavellian of all the Machiavellianisms of capitalism.[58]

As the rest of Liebknecht's analysis emphasised, this reading of the all-encompassing, all-devouring tendencies of militarism was ideally suited to turning Prusso-German militarism into 'a paradigm of contemporary militarism in its forms, methods and effects', because it 'possesses all the evil and dangerous qualities of every form of capitalist militarism'.[59]

But he did not saddle the other West and Central European states with this description. As he pointed out, only military rivalry enforced a degree of standardisation of military technology and organisation. Even Russia, he noted, had been forced to adopt mass conscription and modern armament ahead of its social and economic development. But in the domestic arrangements these states made to police and repress their own populations there was no such pressure towards uniformity. National differences – including differences between the character and organisation of the domestic opponents of the state – continued unabated.[60] Although he agreed with Kautsky that such coercion served capitalist interests, he did not draw any universal principles from this class analysis about how the coercion was carried out.

The question therefore remained how generally applicable were the aspects of German militarism he had highlighted. He had gone farther than Kautsky by claiming that just because German militarism was the most extreme case it should be treated as a model, rather than as an exception. This meant, however, that different selections of these 'forms, methods and effects' would be found elsewhere, but he also acknowledged 'no one has been able to imitate Prussian-German militarism.'[61] Liebknecht would have agreed with Otto Hintze and Max Weber about the paradigmatic importance of the German polity, however much they would have disagreed violently as to what it exemplified. Like Kautsky, both Hintze and Weber emphasised the model quality of its civil administration.

Liebknecht's methodology was also entirely different from Weber's. Rather than following the line of the average, the representative generalisation of Weberian 'ideal-types', Liebknecht chose to draw together *all* those phenomena that were represented in one form of militarism or another. Most of them were, he thought, concentrated in the Prusso-German case. In a popularly written pamphlet, this approach is rather confusing at any theoretical level. It shows how much interpretative 'slippage' the term 'militarism' can undergo. It puts in question Liebknecht's whole construct of militarism as a general system of power. If it meant different things in different places, different subsets of a maximal whole, did it have a common core? Did the Prusso-German model reveal that common core of the ideal type? Or was it simply rhetorically convenient to project the most extreme case as the essence of militarism? To compare adequately, Liebknecht either had to jump to a higher level of abstraction – such as the coercion of 'internal and external enemies' – or he had to seek out a single common factor, like the incidence of troops being used to break up strikes. He attempted to do both. But in neither case was he able to invoke the Prusso-German model as some kind of 'ideal type' which made militarism elsewhere more comprehensible. However much he might reject the exceptional state, he still ended up with it, 'the Prussian-German bureaucratic-feudal-capitalist form – that very worst form of capitalist militarism ...'[62]

In 1907, Liebknecht was still content to define his problem in class terms; the army as an instrument to hold subordinate classes in thrall within the nation, and – taking a leaf out of Marxist theories of imperialism – as a means to pursuing bourgeois interests abroad. But nothing could be less accurate than to rank him, as the ideologists of the old East German regime did, among the minor Marxist deities. Liebknecht's intellectual trajectory led further and further from even this rather political reading of class struggle.

Reflections in prison

After Karl Liebknecht was found guilty of sedition in 1908, he was imprisoned in the old fortress of Glatz.[63] He was allowed to correspond and receive books.[64] Like other political prisoners before and after him Liebknecht turned the frustrations of captivity into a setting for tranquil study and reflection in an otherwise fraught and hectic existence. During this first sentence he started on an extensive course of reading on history and philosophy, making notes towards a manuscript which he reworked again during his second imprisonment in 1916–18. He never finished it to his own satisfaction. Karl Liebknecht was murdered after the abortive Sparticist uprising in Berlin of January 1919, and many of his papers were looted and burned at the same time.[65] But in 1922 a draft of his book was published posthumously under the rather ponderous title *Studies in the Laws of Movement of Social Development*.[66] If Liebknecht would almost certainly have tried to express many of his ideas more tersely and elegantly and attempted to iron out some of the inconsistencies, such drafts almost always also carry a stronger aroma from a writer's intellectual kitchen than does the finished product.

Liebknecht's general preoccupation was the relationship between consciousness and structures of power. The same preoccupation had been evident in his study of militarism. There he had implicitly posited a symmetrical relationship between political power and consciousness. Asserting that structures of coercion depended on belief and consent, he had argued that if the SPD agitated against militarist values, it could undermine first the consent of the soldiers and then the system of coercion itself. Now Liebknecht found his way to stating these propositions explicitly. It was this nexus between psychology and structures of power that led him to reject Marxist theory at the same time as he staunchly defended a radical reading of its politics.

Hitherto unpublished notes show that he became increasingly interested during the first world war in issues of consciousness *per se*, especially in the differences of perspective between actor and observer, or in the example he explored in prison between politician and historian.[67] On the structural side, his *Studies* challenged the Marxist metaphor of economic 'base' and political 'superstructure' in a two-pronged attack. His direct assault on the labour theory of value was not particularly successful, and in any case still remained too much within a Marxist framework to provide much critical leverage.[68] His second line of attack was altogether more fundamental.

The sort of Marxism which the neo-Kantian generation criticised was the kind of historical materialism Plekhanov had popularised in his *Monist Theory of History*.[69] The very title was indebted to Haeckel, and the determinism of material conditions over people, in Marxist terms of the productive forces over the relations of production, had been simple, explicit and paramount. Liebknecht repeated contemporary criticisms that this evolutionary and deterministic framework omitted fundamental characteristics of human social behaviour when he pointed out that 'even economic relations ... always have an intellectual, psychological as well as material nature'.[70] The terms of this neo-Kantian critique foreshadow the neo-Hegelian critiques of orthodox Marxism which Lukacs and Korsch were to advance soon after the first world war.[71]

Although Liebknecht rejected the determinism of orthodox Marxism, he still accepted its evolutionary teleology of social development. How, one might ask, could one preserve the one whilst surrendering the other? Kautsky had asked this question of himself and concluded that the only option was to stay with determinism. For only some trends beyond the reach of conscious human agency, like economic development, could lay down a positively predictable outcome to a history, which was after all supposed to be pushed along by quite unpredictable class struggles. Having rejected such an economic crutch, Liebknecht found himself with no way of predicting in what way society would actually develop. Everything depended, he wrote, on how 'the organism ... chooses and finds the route to higher development.'[72] Evolutionary progress became an ideal rather than a real path, a yardstick against which real development could be measured and found more or less failing. He accordingly applied this criterion to the use of coercive power:

There are two kinds of force: socially dysbiotic and socially embiotic. If force serves social development, it is socially necessary, and therefore socially embiotic. If it works against social development, then it is harmful to society (socially dysbiotic).[73]

These thoughts were still not very far from the Social Darwinist legacy of orthodox Marxism. But even if Liebknecht was still susceptible to evolutionary theory, his emphasis on the causal significance of politics and free will set him apart from most Marxists, including fellow-radicals.

This political emphasis is particularly obvious when he came to cover some of the same ground as he had in his *Militarism*. Gone was any suggestion that class enjoyed any primacy among the various sources of authority. Class was no more significant at an abstract theoretical level in Liebknecht's assessment now than conditions of dependency within a society stemming from 'caste, estate ... profession, sex, age and individual'.[74] What Liebknecht preserved from his earlier account was the distinction between domestic and international types of domination. But even on the international side domination now ran along racial and national lines as well. It followed from his approach that the lynchpin of each relationship of dependency and domination might well lie in a different social sphere, so providing for a kaleidoscopic world in which a great many different relations of power could interact. Such a conclusion had always been a theoretical difficulty for orthodox Marxism, since one particular social relation, namely class, was regarded as fundamental to all others.

In explaining the nature of domination, Liebknecht preserved a second distinction he had maintained in his study of militarism. A true lawyer at heart, he differentiated between motive and means. 'The means', he enumerated,

are among others physical force; economic power; organisational power; social deception (through splendour, pomp, the cloak of secrecy, trickery, bluff, distance, foreign languages {e.g., in church}, affecting the critical faculties especially by completely or partially suspending them); conscious or unconscious influence of opinion (religion, superstition, excitement); cerebral intellectual influence, intellectual superiority (influencing the intellect with the aid and methods of the intellect); dexterity. To this *demagoguery* also belongs ...[75]

At a general level Liebknecht refused to designate any particular instrument of power as being 'decisive in the last instance', since that 'depended on the basis and purpose of the domination'. Further, he argued that reliance on any one particular means in an epoch would tend to make others unnecessary.[76] Turning from society at large to politics in particular, he nonetheless retained his earlier conviction that 'physical force or the readiness to use it' was the ultimate instrument of power.[77] Perhaps this was the criterion that distinguished *states* from other types of domination. If so, Liebknecht never said so explicitly.

Liebknecht had reproduced the intellectual contours of his *Militarism* at a more abstract level. On the one hand, he abided by the minimal definition of state power as control over the means of violence which theorists like Marx, Engels and Weber brought into German intellectual life. On the other hand, he continued to refuse to focus on this minimum alone. He introduced features which were universal in the sense that they might be found in the whole of human history, but which even he accepted were unlikely to be equally important or even necessarily present in any one context. His concern for human agency and motivation convinced him that instruments of coercion could not be created on their own. They needed to appeal to beliefs and values in order to be constructed at all, let alone to be deployed in practice. These were very interesting insights, though they also opened the way for exactly the same kinds of slippage as his Prusso-German 'paradigm' of militarism had done. Such a complete bundle of analytical tools was potentially too exhaustive and wide-ranging to construct a general theory, which necessarily depended on some simplifying and unitary principle. It was just as well that Liebknecht explicitly denied any ambition to construct one.[78]

Conclusion

Karl Liebknecht was the first post-Marxist socialist writer in Germany to regard other categories than class and nation as valid *loci* for explaining relations of oppression. But in so doing, he had also, to some extent, revived terms common to pre-Marxist socialism, which Marx and Engels had sought to subordinate to class analysis. It is not clear whether Liebknecht was aware of this intellectual debt, though the writings of Saint-Simon, Fourier, Owen and Proudhon were known among German Social Democrats. The rise of Marxist economic theory within the SPD had been allied to the party's acceptance that its political strategy would be predicated on a long period of organisational preparation and waiting for revolutionary conditions to mature. It is not surprising that in demanding a more direct and confrontational politics, Liebknecht had turned against the attenuating economics and the fatalistic theory of history.

Such an intellectual debt was strangely appropriate. For he had also revived a pre-Marxist political agenda. By placing the army and democracy so firmly in the centre of his political strategy he had returned to the heritage of the 1860s, the 1848 revolution and the enlightenment. This debt was also almost certainly unconscious. He did not rediscover the tradition afresh but rather repoliticised ideas which had been preserved and adapted into a milder Social Democratic form. Furthermore the character of both army and state had changed radically since 1866, let alone 1780. The generation of Liebknecht's parents had already known that the division was no longer between a standing army of hired mercenaries and would-be free citizens. It remained to explain why such potentially free men submitted blindly to a harsh and alien regime both as its citizens and its soldiers. This was what Liebknecht had attempted to do.

Had Liebknecht actually generated a theory of militarism, or simply an analysis of the role of the military in Germany? Could he justify his definition of militarism as a supreme 'Machiavellianism', an independent system of power designed to hold subordinate classes and nations in subjection? The very contentiousness of what exactly is legitimate coercion militates against any generally agreed definition. To Social Democrats, the answers seemed relatively clear. 'National self-defence' and the policing of 'progressive' laws were legitimate; 'wars of aggression' and the acts of the 'class state' illegitimate. But, as even Karl Liebknecht admitted, these issues were historically relative. It is hardly surprising then that he was unable to develop a general theory of militarism to support his definition of it as a system of power, for, what it was being deployed to evaluate had to be constituted by other, discrete analytical categories.

Liebknecht succeeded rather better as a critic of German militarism and as a critics' critic – in showing the weakness of orthodox Marxism. Liebknecht's 'military pedagogy' introduced a range of psychological concepts about the character of mass obedience and discipline. In the process, he drew attention to the role of belief and ideology in maintaining any army and state.

Orthodox Marxists linked their theory of militarism to their anti-militarist solution in an all too clear way. Since militarism stemmed from the class state, it followed that once the key variable, class, was removed, militarism would vanish as well. Liebknecht found himself in the peculiar position of rejecting the Marxist theory but embracing the most radical version of its politics. In his own theory, Liebknecht had posited politics to be a sphere separate from civil society, subject to its own principles grouped around the spectrum of force and consent. As the epitome of force, militarism therefore found its logical opposite in consent. Since, in his mature work, Liebknecht specifically stated that class power was only one of several bases of social and political power, eliminating class oppression might be a necessary condition for eliminating militarism and force. But he had no reason for supposing that a classless socialist society was a sufficient condition for doing so.

As a contribution to a political debate in the SPD, Liebknecht failed. The party did not throw down the gauntlet and agitate in the army. By forcing the issue into the open and keeping it there, Liebknecht only succeeded in making the party leadership state the limits of its radicalism openly. They might continue to criticise the undemocratic nature of the Wilhelmine state, but they had also made it clear that they were not prepared to *force* the issue of democratic rights. Any advance in the party's anti-militarist programme now depended on its other two elements, cost and national defence.

5   The economics of armament

A few years before Karl Liebknecht raised the banner of youth revolt within the SPD, the party had been urged to respond to a quite different idea of militarism. This version dwelt on armaments rather than the army, on fiscal and economic questions rather than political ones. As we saw in chapter 1, the SPD had traditionally lambasted arms spending as a crushing burden on the poor and for crowding out socially useful expenditure on education, health, insurance and the infrastructure. But this had been only one of several themes in the 1890s.

The Tirpitz plan changed everything. The naval race with Britain which began in 1898 necessitated a quantum leap in German military expenditure. Tirpitz put his faith in Germany's higher levels of industrial output and growth. But, as the SPD warned immediately, German resources were never sufficient to win the race. Britain started with three advantages. It was already the dominant naval power. As an island it did not have to maintain a large army in order to protect its borders. Finally, British governments possessed a powerful and flexible fiscal weapon; a centralised and progressive income tax.

In Germany direct taxation was a right reserved for the federal states. With their generally more patrician governments and restricted parliamentary franchise, the federal states tended to keep such progressive forms of taxation extremely low. The Imperial government thus found itself under the double bind of having to finance its spending out of indirect taxation – committing itself to an anti-consumer politics – and having to persuade the most democratic legislature in the land to pass such measures. Given that military spending stood at about 90% of the Reich budget for a long period of time, it was impossible to finance the 100% increases in military allocations which the naval programme required between 1896 and 1908 by making savings elsewhere. The government tried to reduce spending on social welfare, but this could not achieve any more significant result than providing more grist to the SPD's mill: German culture was being sacrificed to Krupp guns. Nor did the federal structure make it easy for the government to force the states to increase their so-called 'matricular' contributions to the Reich budget. Finally, deficit financing was neither a long-term option nor one in which the government was particularly skilled. In other words, long before the arms race could seriously affect the rest of the economy it ran up against the political inflexibility of the fiscal system itself.[1]

Since its foundation the SPD had campaigned for a direct income tax. This question revealed a supreme irony of German establishment politics. Those – especially Admiral Tirpitz – who were most committed to the naval race with Britain were broadly in favour of such a rational solution to the Reich's finances. Conservatives, on the other hand, had only supported the navy and *Weltpolitik* in the first place because the '*Sammlung*' on which the programme was based provided a new political bloc with which to defend conservative agrarian interests against the growth of the SPD. Whilst conservatives gratefully accepted new tariff barriers on foodstuffs, they were bitterly opposed to any form of property or inheritance tax which would force them to carry part of the burden. National Liberals, the most enthusiastic supporters of Wilhelmine imperialism, were equally opposed to a capital or income tax on industrial and commercial fortunes. Although the Centre party was not in favour of direct taxation either, it had forced the government to pledge in the first naval law (1898) that any fresh finance would not be found by raising indirect taxes. This clause notwithstanding large new tariffs and taxes were levied to pay for the 1902 naval budget. The Centre was right to fear that its rival for mass support, Social Democracy, would reap the benefits of Catholic responsibility for raising the cost of living, as the 1903 general election demonstrated all too clearly.[2] The irony was that the political parties which supported armament opposed the tax reform which would pay for it, and the parties which supported tax reform opposed armament. During the 1900s Tirpitz hoped in vain for a thoroughgoing financial reform, instead of which the government produced endless discussions and exiguous solutions: the reforms of 1904, 1906, and finally under the pressure of dreadnought competition the abortive reform of 1909, which triggered the fall of Chancellor Bülow.

Bülow's successor Bethmann Hollweg accepted new political and new strategic ideas. Following the massive electoral victory of the Left in 1912, one which gave a third of Reichstag seats to the SPD, Bethmann faced the apparently intractable problem of balancing the books. Politically he did not try to forge a cohesive 'bloc' as Bülow had done. Rather, he pursued what he called the 'politics of the diagonal', relying on the parties of the Left – National Liberals, Left Liberals and SPD – to vote through major tax reform in the teeth of agrarian resistance by the Centre and Conservatives; and depending on the parties of the failed anti-SPD

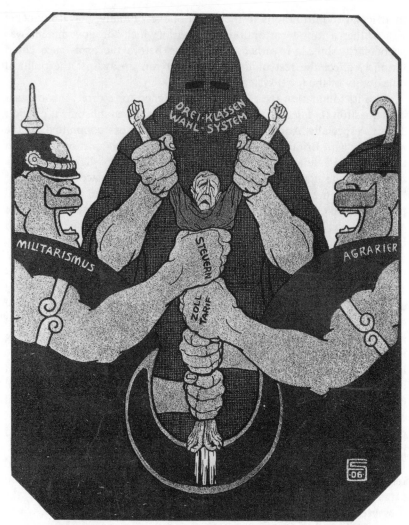

8 Militarism, taxation and suffrage in Prussia, from *Der Wahre Jacob*, 1906

coalitions of the Right to vote through the military budgets for which the tax reform was designed. This new tactic worked remarkably well. The radical Reichstag voted through a financial reform in 1913 which balanced new direct taxation in the form of death duties against much larger indirect taxes. The National Liberals succeeded in persuading the SPD to let the brunt of progressive taxation fall on agrarian rather than commercial or industrial wealth, leaving the Conservatives and Centre cornered and isolated.

For the SPD the political question was whether or not tax reform provided a bridgehead into German politics. From 1904, Social Democrats flagged the electoral importance they attached to the issue by detaching their tax demands from their militia proposals. Fiscal reform was no longer an adjunct to an essentially democratic programme. Tax and social questions now took centre stage.[3] The revisionist Right had already begun to talk about *Kompensationspolitik*, of trading support for the budget in return for social reform at the time of the first Navy Law.[4] By 1908, the Baden and Bavarian Social Democrats were willing to break party discipline and vote for their state governments' budgets.[5] Could a bloc of the Left be constructed which would give the SPD real influence in the Reichstag? Was it worth abandoning the party's proud tradition of opposition, with which so many of its members as well as its leaders identified, for hopes which might so easily be disappointed? In fact, the 1913 tax reform did not create a new bloc. By the time the Reichstag went into recess in May 1914, the Social Democratic delegation was more bitter and isolated than ever. The divisions which prevented any serious alliance between Liberals and Social Democrats had much to do with foreign policy, colonies and war. But in 1913 and in the decade leading up to it Social Democrats did not know how things would work out. It was only obvious that budgetary problems had enormous significance, whether they actually would result in the state's internal collapse – as the party's left hoped – or stimulate major reform as its right wing anticipated.

The intellectual framework in which Social Democrats explored the problem of armament and taxation was Marxist economic theory. Whether they were revisionist critics or orthodox Marxists they implicitly accepted such a general framework. With hindsight this consensus is a little surprising. For Marxist economics dealt with long run 'supply side' questions, growth and crisis, even industrial and labour issues, but not fiscal and financial economics. In fact, on the fiscal questions themselves, Marxist theorists fell back on very classical nostra: budgets had to balance; taxing capital would lower investment and growth; money was an impartial medium of exchange.

It is crucial to distinguish between the realities of German political economy and the intellectual substance of Social Democratic debates. The economic reality was that the arms race placed intolerable burdens on a rather inflexible fiscal system. Social Democratic theorists wrote about the strains arms spending was placing on capitalist development as a whole. This perspective came only too naturally to them. For the foundation of their Marxist belief in socialism was the conviction that capitalism was prone to a final economic crisis from which it could not recover. It was by questioning the central theses of this view that Bernstein had come to the reject the Erfurt programme and the oppositional strategy of the party. But whether or not the German economy was actually severely burdened by the arms race is a moot point.[6] Rapid industrial growth continued until the first world war. Marxist-trained economists were not equipped to theorise about financial and monetary questions. What they did achieve, instead, was to set up many of the basic arguments and criteria with which the arms economy has been addressed ever since.

This intellectual debate began in 1898 with the revisionist controversy and the proposals by Max Schippel and Wolfgang Heine that the party effectively join coalition politics. In 1903, revisionism – at least at an intellectual level – was marginalised. Anathematised at the Dresden party congress, the group found the pages of the *Die neue Zeit* henceforth closed and gathered around the *Sozialistische Monatshefte*, a journal edited by the avowedly imperialist and anti-semitic Joseph Bloch. But the question Schippel had raised returned to the pages of *Die neue Zeit*. In 1900, there had been no immediate prospect of reform. It was merely an idea. By 1910, it was obvious that major tax reform could not be long postponed. This time it was the old champions of Marxist orthodoxy who began to canvass Schippel's intellectual ideas. It became one of the issues which divided them into the so-called 'centrists' – whose intellectual *doyens* included Kautsky and Hilferding and who wanted the party to vote for the tax reform – and the rather heterogenous radical left around Luxemburg, Lensch and Radek, who continued to oppose all parliamentary horse-trading. These new lines of intellectual battle prepared the ground for the centre to vote for the tax reform when it came in 1913. This was a momentous event within the party, the first occasion when it had voted with the government at a national level. The divisions within the party prefigure those of August 1914, with the centre siding with the right rather than the left. But the analogy remains a loose one. Non-Marxist radicals like Karl Liebknecht and Georg Ledebour, who stood out against the war in 1914, approved of voting for the tax reform, because it had been such a long-standing Social Democratic demand. Let us now turn to the intellectual substance of these contending positions. For it is from them that much of the new substance of militarism came.

Military spending and economic crisis

The first salvo in the Social Democratic dog fight over the arms economy was fired by the revisionist intellectual, Max Schippel. In 1898, he published a long and contentious article questioning the legitimacy of the SPD's

militia programme. His trump card was the disdain in which Friedrich
Engels – the party's most renowned military critic as well as its intellectual
godfather – had held militias for long after the defeat of the 1848
revolutions. This unfortunate fact provoked a venomous and pedantic
series of scholastic retorts and counter-claims. Apart from undermining
SPD claims to possess the high ground of military efficiency, Schippel also
attacked the party's economic critique. Kautsky readily conceded that a
militia system in which each citizen was armed might well turn out to be
more costly than a conscript army. But he insisted that the militia was
nonetheless worth its political benefits.[7] What really provoked Kautsky's
ire was when Schippel suggested that existing military spending was not
costly at all. In that case, the SPD's entire focus on its fiscal burdens had
to be mistaken.

This revisionist onslaught proved so hard to refute because of the
precision with which Schippel had turned Kautsky's own intellectual
weapons against him. As we saw in chapter 3, Kautsky had based his
prediction of a capitalist 'breakdown' crisis on a chronic shortfall of
demand. Given the unequal distribution of the national product between
workers and capitalists, the capitalist class and its hangers on could never
consume their entire portion. And the surplus product that remained
would, in the language of orthodox Marxism, trigger a crisis of 'under-
consumption'. Kautsky himself had already suggested in the 1880s and
1890s that imperialism served as a safety valve, a way of getting rid of the
surplus product in markets which lay beyond this vicious circle.[8] By the
early 1900s, this explanation of the 'inevitable crisis of capitalism' had
become so widely established – largely through Kautsky's own writings –
that it appeared as far afield as Jack London's *Iron Heel*.[9] Even after it had
been subjected to considerable criticism it continued to be canvassed by
Rosa Luxemburg and, in the post-1945 period, by economists like Paul
Sweezy and Paul Baran.[10]

With these ideas in mind, Schippel claimed that the real cost of
armaments ought not to be measured by their effect on capitalist
development as a whole. At this point, like a good conjurer he drew
Kautsky's theory of under-consumptionism out of the hat and pointed out
that state spending on arms helped to compensate for shortfalls in demand.
In this prematurely Keynesian view, the problem did not hinge on the arms
race at all but on who paid for it. 'Every society facing "over-production"
is not burdened but rather relieved if production relatively falls and
consumption relatively increases.' Armament was a perfect solution to
crisis precisely because it added nothing to economic productivity. As
Schippel continued, 'The enormous expenditure in all modern societies for
unproductive purposes, above all on the part of the state for military

purposes, is not a strengthening but a weakening of the *general* economic pressure ... the general economic effect of *these enormous unproductive expenditures has, purely economically, become a condition of existence for modern society.*'[11]

Schippel concluded that the SPD had no rational, economic basis for opposing military budgets in principle, only pragmatic, negotiable objections to the way the tax burden was distributed. 'The capitalist "state"', he asserted, 'does not have the means to aid capitalist society; by pumping up taxes from its lower classes it is likely to go beyond its own "financial" strength as well as the patience of its citizens.'[12] The trajectory towards the 1913 tax reform was already proposed. But if the SPD had accepted this view, it would have surrendered its claim to represent the general social good and the new society and emasculated itself into, in Bebel's words, 'just another interest group'.[13] In his rejoinder to Schippel, Kautsky was predictably hampered by his own role in pioneering the theoretical framework in which Schippel had made his case. The oracle of orthodoxy was reduced to posing a number of sceptical, if nonetheless acute, questions: (1) Were countries without a standing army, like Switzerland and the USA, poorer or suffering from higher unemployment than those with standing armies, like Italy and Austria? (2) Could personal consumption not be raised further such that military expenditure was necessary to generate demand? (3) What effects did military expenditure have on the personal consumption of the masses? (4) What effects did heavy domestic tax burdens have on industry's competitiveness on the world market? (5) Would the demobilisation of the standing armies increase unemployment and create an economic crisis?[14]

Kautsky did not answer his own questions and perhaps he could not do so, for he subscribed to the same dubious underlying assumptions as Schippel. The Russian populist Vorontsov had recognised a decade earlier that this sort of under-consumptionist argument depended entirely on a case in which the military bill was footed by the bourgeoisie. After all, it was the bourgeoisie's share of the social product which was not being consumed. Where taxes were levied on mass consumption the only result would be to depress working-class living standards further. Aggregate demand remained unchanged and the surplus product unabsorbed. But this, as Luxemburg realised by the time she wrote her *Accumulation of Capital* in 1913, was just what happened in Germany.[15] The distribution of the tax burden which Schippel wanted to dismiss as a matter of secondary importance was the central political issue. Simply – and in the early 1900s none of the participants yet realised it – this version of Marxist economic theory could not elucidate the problem.

The second unreflective assertion Schippel had made was to assume that armaments were 'unproductive'. Only thus could the military sector be regarded as a buffer against crises. By 1907, Kautsky found himself advancing precisely the same arguments though to a rather different moral and political effect. In a tract on socialism and the colonial question, arms production took on the contours of a maw sucking in materials and human beings, the moloch so beloved by Social Democratic cartoonists. Kautsky listed three methods of preventing crises of under-consumption, which he still believed to be the main problem facing modern capitalism. One was to export capital, a variation on his original theory of imperialism; another was to limit competition through oligopoly, so removing the micro-economic causes for rising productivity; and the third was to waste productive capacity. 'A very effective way of doing this is by the arms race on land and sea ... '[16] Kautsky banged home his conclusion that 'the abolition of militarism, like that of cartels and trusts, is today only possible through socialism'.[17] After their defeat in the 1907 elections Social Democracy groped for new slogans to attack the nationalist Right head on. The choice was no longer, according to some SPD publicists, between protectionism and free trade but – borrowing the slogan of Joseph Chamberlain – 'between imperialism and socialism'. Kautsky's theory made sense of such claims. Hilferding's talk of a 'new stage' of finance capital contributed even more explicitly to this belief that capitalism had reached its *fin de siècle*.

Schippel and Kautsky had painted with a broad brush. Neither had questioned whether the arms industry could actually fill the canvas they had prepared for it. Irrespective of whether or not it was supposed to be a buffer or a burden, was military expenditure actually large enough to have a serious effect on capitalist development? And was the military sector 'unproductive'? Eduard Bernstein tackled the first of these questions. Rosa Luxemburg would address the second.

Bernstein pointed out in 1899 that the size of the military budget remained a relatively small percentage of national income. However great the sufferings that indirect taxation might impose on the German working class, these had to be distinguished from the impact of military expenditure on the economy as a whole.[18] This distinction between fiscal questions and growth ought to have served as a salutary warning, and headed off much of what Kautsky and the radicals subsequently wrote. Bernstein himself tried to answer Kautsky's question about whether conscription increased or decreased unemployment. To do so he drew on David Ricardo's idea of the war economy.[19] Ricardo, writing soon after the Napoleonic Wars and the imposition of the first income tax in English history, had regarded a war as potentially beneficial to industrial growth. By taxing the rich luxury consumption was held down, so diverting resources from handicrafts to the industrial suppliers of the army. The net result, Ricardo said, had been to stimulate growth in output and productivity and reduce the level of unemployment. Conversely, the end of the war would, as the experience of England in 1815 had demonstrated, make the part of the population mobilised for the war 'redundant, and by its effect on the rest of the population, and its competition with it for employment, will sink the value of wages, and very materially deteriorate the condition of the labouring classes'.[20] Bernstein found this account very persuasive, though he followed Marx in rejecting Ricardo's theory of subsistence wages. In Bernstein's Germany as in Ricardo's England, unemployment was high and the labour market slack; conscription might reduce the intense competition for jobs but it would certainly not hold back civilian employment. As we shall see this Ricardian thesis would be called into question at the end of the 1900s, once renewed growth led to a tighter labour market and higher wage levels.

Much of Bernstein's intervention was given over to an over-ambitious and confused examination of Schippel's main thesis. Almost incidentally Bernstein commented that the real economic effect of militarism was to 'direct production along the wrong path'. Military contracts allowed for high profits and wages because of monopoly pricing. Domestic heavy industrial suppliers were induced away from producing for markets where they faced more competitive pricing (e.g. railway locomotives), and towards naval and military projects.[21] This was a telling insight, although he did not elaborate it further. Moreover, Bernstein was no more critical than Schippel or Kautsky of the idea that devotion of social production to militarism was 'unproductive'.

Rosa Luxemburg attacked Schippel principally for his political views, for forgetting Social Democracy's mission to bring democracy to Germany and to replace the standing army with the militia. Her own thinking was too strongly imbued with the same under-consumptionist arguments as Kautsky and Schippel subscribed to for her to able to stand back and present a different economic perspective when the revisionist controversy was at its height.[22] Not until she wrote *The Accumulation of Capital* in 1913 did she make the attempt. In the concluding chapter she set out to demonstrate why militarism was an important 'province of accumulation' in its own right and what its effects on the rest of the economy were. Now she challenged one of the key assumptions of the debate so far; that armament production was inherently 'unproductive'. She showed that it was wrong to elide what might be socially undesirable with what was economically 'unproductive'. What defined labour under capitalism as 'productive' in Marxist terms was that a commodity was produced for sale on the market:

As far as the individual capitalist is concerned ... there are only commodities and buyers, and it is completely immaterial to him whether he produces instruments of life or instruments of death, corned beef or armour plating.[23]

It therefore also did not matter that the commodities were sold to the state, as long as they possessed and realised an exchange value. They had to pass through the market. That was all.

The main thrust of Rosa Luxemburg's investigation aligned government taxation policy with the profitability of producing arms. In a book which appeared just when Bethmann Hollweg had persuaded the Reichstag to agree to large increases in spending on the army, Luxemburg's final chapter could hardly have been more topical even though it remained on the same formal theoretical plane as the rest of the work.

Unfortunately, her argument was also internally self-contradictory. She asserted that the rate of surplus value and thus the rate of profit rose, if, as in the German case, armaments were paid for by taxing workers' wages. To the German worker, of course, it scarcely mattered whether wages were lowered by the employer or the state. But Luxemburg elided the two, erroneously assuming that somehow the individual capitalist benefited directly from such government taxation and so reaped super profits.[24] This was obviously not be the case, since the same amount of wages was being advanced by the employer.[25] Indeed, from a purely economic point of view all she had actually done was to show that industrial capitalists had an interest in forming a sort of anti-corn law league against the dominant alliance of 'rye and iron'. As a Marxist radical she did not of course draw this conclusion. Other commentators soon would.

Starting from a completely different point on the circle, she had reached the same point as Schippel. Where he had begun with the conundrum of 'over-production', she had commenced from the dynamics of the process of accumulation. Both had ended up concentrating on and attributing a positive economic role to government fiscal policy. The arms sector itself was only incidental to their theories. Armour plating mattered more than corned beef only because this was where the lion's share of the budget went. Like August Bebel, Wilhelm Liebknecht and Max Schippel all she was ultimately left with was the conviction that workers would not endure an ever greater tax burden indefinitely.[26] Since the 1890s this had been staple Social Democratic electoral propaganda.

Monopoly prices and economic growth

The one area in which Luxemburg and Bernstein had concurred was in considering the chief attraction of armaments contracts to reside in the guarantee of enormous and stable demand at monopoly prices. What was peculiar about the demand generated by the state for arms was that it did not come from 'fragmented private buyers'. 'The state's demand is characterised by security, massiveness, and the favourable, usually monopolistic, setting of prices, which makes the state the most privileged customer and makes contracts with it the most desirable for capital.'[27] Luxemburg, however, added one new and crucial point that Bernstein had not made but which had been implicit in Ricardo: the effect of the arms race on industrial productivity:

... the most important advantage of military contracts over state expenditures for cultural purposes (schools, roads, etc.), is the endless technical innovations and the ceaseless growth of expenditures. Indeed, it is an ever-increasing source of capitalist profit and erects capital as social power which the worker comes up against, for example, in the factories of Krupp and Stumm.[28]

She did not develop this theme further, but the young economist and protegé of Rudolf Hilferding, Gustav Eckstein, did. Like Luxemburg, he considered arms manufacture to be productive. But unlike all the previous contributors to the discussion he did not hold to an under-consumptionist theory of crisis. As we shall see this intellectual break with traditional crisis theory allowed Eckstein to consider the relationship between the arms sector and the rest of the economy in quite new terms.

In the early 1900s, the under-consumptionist case was subjected to devastating criticism by the Russian economist Michael Tugan Baranowsky and the Austrian Eugen Böhm-Bawerk. Austro-Marxists like Hilferding and Otto Bauer introduced their critique to German Social Democrats. It showed that the surplus product need not mount up until it produced a chronic crisis, but could simply be reinvested as capital. Technological and productivity growth could potentially continue unabated. Whereas the under-consumptionists had built their case on a reading of Marx's 'General Law of Capitalist Accumulation' in *Capital*, 1, the new school turned to his 'schemas of expanded reproduction' in *Capital*, 2.[29] In these schemas Marx had divided industry into two 'departments', one producing capital goods and the other wage goods, and shown that their mutual demand for each others' products could sustain growth potentially indefinitely. From this standpoint, crisis would depend on market failure, on the two departments losing their synchrony and growing in disproportion to each other. By the time Hilferding's *Finance Capital* appeared in 1910 'disproportionality theory' had supplanted under-consumption as the main explanation of capitalist crisis.[30]

Eckstein followed Tugan and Hilferding in discounting all under-consumptionist theories of crisis.[31] He therefore had two reasons for rejecting Schippel's whole line of enquiry. Capitalism did not need to waste resources to survive, and the arms industry was not a waste of economic resources anyway. Instead, Eckstein divided the economics of state intervention into two halves which corresponded to fiscal supply and demand. On the fiscal supply side came the impact of different types of taxation. On the demand side, he placed the effects of state expenditure on arms. He and Luxemburg were the only writers to address themselves to this aspect of the problem and, as we shall see, he did so more successfully and rigorously.

On the tax question, Eckstein considered two different situations, one in which workers alone were taxed, and one where the burden was shared between workers and capitalists. Taxing workers alone, Eckstein noted, reduced their personal consumption but had no immediate effects on output or accumulation. In this he agreed with Vorontsov rather than Luxemburg.[32] Taxing both classes, on the other hand, would reduce the rate of accumulation because it lowered surplus value, the rate of profit and hence the capital available for fresh investment.[33] If the under-consumptionists were premature Keynesians in their view of state-generated demand, then this sort of Marxist view of taxation was definitely part of pre-Keynesian classical and neo-classical economic orthodoxy. There was not any distinctively Marxist theory of monetary and fiscal policy. It also accorded well with Social Democrats' old Radical preference for free trade and low levels of taxation.

Eckstein then introduced a third scenario, a reduction of the workforce through conscription. This was the obverse side of the coin passed out by Ricardo and Bernstein. They had talked about reducing unemployment through military service. But they had not considered the possibility of a labour shortage. In the rather tighter labour market of 1912–13, Eckstein obviously felt entitled to pose the question. He argued that conscription would have more negative immediate consequences on output and accumulation than taxation. Production would have to be scaled down and spare capacity would mount.[34] It is true that the full knock-on effects would only occur in a full-employment economy which even late imperial Germany certainly was not, but the point was a significant one.

These conclusions about the short-run effects of taxation and conscription were based on a static analysis. In fact, like the other contributors to the debate, Eckstein dealt with all the serious dynamic questions outside the rather decorative framework of Marx's reproduction schemas. Over the longer term, Eckstein argued that taxation to fund military expenditure was having adverse effects on both working-class living standards and the path of capitalist development. For the working class, an increasing tax burden was driving down the standard of living, which presumably led to the kind of decline in public health Bebel had agitated against since the

1890s. If carried far enough this would obviously result in a fall of labour productivity. 'The expectation', Eckstein wrote, 'that has been so frequently expressed that the financial burden of armaments must soon lead to the breakdown of the capitalist states is only correct in so far as the proletariat's labour power is harmed by the tax burden.'[35] But, as both he and Rosa Luxemburg pointed out, a tight labour market and successful trade union struggles made even this a very unlikely scenario.[36] Having disposed of the question of crisis and breakdown, Eckstein now turned to the problems of growth and monopoly.

Taxing capital over the longer term, Eckstein observed, would adversely affect accumulation of small capitals far more than big ones. With their smaller turnover small capitalists consumed a relatively larger proportion of their profits than did large ones. Fresh investment by small capitalists would be constrained by such tax burdens as much as by sudden increases in their own personal expenditure. Big capitalists were also freer to direct their investment purely on the basis of the prevailing rate of profit. They would therefore be able to carry the weight of taxation by a slight reduction of their own personal consumption rather than by reducing their level of investment.[37] Bebel had also insisted back in his attack on the military budget of 1893 that taxation accelerated the centralisation and concentration of capital, those Marxist hallmarks for the rise of oligopoly.[38] So new taxes would allegedly ruin small businessmen.[39] It is interesting that Eckstein did not consider that large investors might take the rate of taxation into account when calculating their returns. In his pre-'rational expectations' world, the idea that taxation might lead to a flight of capital did not strike him. It did, however, occur to the commentators on German armament in the British Foreign Office at this time.[40]

Instead, Eckstein drew attention to the common political interests between the smaller capitalists and the proletariat in resisting higher taxation. Like David Ricardo, Eckstein assumed that a wealth tax – like the very one the SPD helped to vote through in 1913 – would reduce demand for luxury goods (assuming that capitalists reduced their personal consumption), so that the rising output of 'mass products' for the military would be at the expense of handicraft production of luxury consumption goods.[41] So much for the effects of taxation; let us now turn to Eckstein's consideration of the effect of state spending on armaments upon economic growth as a whole.

Here we find a general consensus ranging from Eduard Bernstein to Rudolf Hilferding, from Karl Kautsky to Rosa Luxemburg and Gustav Eckstein, that heavy industry benefited inordinately from the arms race. Selling to a single buyer, the state, allowed the already strongly cartelised heavy industrial sector to charge monopoly prices and secure guaranteed long-term contracts in return. If heavy industry benefited most from a large military establishment, then this introduced a political distortion into a 'natural' pattern of growth. In the absence of militarism, rates of investment would be more balanced between sectors, leading to higher growth in manufacturing and agriculture.[42] Hilferding had already argued in *Finance Capital* that technological innovation and productivity growth tended to be much higher in heavy industry than in the rest of the economy.[43] State spending on armaments could then be regarded as a way of preventing this unbalanced growth from precipitating a disproportionality crisis in the economy as a whole.

But Eckstein preferred to concentrate on the idea that economic development was being simply directed along the wrong path. By 1913 there was also a general consensus that manufacturing industry and agriculture were paying the price for this over-rapid development of heavy industry.[44] As Eckstein put it, 'The capitalist country turns into a large factory, which draws its raw materials and consumption goods for its workers to a large extent from foreign countries which are still not developed from a capitalist point of view and exports its industrial products.'[45] By 1912–13, 'centrist' Marxists like Kautsky, Hilferding, Bebel and Bauer had reconstructed their theory of imperialism around this tenet. Imperialism only benefited heavy industry. Only it needed to export its surplus production and excess capital to protected colonial markets and import agricultural products and handicrafts in return.

The political conclusion which the SPD leadership drew from this line of reasoning was that 'militarism' and 'imperialism' did not benefit capitalism as a whole. They certainly were not the functional necessities to capitalist development which orthodox Marxists had once believed.[46] As we shall see in the next chapter, the party leadership hoped that it might be able to persuade the 'progressive and pacifist bourgeoisie' to join a broadly-based movement in favour of peace and disarmament. If the party could thus isolate the magnates of heavy industry as the villains of the piece, then it would have succeeded in undermining popular support for Wilhelmine *Weltpolitik* and could return democratic and social change at home to the top of the political agenda. This was the hope and the strategic aim. On the intellectual front, Eckstein was obviously contributing to this new pacifist orientation when he suggested that low defence spending had contributed to the unrivalled growth of the USA and insisted that high military spending only served very narrow sectional interests.[47]

The military–industrial complex

As if on cue to endorse this general conclusion a most spectacular arms scandal broke cover in Germany. Just when it seemed that discussion of the economics of armament had become a dry affair accessible only to the party's Marxist educated intellectuals, Karl Liebknecht shocked the Reichstag and provided banner headlines for the press. The scandal concerned the lobbying methods of Krupp, the flagship of German industry and *the* contractor for the high seas fleet and the army. In the winter of 1912–13, Liebknecht came into possession of documents showing that Brandt the head of Krupp's Berlin office had bribed seven officials at the War Ministry in order to obtain inside information on the tenders of other suppliers. Brandt sent his reports to Eccius, one of the directors of the firm at its headquarters in Essen, where they were filed in an armoured safe as 'top secret'.[48] Liebknecht received copies from an anonymous source, most likely a rival firm. After sending these reports to the Minister of War, Heeringen, in November 1912, and conscientiously waiting five months for official action, Liebknecht himself revealed his information to a stunned Reichstag.[49]

The Krupp scandal provided the SPD with a field day. Party publicists had long claimed that military suppliers had a vested interest in the arms race,[50] but this could all still be dismissed as inflammatory speculation. The party had had very few hard facts to go on. Liebknecht demanded that the guilty parties, Krupp and the Deutsche Waffen und Munitionsfabrike, should be barred from receiving future contracts in line with official government policy.[51] To have enforced this norm against Krupp would have literally halted German armament. Instead, the government immediately agreed to establish a Reichstag Committee of enquiry to investigate what Liebknecht had dubbed Germany's 'Panama scandal'. Liebknecht, however, was kept off the Committee, which the SPD then boycotted. On 4 July, Heeringen resigned over the affair.[52]

As Liebknecht dug deeper he showed how far the roots of the German arms lobby reached – into the French and Russian press as well as the German. He revealed how the arms lobby had deliberately planted disinformation in the French press in order to scare Germany into further armament. Every leading Social Democrat added his or her voice to the clamour against what Liebknecht called the 'International of the arms industry' and what we have come to know as the 'military–industrial complex'. Even Eduard Bernstein joined the clamour against the arms lobby with its press, connections with the great financial houses and its friends in the ministries and general staffs.[53] But Bernstein saw the problem in much the same Cobdenite and pacifist terms J. A. Hobson was canvassing in Britain, and towards which, as we have seen, moderate Marxists like Kautsky and Eckstein now leaned.[54] On the radical Left around Rosa Luxemburg, the Krupp scandal also changed nothing. It was one more piece of evidence that German capitalism was irredeemably militaristic and imperialist.

Once again Karl Liebknecht was the odd theorist out in the party for attaching significance to the actual political facts he had come across. From them he constructed a rather conspiratorial if carefully documented account of the pro-armament lobby. First, he extended the line of enquiry opened up by the Krupp scandal and showed that high-ranking military and civil personnel systematically 'retired' to well-paid positions in the arms firms they had been responsible for giving contracts to. Then he turned to the extent to which the arms industry itself was organised. Not only was domestic heavy industry heavily cartelised, as Hilferding and others had already shown and Liebknecht now demonstrated afresh for the armaments producers. But, as he revealed, these cartels, joint-stock companies and trusts also reached across national borders. The German armaments firm Dillinger was largely French owned. Dillinger in turn had a major holding in the conservative *Post* newspaper, famous for advocating strong-arm measures at home and abroad. He showed a similar interpenetration of capital between a number of German and French, German and Russian and Austrian and French firms, all supposedly on opposite sides of the international alliance system. German, French and British firms had jointly equipped the Putilov armament works in St Petersburg, while an Austro-German firm had sold 200,000 rifles to Austria's enemy Serbia. The most conspiratorial case of all Liebknecht's allegations related to the Nobel trust, which he claimed spanned seventeen countries and 33 arms companies.[55]

The point that Liebknecht was trying to make was that governments had lost a great deal of control over the arms race not only because they could not stop it, but because the arms suppliers had subverted control.[56] Whereas Kautsky and Hilferding had regarded international joint ventures and cartels as a pacific force, which could overcome the armed confrontation of nation states, Liebknecht was now arguing that the international arms trade revealed the opposite forces at work. Vested economic interests were also much more prominent now in Liebknecht's account than they had been in his *Militarism*. But the links and structure of the system he was describing still had more to do with the sorts of networks of power he had begun to think about in prison than with any Marxist conception of the 'capitalist system'.[57]

It was this sharper political edge to Liebknecht's enquiry which caught the attention of the Radicals and socialists in France and Britain. Plans were made with André Morizet and John Newbold for joint studies of the munitions industry in Britain, France and Germany.[58] The first world war interrupted this collaboration but Newbold at least managed to publish his contribution in the middle of the war. Although the British Foreign Office rated the importance of the Krupp scandal rather lowly,[59] it signalled the beginning of the study of what we have come to call the 'military–industrial complex'.

Conclusion

A fault-line runs between this intellectual discussion of armaments and the SPD's political preoccupations. If the principal goal of the SPD publicists was to target high taxes on the consumer, then its economic theorists consistently missed that objective. Marxist economics – even in its re-visionist versions – consistently transposed policy and fiscal problems into structural questions of capitalist development and crisis. What is more – and this is perhaps the ultimate irony – the marginalist revolution in neo-classical economics which had been under way since the 1870s provided a perfectly satisfactory framework in which the SPD's case against excessive taxes could have been put. As a negative good, defence and security should not cost more than the margin of risk which they offset. Eduard Bernstein stumbled nearest to such a formulation, as he strained to include 'the necessary defence of the country' within his analysis. But Marxist economics simply was not conducive to substantiating Social Democratic claims that Germany could fulfil the requirements of territorial defence more cheaply and equitably than under the policies prescribed by the Imperial government.

Much of the Marxist debate was already directed in search of an ultimate 'fetter' on growth which would precipitate some inexorable and insoluble crisis of capitalism. As long as the party's leading theorists remained wedded to under-consumptionist explanations of economic crisis they subordinated any analysis of the arms race to this prior *idée fixe*. They compounded this problem by insisting on the 'unproductivity' of the military sector as if the same steel mills in Essen which rolled railway track suddenly became unproductive when they turned out socially undesirable commodities like howitzers. It was not until Rosa Luxemburg overturned this assumption and Gustav Eckstein rejected the more fundamental under-consumptionist paradigm that a more nuanced and plausible view could emerge. This view focused on the unbalanced growth of heavy industry, the monopoly position of the armaments' industry, the dangers of over-taxation and a potential conflict of economic interests within the establishment.

Almost all the contributors failed to supply any empirical data, except for Karl Liebknecht, and he was not an economist.[60] As economists they also lacked rigorous analytical tools. Even the comparative statics that Eckstein and Luxemburg presented in their reproduction schemas contained arithmetic errors. Again they might have avoided traps if they had used the techniques of algebra and calculus pioneered by the neo-classicals, rather than sticking to Ricardo's and Marx's method of arguing via arithmetic examples. But the only Marxist economist to seriously engage with marginalism at this time wrote it off as *The Economic Theory of the Leisure Class*.[61] These minor problems mask the much greater ones of using the labour theory of value and the key elements of Marxist growth theory, the organic and technical compositions of capital, the rate of profit and relating the general equilibrium model of *Capital*, 2 to the disequilibrium model of *Capital*, 3. But for all that, specific questions asked about military economics which were raised in the decade and a half prior to the first world war have continued to be formulated in much the same terms long after the original preoccupations have been forgotten and the general framework of Marxist economics has gone out of fashion.

The questions which came to the fore were vital. What is the scale of the military sector? What are the linkages between the military sector and the rest of the economy? Does arms expenditure raise or lower the rate of productivity growth and the rate of profit? Does the military sector serve as an 'engine of growth' or does it retard development elsewhere? What are the effects on levels of consumption and employment? To what extent do military industries operate as independent agents, influencing their own governments' policies on armament and the international arms trade? Although only Kautsky left these questions in an interrogatory form, it is the questions and underlying ideas rather than the grander theory which have remained just as topical today as when they were first posed.

In the 1950s radical American sociologists recreated much of this perspective under the general heading of studies of the 'military–industrial complex'.[62] Knowing only Luxemburg's work, they were necessarily unaware of the relationship between the sort of sophisticated Marxist critique of 1912–13 and that of Marx's *Capital* or Karl Kautsky's *Class Struggle*. By the time Eckstein was writing, crisis theory had been narrowed to the issue of market failure and the imperatives of planning. To deal carefully with armament as a specific problem was only possible once attention had turned away from sweeping and simplistic explanations of the general crisis of capitalism. In political as well as intellectual terms the new attention accorded to military economics was predicated on a less stark juxtaposition of the alternatives. It was no longer simply 'imperialism or socialism'. The 'progressive and pacifist bourgeoisie' could join the peace movement and prevent world war; the arms race could be curtailed without undermining the viability of the whole system. Capitalism, as Hilferding would put it a few years later, could be 'organised'. The political and intellectual framework was already being created on which Social Democracy would erect its democratic reform politics during the Weimar Republic and, indeed, after Nazism.

6 The tides of pacifism, 1907–14

Historians no less than contemporaries have been fascinated by the SPD's *volte face* on 4 August 1914 when the parliamentary party endorsed the first world war. To some it signified the triumph of nationalism over international class solidarity; to others of reform over revolution. Both Social Democrats and Communists traced their ideological differences back to this vote. The causes of the switch from intransigent opposition have been at least as much a matter of dispute, but the most influential interpretations have focused on the attenuation of that intransigence during the previous decade and a half. Revisionist ideas, reformist political practice – especially in Southern Germany – and the increasing influence over the party of moderate trade union leaders have all been canvassed. In the Weberian view the SPD acquired vested interests through its very organisational success; their survival became more vital to the new generation of professional politicians and functionaries than its political programme. Social historians have discussed whether or not an 'embourgeoisement of the proletariat' took place.[1]

All of these accounts are persuasive up to a point. They also all share two flaws. First, they suggest some sort of gradual linear development from radicalism to reformism. But even Reichstag delegates on the right-wing of the party, like Gustav Noske, could turn radical on the old-fashioned issues of military interference in civilian life raised by the Saverne affair in 1913. Politically, the party also oscillated more and proved less tractable than would fit these linear trends. It was radical on the back of the mass mobilisations of 1905, 1910, 1912 and the spring of 1914, and more moderate in 1907 in the face of electoral defeat and again in 1913 with the prospect of coalition politics over the tax issue. Yet, however divided and increasing restless for change the party may have become, the centrist leaders still held it together – just. The second flaw in these accounts of the vote for war credits is that they focus exclusively on trends in domestic politics. That may have been where the SPD's principal concerns and traditional strength lay but the vote for war was nothing if not a triumph of foreign over domestic policy.

The July crisis and the declaration of war involved the SPD in not one *volte face* but two. The obvious and glaring turn was from calling for peace demonstrations in late July as 'a flaming protest against war and war-mongers' to supporting the war on grounds of 'national defence' a week later. Less obvious but of great significance was an earlier swing from regarding war as inevitable to striving to prevent it. During the 1890s and early 1900s, it had been an article of faith for Social Democratic leaders that the labour movement could not prevent wars and that to seek to do so was tantamount to anarchism. In 1911, they staged the first mass peace demonstrations in European history. In 1890 or 1900, it was perfectly evident that the party regarded virtually any war against Russia as a matter of 'national defence', of German 'culture' against Russian 'barbarism', as we saw in chapter 2. The turn to pacifism clouded this picture. The mass activity which accompanied this new pacifist commitment also distracted attention from what Social Democrats would actually do if they failed to prevent war. Many of the Reichstag deputies who assembled for the Social Democratic caucus on 3 August did not know which way they would vote, confused by the rush of events and their own contradictory values and aspirations.

The turn to pacifism was clearly a complicating factor in a number of ways. It was an abrupt departure from Social Democracy's pessimistic realism in dealing with great power conflicts. At the same time, it tapped the humanitarian and idealistic resources of the movement to the full. If the SPD was becoming more conservative at this time, then this was a very zig-zag and uneven progress. Again, how 'militarism' was reinterpreted and divined is highly indicative. We have seen how in domestic politics the meaning of militarism shifted from a radical democratic attack on the authoritarian state to a narrower focus on the economic interests involved in armament and a more fearful concern for the 'mass psychosis' engulfing a civil society increasingly dedicated to marching, wearing uniforms and consecrating flags. The turn to pacificism completed this move away from the original radical identification of militarism with the authoritarian state. Henceforth the central motif would be war.

Pacifism followed from a radical rethink of party strategy in the wake of Social Democracy losses in the Reichstag elections of 1907. Although the SPD vote remained virtually the same, the party lost half its Reichstag seats, down from 80 to 40. This came as a tremendous shock to a party whose confidence in its own inexorable rise had been validated by gains in every election held in the last twenty years. Something had gone badly wrong. The election itself had been a snap one, called in the depths of winter by a Chancellor furious at criticism of German colonial policy. The SPD and the Centre had both turned the atrocities committed by the

German troops who repressed the Herero uprising in South West Africa into a national issue.[2] Chancellor Bülow successfully turned the table on the opposition and fought the election on nationalist and colonial issues. Having gone to the polls confident that its traditional case against the expenses of *Weltpolitik* would receive a sympathetic hearing from German consumers, the SPD was astounded by the result. Its campaign had been efficient. The same message had worked in 1898 and 1903. What had gone wrong in these 'Hottentot elections'?

The party leadership and activists passed introspective evenings wrangling over the problem – had the party gone too far to the left or too far to the right – and denying in public that there was a problem. The principal change since the days when Bismarck had played the nationalist card against the SPD was the rise of mass politics on the radical Right. Germany's 'place in the sun' found more than just an echo in the mass organisations of the Right, the army associations (*Kriegervereine*), the Navy League, the Pan Germans and the Imperial League against Social Democracy. Populist politicians had gone several steps further and begun to attack the Wilhelmine establishment itself for being soft on the labour movement, too conciliatory in its foreign policy. From 1890 until 1905, mass politics had been largely in the SPD's favour. Now it faced an aggressive and belligerent nationalism for which it was relatively unprepared. The old economic arguments about the unprofitability of Germany's colonies and the costs to the German tax-payer sounded routine and increasingly irrelevant in the face of this rising crescendo of rhetorical violence.[3]

The party might predict and deplore Anglo-German naval rivalry.[4] The SPD went to the polls in 1907, blaming the government's haphazard and universally aggressive foreign policy for uniting such long-standing enemies as Britain and France and alienating Italy. True to its Cassandra role, the party forewarned of the Anglo-Russian entente which was to be signed later in the same year.[5] But the SPD received no more thanks than Priam's daughter. Nor did these accurate analyses of international relations lead to obvious policy conclusions. Eduard David and some of the revisionists within the SPD began to echo the nationalistic rhetoric about Germany's 'encirclement'.[6] The Left preferred that the party continue to ignore international relations.[7] The party leadership officially called for an end to the naval race and a conciliatory policy towards Britain as the only means out of the Reich's self-inflicted isolation. August Bebel himself made secret contact with the British Foreign Office, urging Britain to outbuild Germany's fleet, so that fiscal constraints might finally prevail over dreams of sea power.[8] He must have been deeply gratified when the German government was forced to just such a compromise in 1912. Apart from the danger of being tried for treason, Bebel could not afford to shock the pacifist sentiments of the Second International by publicising these diplomatic moves. Keir Hardie was already pressing for the International to adopt a pro-disarmament policy at the time Bebel was urging for more rapid naval construction in Britain.[9]

The SPD's long-standing objection to the 'big navy' as a dangerous extravagance in the face of Germany's need for continental defence might have the endorsement of Bismarck and the elder Moltke. But these architects of German unity had other more direct successors in conservative and army circles who thought the same, including Moltke's nephew. When enthusiasm for the navy began to wane in Germany, it was the younger Moltke and the General Staff who would reap the benefits, not the SPD. The SPD may have shared Bismarck's belief that a continental strategy meant no more than defending the territorial integrity of the Reich, but by 1910 a 'continental policy' had come to mean expansion eastwards, compensation in Europe and the Balkans for the colonial power not yet attainable overseas. But even at the height of Wilhelmine navalism Social Democracy was in disarray. The traditional emphasis on domestic politics had been upstaged by international conflicts of the worst kind. Secret conversations in Zurich between the veteran leader of the movement and an honorary British Consul appropriately named Angst were no substitute for a new policy. Each faction in the party tried to find a different opening. But the SPD's old strategy led no farther.

Social Democracy also faced a renewed domestic challenge which fundamentally undermined its traditional anti-militarist programme. In 1909 the Munich Military Association was launched in order to combat Social Democratic influence over the young and to provide an antidote to the 'increasingly dominant fantasies of "eternal peace"'.[10] Its membership grew to over 10,000 by 1914. Prussia soon imitated the Bavarian initiative and in 1911 Field Marshal Colmar von der Goltz obtained royal blessing to establish the Young Germany League. War games, gymnastics and nationalistic talks, it was hoped, would win the loyalty of young workers where explicitly anti-Social Democratic and religious appeals had failed in the past.[11] By 1914 the League had some 67,000 active members, their units often being drawn from the continuation schools for young workers.

This development challenged Social Democracy more directly than probably any other type of 'social militarism'. True the Young Germany League soon antagonised Catholic and Protestant sensibilities for not respecting the sabbath and alienated the nationalistic German Gymnasts by replacing its instructors with army officers in the continuation schools. But to Social Democracy it began to be clear for the first time that the jingle 'He who has the youth has the future' did not necessarily lead to an optimistic conclusion. How could Social Democrats go on demanding civilian gymnastics and military training as the cornerstones of a citizens' militia? In such circumstances the militia itself had become a political liability to anti-militarists. Wilhelmine nationalists had finally succeeded in constructing more potent metaphors of the 'people in arms'.

From national defence to pacifism

Launching a pacifist counter-offensive may have been a logical response to the threat of nationalism and war but it was not an easy one. Not only did Social Democratic leaders often fear beings branded 'traitors to the fatherland', but they also had to overcome their own reservations about the efficacy of pacifist action. In 1907, the SPD was also put under direct and intense international pressure from the French Socialist Party and the British Independent Labour Party to embark on a pacifist programme.

German party leaders had always been hostile to the International acquiring any independent executive authority and remained rather suspicious of the other national sections, doubting their organisational ability and political acumen. This simmering impatience duly surfaced at the Stuttgart congress of 1907, when the old plan to call a general strike in order to prevent war was once again tabled. This time its sponsors included not just anarcho-syndicalist sympathisers like Gustav Hervé but also Edouard Vaillant, who had been among those to insist most strongly that the general strike was impossible back in the early 1890s.[12] The general strike demand continued to be tabled by Vaillant and Keir Hardie till 1914 and the German and Austrian Social Democrats continued to refuse to endorse it.[13] If the French failed to convince the Germans over this tactical question at Stuttgart, they nonetheless scored a strategic victory. The SPD had committed itself to adopt a pacifist strategy. Something had to be done to prevent war. This wrought a great change in the party. As it redefined its strategy, so too the dividing lines between Left and Right changed. In 1900 Luxemburg had delivered an unchallenged address to the International in which she had said war could not be prevented. By 1910 she wanted the party to go all the way and endorse the general strike motion itself.[14] The new divisions reflected a new, if somewhat submerged, consensus between the different factions of the party around the pacifist objective. This was no mean feat considering the sharp divisions of 1907.

The first joint peace rallies were called in Britain and Germany in 1908 to protest against the colossal rise in the naval race marked by the dreadnought. The meetings were small-scale and the tone hesitant compared with those that would be held in the years 1911–12. The second Moroccan crisis of 1911 set the alarm bells ringing. It inspired nationalist

9 'Progress in Prussian schools', from *Simplicissimus*, 1911

groups and much of the press in France and Germany to a new pitch of
hysterical belligerence. It also provided the first occasion for full-scale
peace demonstrations in Germany. The enthusiasm in Germany was so
great that the rallies continued throughout the autumn in order to protest
against the Italian government's Tripoli expedition, an act about which the
Italian Socialist Party itself had very little to say. The response in Germany
was also far greater than in France. While the joint SFIO–CGT rally at the
Aéro-Parc in Paris could only muster some 3,000 to 4,000 participants –
and tried to make up for their paucity in numbers by the radicalism of their
slogans – the main SPD rallies were enormous by any measure. On Sunday
20 August, 30,000 turned out in Leipzig to hear Luxemburg and her fellow-
radical Marxist Paul Lensch, and 100,000 gathered in Berlin,[15] while on the
Monday evening the South German reformist Ludwig Frank packed the
beautiful Niebelungen Hall in Mannheim to overflowing.[16] Protests were
also held in Halle, Brunswick, Elberfeld, Barmen, Jena, Essen, Lausitz,
Gotha, Augsburg, Strassbourg and Schwerin. The organisers often took
over the largest meeting place in the town and they still had to turn away
hundreds or even thousands of people. Many of them hung around in the
nearby pubs and beer gardens so they could join in impromptu street
marches afterwards. Sometimes these ended in minor scuffles with the
police.[17] But for the most part the atmosphere was good-natured. The

Prussian police took elaborate precautions but in the end they left the crowds in the mild-mannered but extremely efficient hands of red-armband-wearing Social Democratic stewards. The climax of this series of anti-war demonstrations was reached again on a Sunday, 3 September, when some 250,000 flocked to the Treptower Park in Berlin.[18]

The peace demonstrations were the biggest gatherings ever organised by the pre-war SPD. They far outstripped the May Day celebrations, which in any case had lost much of the agitational edge they had enjoyed when they were first started in 1890. Instead, May Day had become a cultural festival redolent with beautiful gymnastic displays, beer, choral singing and dancing.[19] It was also often – as in most of Prussia in 1911 – confined by the police to clubs, pubs and meeting halls.[20] Even the famous Prussian suffrage demonstration of 1910 had not exceeded the 150,000 mark in Berlin. There can be little doubt, however, that the suffrage campaign and the peace movement fed into each other. At the Treptower Park rally of 1911, Karl Liebknecht warned against the dire link between repression at home and expansion abroad.[21] By the time the next mass peace protests were called in the autumn of 1912, the SPD explicitly linked the suffrage campaign – which had once again dominated the political agenda in the spring – to the right of the German people to decide democratically in favour of war or peace.[22] No doubt, too, the anti-war movement was assisted by parallel protests against the rising cost of living and the increasingly aggressive anti-trade union tactics of big industry, but again they far outstripped the strike movements in scale.

The peace movement reached its peak in late 1912. The outbreak of the Balkan War spread terrible alarm, raising the spectre of war between Austria and Russia. It was the first clash on the European continent since the Russo-Turkish war of 1877, and – in an age of rival alliance systems – socialists had become so used to the idea that the era of limited wars was over that they rightly felt themselves to be on the very edge of world war. Even the Prussian police admitted that huge rallies were staged in virtually every major city in Germany.[23] Again they built up to a mass gathering in Treptower Park on 20 October to which some quarter of a million people came, followed by another set of smaller simultaneous rallies in London, Paris and Berlin on 17 November.[24] To heighten the sense of inter-nationalism, socialist leaders were exchanged, Jaurès speaking in German (because of the legal restrictions on speaking foreign languages in public) in the closed meetings in Berlin.[25] A week later the extraordinary Congress of the Second International met in Basle, greeted by the protestant clergy who handed over their cathedral to the delegates with the red flags.[26]

The scale of the turnout begs the question of middle-class support. The Liberal parties had done anything but endorse the peace movement.

Indeed the National Liberals remained one of the more belligerent and expansionist-minded parties in German politics, undermining Social Democratic political hopes in the 'pacifist bourgeoisie' at a parliamentary level. But both the numbers at the rallies and the description of the participants indicate that many middle-class people did take part.[27]

During 1913 the peace movement collapsed. Few rallies were held and fewer people attended.[28] Contrary to all expectations, the Balkan wars had turned out to be limited, and Social Democrats started to believe that their own lobbying for peace had a restraining effect on the great powers. The spirit of reason had prevailed. It was only in retrospect that 1913 with its army increases in Germany and reintroduction of three year conscription in France appeared as the last frantic round before governments plunged into the first world war. At the time, the SPD and SFIO congratulated themselves on having issued a joint manifesto against the new cycle of the arms race.[29] The series of compromises between the great powers set in motion by the Anglo-German agreements of 1912 and the short-lived period of domestic parliamentary co-operation between Liberals and Social Democrats which culminated in the 1913 tax reform sowed illusions of peace and stability. Perhaps too, people were tired of demonstrating; as anarcho-syndicalists learned in Central Italy at about the same time, there was a limit to the number of times people could called out unless something positive was achieved.[30]

In some ways the popular appeal of the peace movement must have come as a pleasant surprise to Social Democratic intellectuals and leaders. Not much had yet been written about mass psychology. Psychology itself was a new subject. Marxist intellectuals had discussed workers' 'class consciousness' in the rationalist language of classical liberalism, occasionally venturing into social Darwinist debates about the relative importance of social versus individualist 'instincts'. But it was only with the rise of nationalist and jingoistic mass politics that liberal and socialist intellectuals turned to psychology. In their schema of 'progressive reason' war, racism, demagoguery or national hatreds were reactionary, violent and anti-enlightenment. Accordingly non-rational grounds for these values had to be found. As we have seen, Social Democrats, like Karl Liebknecht talked about 'mass hypnotism' and 'mass psychosis' from the early 1900s.[31] It must have come as something of a relief then to find that so many people were willing to fill Germany's squares, parks and meeting halls to protest against war. But the very success of the peace movement also encouraged a rather smug reading of how far socialist peace protests had actually influenced their governments. The International was nominated for the Nobel Peace Prize in 1913, and the boast of the Dutch socialist Troelstra that governments had 'managed to find the address of the International

Socialist Bureau in their anxiety to avert war' went the rounds of the European Left.[32]

Programme and policy

The socialist peace movement entailed a merger of programmes and techniques. There was nothing particularly new or socialist about the programme. The Copenhagen Congress of the International endorsed a motion drafted by the Austro-Marxist Karl Renner in favour of international arbitration, general disarmament and an immediate convention to limit navies; the abolition of secret diplomacy and publication of all treaties.[33] International appeals for disarmament and arbitration instead of military rivalry and war had an unbroken history going back to Richard Cobden and the first Peace Society. But the peace societies, especially in Germany, were small genteel associations which had little or no popular legitimacy.[34] What the parties of the Second International could give to the peace movement was their ability to mobilise people in their tens and hundreds of thousands, even millions. This capacity gave the socialist peace movement its particular legitimacy and led to the development of a distinctive political style and technique.

Pacifism may not have been new but it was new to Social Democracy. Although Social Democracy had always abjured violence, bloodshed and war at a general level, it had previously eschewed pacifist politics. The peace movement may have given a practical outlet for idealistic values which had been long held in check.[35] But it was not easy to integrate pacifist ideas with conventional Marxist theory or with SPD foreign policy. In order to achieve a new theoretical synthesis the idea of militarism had to be wrested from its traditional identification with the remnants of the absolutist state. The dichotomy between the citizens' militia and the absolutist standing army was replaced by a new polarity between disarmament and world war. Kautsky found himself under challenge here from radical Marxists like Anton Pannekoek, Karl Radek and Paul Lensch, who refused to surrender the old militia ideal or to believe that disarmament was feasible under capitalism. Within the party as a whole, however, only the Bremen Left clung to the end to the idea that the militia provided the only plank in the anti-militarist platform.[36] Even Rosa Luxemburg herself shifted ground to a preventive strategy.

The real issue under dispute here was whether or not Social Democracy could find political allies within the middle class. The radicals subscribed to the thesis that the bourgeoisie formed 'one reactionary mass', because – as we saw in the previous chapter – they considered colonialism to be essential to capitalism as a whole. As late as 1910 Kautsky substantially agreed and condemned it as 'utopian to believe that bourgeois pacifist conferences or visits by friends of peace to foreign governments can abolish the danger of war and introduce disarmament and submission to international courts'.[37] But during the next three years Kautsky changed his mind and tried to explain why Social Democrats could co-operate with these bourgeois 'friends of peace'. As ever he explained political alliances in the same language of economic class interests which radical Marxists and revisionists also used. Kautsky contended that international joint stock companies were superseding national enterprises as the dominant form of capitalism. He concluded that there was no longer any over-riding functional reason within capitalist development why national bourgeoisies should compete for colonies. Inter-imperialist rivalries and bellicose policies, as we saw in the last chapter, were no longer supposed to be associated with imperialism as a whole, but rather with the interests of that section of the bourgeoisie which was involved in armaments and protected sectors of the national economy.

In German terms the guilty parties were the heavy industrialists and agrarians of the National Liberals and Conservatives. Export-earning manufacturers and international investors associated with the Left Liberals and sections of the National Liberals, especially in the Hansa cities, were now supposed to come over as the 'pacifist bourgeoisie'. Although by the end of 1913 Kautsky himself was disappointed by the scant enthusiasm of the German bourgeoisie for disarmament, his theory of 'ultra-imperialism' was of profound ideological importance in the reorientation of the SPD towards the peace movement. The high point of the 1912 Party Congress was an oration by Bebel's new co-chairman Hugo Haase which delineated all the main elements of this new orthodoxy, relegating Luxemburg's sharp resumé of the traditional view of imperialism to the radical sidelines.[38] The point was not to suggest that war was unlikely, only that it was not inevitable. If it was not inevitable, then it was worth throwing the entire organised weight of the labour movement into the scales against it. To prevent further damaging public wrangling, the party executive organised a censorship of the radical Left within the party press. From March 1913 this assumed a systematic form.[39]

However economistic the language, the tactical divisions had been sharply drawn once more within the party, this time around different varieties of pacifism. The radicals wanted to link the struggle for peace to political revolution, relying solely on the mass action of the 'proletariat'. The party leadership strove to break down the isolation of the movement and regain the political initiative without abandoning its programme; hence the attempt to win liberal allies, to use the mass support of the party without provoking an open confrontation with the authorities. The immediate goals were the same as the radicals': suffrage reform in Prussia and international disarmament. Some left-wingers, like Karl Liebknecht, wanted to combine the radical tactic of the mass strike with the quest for liberal alliances. But behind the sharp tactical differences lay a greater consensus about basic strategy than had existed in 1905–7, or would exist after the war broke out. Even Bernstein and the South German reformists backed the suffrage campaign in Prussia and the creation of an international peace movement.

The tactical sticking point between the leadership and the radical Left was the mass strike. In part the division revisited the old problems of legality, consensus and violent confrontation with the state; whether or not Social Democracy should invite or could survive such an encounter. Kautsky expressed the general view of the leadership when he dismissed such an anti-war strike as 'heroic folly'.[40] The ebb and flow of popular moods was observed by Jaurès' deputy Marcel Sembat. He admitted bluntly in 1913, in a best-selling book on the peace issue, that

the possibility of an insurrection is a powerful way to exert pressure and an excellent threat. But when the time of threats is passed? When war is declared? ... What is to be done?[41]

Under fire from the Centre party, Hugo Haase had to admit equally frankly to the Reichstag in December 1912 that 'none of us thinks of making a revolution in order to prevent war'.[42] Instead, from 1911 onwards the SPD executive kept the peace movement under close control; it issued printed resolutions for the public meetings to pass.[43] These merely urged people to join the SPD as the only party that genuinely worked for peace and warned the government that the population would not support foreign adventures.

In part, too, the rejection of the pacifist mass strike rested on assumptions about national interest and foreign policy. Sembat concluded that socialists would defend their countries rather than leave them open to attack. And in fact, the SFIO conducted its campaign against the reintroduction of three-year conscription in France in 1913 under the slogan 'For national defence!'[44] In May 1914, Hugo Haase formulated the SPD's last memorandum on the general strike, in preparation for a further round of the Keir Hardie–Vaillant resolution at the International Congress scheduled for Vienna in August. After reviewing all the organisational weaknesses to which even the SPD would be prey, he returned to the central problem of policy:

One nation gratuitously attacks another. To prevent the attack, the socialists of the aggressor country call for a general strike but fail to win the support of the masses. Should the socialists of the invaded country, who might command much more powerful working class organisations, now be compelled to organise mass strikes in their country, and in this way virtually ensure the triumph of the aggressor?[45]

In his careful lawyer's prose, Haase was simply rephrasing Plekhanov's growl of 1893: A general strike 'would disarm the civilised peoples and surrender Western Europe to the Russian cossacks'.[46]

There could be little doubt against whom Haase's anxieties were directed. During the decade 1905–14, Social Democratic commitments to national defence remained closely calibrated to their degree of Russophobia. The SPD had delighted in Japan's victory over Russia – although Japan was actually the aggressor[47] – and Bebel had told the Reichstag that he was now convinced that 'the spectre of a war with Russia and France which has hung over Europe like a heavy storm cloud for the last three and a half decades has been banished for many, many years'.[48] With the outbreak of the 1905 revolution, most Social Democratic leaders accepted that the Russian threat had vanished. Even in the wake of the counter-revolution, many continued to assert that Russia was militarily and politically too weak to pose a danger to Germany, so that national defence no longer had any meaning. The conflict with Britain and France could be written off as 'imperialist rivalries' in which the SPD had no interest to defend.[49]

By the time of the second Moroccan conflict, however, most Social Democratic observers had come around to a more sombre view and regarded Russia's defeat in East Asia as having made strategists in St Petersburg look for compensation in the Balkans.[50] Only the radical Marxist Left – principally Konrad Haenisch and Paul Lensch – continued to claim that Tsarism no longer posed a threat and when the war actually broke out they moved faster than anyone else to a position of belligerently anti-Russian nationalism.[51] At a popular level, the coverage of the tsarist counter-revolution in the Social Democratic press, with its images of mass hangings, saw to it that Russia remained firmly identified with barbarism and political reaction. In this, at least, all sections of the party were agreed, with the left especially vociferous and ready to renew the accusations of barbarism whenever there was the slightest sign of Russo-German rapprochement, as for example during Nicholas II's visit to Berlin in 1913. New research on the pub surveillance reports compiled by the Hamburg political police suggests that such anti-Russian attitudes were strongly held by working-class customers. And the terms in which they expressed their opinions reproduced the images and arguments put forward by Social Democracy over the previous two decades to a very high degree.[52]

With the revival of anxieties about Russian expansion within the party leadership, a number of radicals and socialists again began to canvass the

Saint Simonian alliance of the 'advanced' countries – Germany, Britain and France – against the 'backward'. In practical terms, all the SPD could do was to use the International Socialist Bureau to co-ordinate the peace movement in the three countries.[53] But the problem of how to balance pacifism with national defence against Russia remained.

The outbreak of the first Balkan war prompted the French, German and British party leaders to clarify pacifist policy. At Basle they agreed in effect to throw the unequal weight of the labour movements on the uneven scales of the alliance system. The SPD was to lobby the German government to restrain Austria in the Balkans, while the French Socialist Party and the British Independent Labour Party were to press the French and British governments to refuse to support Russia. At the same time, the British and German organisations committed themselves to pushing their respective governments towards an understanding that would end the arms race.[54] In Basle cathedral this sounded very encouraging but back home the SPD now had to balance its pacifism against its own Russophobia. Unless 'national defence' was turned into a precise and operative method of assessing foreign policy, the SPD had no basis for telling the German government which policies the party would oppose, nor in what spheres the Reich ought to restrain its Austrian ally.

The first opportunity to put the SPD's views on the record came quite soon, in the Reichstag debate on 3 December 1912. True to the party's appeasement of its factions, Georg Ledebour spoke for the left and Eduard David for the right of the party. What each of them said turned out to be of enormous significance. Not only were the circumstances in July 1914 analogous but the two men would each play a key part in the hasty debate on war credits. In fact, in 1912, they both made very similar points. Both stated categorically that they would not support any Austrian aggression against Serbia even if Russia were to come to the aid of the latter. Ledebour accused the Imperial government of 'extending *carte blanche* to the allies of the German Reich, especially Austria, to embark on whatever policy Austria holds to be in her interests'. David acknowledged in one breath that the government had 'kept to the letter of the treaty' and emphasised in the next that the SPD interpreted it purely as 'a defensive alliance against Russian threats' and that only in the event of such an attack would Social Democrats participate in national defence.[55] Although Rosa Luxemburg and the Mulhouse party branch persisted in rejecting David's use of the defensive–aggressive polarity, such criticisms were now a fringe affair.[56] The speeches of December 1912 remained official SPD policy until August 1914.[57]

By the time Europe was plunged into the crisis of July 1914, German Social Democracy had effectively altered its anti-militarist programme in a number of fundamental ways. It had embraced the preventive tenets of a peace movement, instead of leaving war to the fates which governed capitalist development. This change necessitated a wholesale shift from an essentially domestically focused anti-militarist programme which it had formulated so effectively in the 1890s to an international one, from the militia to disarmament. It also entailed more direct responses to foreign policy, a subject of which Social Democrats had generally fought shy, and the mobilisation of large numbers of people for peaceful civil protests – pursuing in a more active but nonetheless controlled way the traditional Social Democratic strategy of trying to mobilise civil society against the state. The party observed the traditional legal limits and even when it took to the streets, public squares and parks scrupulously avoided any showdown with the authorities. If prevention failed, then the SPD spokesmen warned that they would decide their stance on the basis of national defence. The term had to be operationalised and inserted more carefully if still not unambiguously into the given alliance system.

All of these policy shifts are clear enough in retrospect, but at the time the pattern was far more confusing. Each one of the changes was challenged and argued over at the same time as the party was in the midst of completely different controversies; whether or not to approve the 1913 tax reforms; how to win suffrage reform in Prussia.[58] On top of this old elements of the anti-militarist programme continued alongside the new. The press still publicised the abuse of conscripts. The Bissing order and the Saverne incident reawakened the old democratic anti-militarism.

All of these variegated threads mingled in the midst of a generational crisis in the Social Democratic leadership. Paul Singer and August Bebel had served as the party's co-chairmen since the party had been re-established in 1891; they had been part of its leadership from the beginning. In 1911, Singer died and Hugo Haase was elected – with the support of the centre left – to replace him. Although Haase was an intelligent, independently-minded lawyer who would prove during the war to possess great moral courage, he inevitably lacked the contacts, experience, self-confidence and moral authority of Singer. Because Haase became co-chairman of both the party executive and the parliamentary *Fraktion*, he also had little time to keep tabs on his other co-chairman of the party executive, Friedrich Ebert. Ebert took over much of the day-to-day running of the party organisation, having risen through its ranks, and he increased his own network of contacts and supporters within the apparat in the process. When Bebel himself, after years of illness, family worry and increasing withdrawal from day-to-day activity, died in 1913, the parliamentary party was so divided that it took two ballots before the centrist Philipp Scheidemann was narrowly elected over the leftist Georg Ledebour to co-chair the *Fraktion*.[59] Thrust now into the position of the senior party leader, Haase lacked Bebel's charisma as a public speaker, his heroic and extraordinarily resilient record, his brilliance as a publicist, or his capacity to argue around his dissenting colleagues.

At such a conjuncture, it is not surprising that a sense of drift in party policy should communicate itself to many Social Democratic sympathisers. As Rosa Luxemburg noted with anguished acidity as Social Democracy stumbled into 1913,

The Basle Manifesto only recognises the international action of the proletariat to protect the peace and membership of the triple alliance endorses capitalist diplomacy; the central newspaper [of the party] comes out in favour of two year service and the abolition of one year volunteers and the parliamentary party in favour of one year service; a few months ago a pro-disarmament policy and now again the old militia policy – one must admit that such a muddle is not suited to triggering strong, committed and convincing agitation, that on the contrary it leads to uncertainty and a weakening of the mass movement and to an extent confuses our own agitators and makes them ineffective.[60]

August 1914: from pacifism to national defence

The two weeks separating the Austrian ultimatum to Serbia on 23 July 1914 and the vote in the Reichstag for war credits on 4 August have long absorbed historians of high politics. The view from below is still rather fragmentary. We know little about what the people who demonstrated for peace thought and expected. Neither the SPD press nor the police reports are much help here, focusing as they both do on bare numbers who turned out and the set-piece speeches and resolutions, with tantalising curt asides about the mood of the crowds.[61] The key question about the July crisis which has to be answered in this study concerns the connection between the preventive strategy, which the SPD continued to pursue till the last days of July and the decision to support the war in the interests of national defence, which the party leadership took in the first days of August.

The SPD executive met on 26 June, the day after the Sarajevo assassinations. Haase was one of the few European political leaders to predict that this event would lead the great powers to the brink of war. The strains within the party leadership immediately became clear. Ebert violently disagreed with Haase's analysis, though the executive as a whole at least finally agreed to recommend that the Congress of the International scheduled to take place in Vienna in August ought to be postponed. Social Democracy was no more prescient than anyone else not privy to the quiet workings of the European chancelleries. Many socialists, as well as monarchs and leaders of other parties, were in the midst of their summer holidays when the Austrian government delivered its savage ultimatum to Serbia on 23 July. Karl Liebknecht was hiking in Switzerland. Ebert, Scheidemann and Molkenbuhr were away too when the executive met again on 25 July. As a result Haase had a free hand to draft the SPD's categorical rejection of Austrian policy, calling on the German government to exercise restraint over its ally and instructing the party to stage immediate mass protests everywhere in Germany. Even if the rest of the executive had been in Berlin it is unlikely that they would have proposed anything very different.[62] Ebert himself approved of the statement when he read it.[63] Eduard David, who in early August was to be the prime mover of Social Democratic approval of war credits, on 29 July himself repeated his call of December 1912 for Germany to force Austria to negotiate peace with Serbia.[64]

In many ways, the stage seemed set for a rerun of the events of November and December 1912 and the SPD accordingly adopted similar tactics. When Haase had been invited to the Ministry of the Interior on 26 July for discussions on the SPD's stance in the event of war, he continued to insist that David's speech of 3 December 1912 provided the basis of the SPD's interpretation of the Austro-German alliance. Germany ought not to support Austrian aggression even if Russia did come into the war on Serbia's side. An emergency meeting of the International Socialist Bureau was held on 28 July; Haase successfully proposed that the congress be held in Paris and brought forward to 9 August with 'war and the proletariat' at the top of the agenda. He obviously envisaged another Basle Manifesto.[65] No one mentioned the possibility that a general war might actually break out before then.[66]

The peace demonstrations which the party held on 28 and 29 July were impressive. In Dusseldorf, 15,000 to 20,000 packed twelve giant rallies and then marched and sang through the streets.[67] In Berlin, between 30,000 and 60,000 attended 27 meetings, afterwards thronging into Unter den Linden, the respectable heart of the city, where their rendition of the 'Internationale' and other socialist songs held its own against the 'Watch on the Rhine' of the excited nationalists who had already filled the cafés and pubs – until the Prussian police intervened.[68] As many as half a million people may have demonstrated against the war across Germany at the end of July.[69] The demonstrations were, however, both smaller and quieter than those of 1911 and 1912. Not more than a half of the party members in Berlin attended the anti-war meetings, and the orderly, solemn nature of the protests contrasted in the minds of the Mannheim authorities with the unruly 'bourgeois-patriotic' demonstrations.[70] Again as in 1912, the SPD leadership stated that it would rally to Germany's defence in the event of a Russian attack.[71]

Some historians have laid the comparative weakness of the movement at the door of the false confidence of 1913 that peace would prevail and imperialist rivalries could be settled quietly.[72] There is obviously some mileage in this case. But the sense of drift and confusion in Social Democratic politics may have affected the turnout also. Other historians, however, have also noted that a new period of sharper confrontation had begun in the spring of 1914 because of the failure of the Liberal parties and the government to deliver suffrage or social reform.[73] But this new polarisation had not yet spilled over into either mass action or foreign policy questions before the July crisis broke. This leads us back to the more mundane question of timing. The great demonstrations of 1911 had marked the climax of a general movement of domestic protest which had started with industrial disputes and suffrage demonstrations. It had culminated in the Social Democratic landslide in the elections of 1912. Again in 1912, suffrage demonstrations merged with the peace movement. But in 1914, there had been no protest movement to build upon; the marching season in German cities was spring and autumn. The preparation time was also much shorter. A mere two weeks separated the Austrian ultimatum from the declarations of war. How were people to know that this time the war scare was real?

Bethmann Hollweg admitted that demonstrations had occurred in every German city, but he had already taken steps to prevent Social Democratic opposition going any further. He gauged the attitude of the party's leadership accurately by dwelling on the need, as his confidant Rietzler apparently noted, 'to put Russia utterly in the wrong'. Feigning German passivity in the face of panslavic warmongering in St Petersburg, Bethmann even encouraged the SPD to demonstrate for peace, whilst warning them to tone down any Russophobic rhetoric lest it inflame passions further. Above all he persuaded the Kaiser to delay issuing mobilisation orders until Russia had done so.[74] Bethmann's delicate tactical game completely outplayed the shrewdest and most uncompromising Social Democratic observers. Rosa Luxemburg thought that Germany did not want war. Karl Liebknecht later concluded that the government's 'refined diplomatic game which succeeded in making tsarism the scapegoat during the decisive days caused such enormous confusion in public opinion' that the SPD could not have done much more to prevent war; certainly not have called a mass strike or asked soldiers to desert even if it had wanted to.[75]

For his part, Bethmann also had to prevent Wilhelm II and some of the generals from using a state of siege to arrest all the Social Democratic and trade union leaders, whom the Prussian Ministry of War had named on its 'B lists' in 1912.[76] Bethmann was assisted by Falkenhayn, the Minister of War, although neither man's authority extended over the army, which would theoretically take control of civilian government in time of war or a state of siege. In a circular to the commanding generals they stressed the patriotism of Social Democracy, while to the Kaiser Bethmann shrewdly drew attention to the strong-arm measures used by the police to curb the anti-war demonstrators. That generals once let off the leash would tolerate Social Democracy was no more a foregone conclusion than that the SPD would vote for war credits.[77] The SPD executive took no chances and on 30 July sent Ebert and Braun to Switzerland with part of the party's treasury.[78]

On 31 July, Russia issued mobilisation orders. The Kaiser declared a 'state of threatened war', prohibiting further demonstrations. For the first time, the SPD leadership discussed what it should do now that prevention had failed. Should it vote for or against war credits or abstain in the emergency session of the Reichstag which had just been called? This was the moment when the pacifist politics of the last six years unravelled. A joint meeting of the executive and the leadership of the parliamentary party was held. Its confusion is reflected in Eduard David's diary. Haase stuck to his position that the party should reject war credits on the defensive grounds of David's own December 1912 declaration. Only Georg Ledebour supported him strongly. Most delegates were undecided, while David who now started to canvass actively for a 'yes' vote blandly asserted that his own earlier position was no longer tenable.[79] One temporary exit from their dilemma was to seek a common front with the French party and Hermann Müller was despatched to Paris. He returned on 3 August in the middle of the fateful final caucus debate attended by the entire parliamentary party plus prominent non-parliamentarians like Kautsky. His report that the French would probably vote in favour of war credits was obviously a blow to advocates of a 'no' vote such as Haase, Ledebour, Lensch and Liebknecht. But the decisive shift of ground had already taken place. Another combined meeting of the executives of party and *Fraktion* had been held on 2 August, where the weight of patriotic demonstrations following the 1 August declaration of war on Russia had made their impact. The meeting had agreed by four to two to vote for war credits, but had delayed a final decision until the entire delegation met on 3 August.

Key right-wing figures, most notably David, Südekum and Frank, all lobbied intensively during these few days to win over the waverers, leading some historians to stress the caucusing of the right-wing reformists, and Frank's preparations of a list of 20 or 30 parliamentarians who were ready if need be to break party discipline and vote for the credits come what may.[80] It is equally true that the left was badly organised as a faction. Karl Liebknecht only returned from his holiday on 3 August, astonished that the party was thinking of voting in favour at all. But by this point, key centrists like Scheidemann and Kautsky, who had at first supported Haase, had been won over. What is more striking in retrospect is the way Social Democratic leaders shared information among themselves and sought a compromise right up to the last moment, as well as the willingness of the right to await the verdict of the entire delegation. These aspects all suggest a considerable degree of trust and respect for inner-party democracy.

Far more decisive than the factional organisation of the right was the general swing of political mood once war had been declared on 1 August. This is particularly sharply borne out by the testimony not only of those who opposed the vote, like Dittmann, but also the expectations of Müller when he set off to Paris to negotiate with the French.[81] In other words, the Chancellor's tactic of quietly stoking up Russophobia had worked. Indeed such was the new bond of trust forged between Chancellery and SPD that at the last moment the party leadership retracted a sentence condemning all military aggression from the draft of its Reichstag declaration because the Chancellor warned that the British might read it as a repudiation of the German violation of Belgian neutrality. In fact, the attack on Belgium and France did not feature in Social Democratic deliberations at all. The whole focus was on the war with Russia.

Both Haase's opposition to war and David's endorsement of it could be logically deduced from earlier Social Democratic policy. Austrian aggression against Serbia led Haase to repudiate any German involvement. The diplomatically crucial, if militarily irrelevant, fact that the order to mobilise was issued a day earlier in Russia persuaded David and many others that Germany was under attack, regardless of the fact that Russia would take much longer to mobilise. Bismarck in his time had doctored the Ems telegram to justify the Franco-Prussian war. Now the government published a *White Book* of the telegrams exchanged between Nicholas II and Wilhelm II to demonstrate the purity of German intentions. These also appear to have been accepted at face value. Although Wilhelm Liebknecht had subsequently denounced Bismarck's fraud in a widely circulated pamphlet, there had been a more recent precedent to guide government action. In the 1912 crisis, the Bavarian Ministry of War had confidentially 'shared' bogus information with Social Democratic leaders about the threat of a Russian attack on Germany, producing the immediate – and thereafter predictable – public response that the SPD would 'defend the fatherland'. This was the occasion which led Kurt Eisner, the future leader of the Bavarian Council regime, to renounce his opposition to all imperialist war and embrace national defence.[82]

Gullible as such events may make Social Democratic leaders appear, in fact these were risks the party could not avoid in the pursuit of its own version of German foreign policy. If the party leadership was to distinguish

10 'In the name of culture', from *Simplicissimus*, [3 August] 1914

reliably between aggression and self-defence, it had to trust its own ability to sift the information it had. As soon as the Second International committed itself to a strategy of preventing war in 1910, the member parties had an inbuilt need to believe that their own governments wanted peace: that after all was the only way of measuring the success of the peace movement. At the height of the July crisis such resolute opponents of war as both Jaurès and Haase were taken in to the extent that each vouched to the other for his own government's pacific intentions.[83]

The July crisis was unlike 1912 not just because industrial relations were not quite so violent, nor only because Social Democrats had begun to believe in the reality of their own pacifist slogans. Above all else, the dress rehearsal had instructed their governments on how to manage public opinion at home. The crisis was quickly brought to a head. In France no less than Germany, the same measures were taken. Standing orders to round up and arrest activists and labour leaders and close down their publications were set aside, and public opinion was worked on to fit the socialists' own treasured criteria of national defence. Just how successful the German government was in winning over the Berlin rank and file as well as the leaders of the labour movement we may guess at. Klara Zetkin, that *doyenne* of the anti-war Left, wrote to her close allies and friends, Rosa Luxemburg and Franz Mehring on 5 August, stressing the utter foolishness of issuing any public protest because it 'would only reveal how isolated we are now ... A protest [meeting] would completely wreck our wing of the movement – i.e., within the masses, I'm not thinking of the leaders – and would hinder us in our cause for a long time to come.'[84]

Conclusion

Support for the war was the logical consequence of the SPD's long-standing fear and hatred of tsarist autocracy and its equally traditional commitment to national defence. The peace movement had overshadowed but never replaced these positions. It is impossible to guess how the party would have acted if the government had not tried so hard to paint Russia as the aggressor. Perhaps it would have made little difference under the immediate impact of events. Perhaps it would have hastened the rupture in the SPD which took shape during the following year, once many of the leaders of the former centre-left realised that the war was after all an expansionist one.[85] By then these leaders of the former majority found themselves in the expelled minority. Given the resolve of Ludwig Frank and his friends to support the war whatever the party did, it is clear that a 'no' vote would have split the party immediately, though in that case the pro-war faction would have been the minority which had to leave.

But here too there is no certainty about how the different sides would have fared. Frank's faction alone had a strategy in which supporting the war had a tactical place. The General Commission of the trade unions simply hoped to defend and extend their organisational empires by co-operating with the government, and on 2 August initiated their own contacts to this end ahead of the *Fraktion* vote.[86] But Frank hoped to use the concession of supporting the war as a lever to extract democratic reform, thereby opening the way for Social Democracy to enter the state rather than merely command a third of the seats in the Reichstag. As he succinctly put it, 'We will win suffrage in Prussia by waging a war instead of a general strike.'[87] Although Frank himself was the first member of the Reichstag to be killed in the war, his strategy was taken up by key former centrist leaders, such as Friedrich Ebert and Philipp Scheidemann, as well as more straightforward nationalists such as Eduard David. After 4 August we can speak of a 'vanguardism' of the right.

At the time there is overwhelming evidence that the bulk of delegates were in the grip of strong and conflicting emotions. Although much of what they experienced is doubtless related to the nationalist war hysteria of the 'August days', it might not have disoriented them so much if they had themselves known clearly what they should do. They did not know this. All the values, emotions and symbols involved in shifting from a pacifist strategy to a bellicose tactic were in conflict. Social Democrats nearly came to blows in the lobbies of the Reichstag, because some right-wing members of the delegation had applauded the Chancellor's declaration too vociferously. A wrangle arose over whether or not to stand for the *Kaiser Hoch*, the cheers for the Emperor at the end of the session. In the past the SPD had quietly left, or even as recently as May demonstratively sat through the proceedings to signal their opposition. Now they persuaded themselves they too should stand because the cheers were also for the 'fatherland'.

When Social Democrats began to justify why they had voted for war credits at the outset of the first world war, they often became confused about whether they were explaining why they had been unable to prevent war or had not continued to oppose war. As Karl Liebknecht contemptuously remarked, 'We can't enforce the peace – so, we join in the war fever.'[88]

The tragedy of 1914 had a long gestation. For Social Democracy the crucial criteria were national defence and Russophobia. Both derived from a strategy worked out in the 1880s and 1890s. They had become articles of faith. They had also served as tactical means to assert a primacy of domestic politics; they had helped the party to hem the government in, rather than allowing it to use foreign policy adventures as a distraction from domestic issues. International May Day, and later the whole pacifist strategy of the Second International, had fleshed out this image of an alternative to nationalist confrontation at a time when jingoistic metaphors, publications and organisations were in the ascendant. But as an actual policy, national defence – and the Russophobia which underpinned it – had never before played a central and active role in Social Democratic strategy. That had been based on gradually winning hegemony in civil society, through the party organisation, press, trade unions, cultural associations and parliamentary activity, what Kautsky called a 'war of attrition'. The centre and left had always clashed about how aggressively to pursue this strategy, in particular whether or not to remain off the streets and within the law. It was not just that the symbolism of the movement ran completely counter to cheering the Kaiser. More seriously, those centrists interested in promoting the organisational power of the party could now only do so by accepting the utterly different strategy of the reformist right. Those historians who have depicted the gradual rise of revisionism and reformism in the pre-1914 party have tended to exaggerate the influence of the Right. Its day came after 4 August, not before. The SPD's declaration in favour of war credits was so halting not only because it went against so many pacifist and internationalist convictions, but also because it had no place in the hitherto dominant centre left strategy.

By 1911 the old radical democratic anti-militarism of the 1860s had been completely eclipsed by new issues and ideas. The military–industrial complex, the militarisation of civil society and the threat of world war had transformed the meaning of militarism and given it reference points and theoretical ideas which it carries to this day. The war itself destroyed this new anti-militarist politics. It had to be pieced together again after 1918. Intellectual dissidents like Heinrich Mann and Ludwig Quidde stood by their pacifist convictions. Left-wing radicals like the Spartacus group tried to hold to the old party programme. With the coming of the war 'militarism' was also invoked as a positive virtue for the first time. The flag-wavers and cheer-leaders no longer had to find other words to describe their ethos of the heroic, teutonic warrior. Militarism appeared to have overcome its own pathology.

Conclusion

Bismarck's methods and ideas fascinated, absorbed and overshadowed succeeding generations. His enormous success in remaking and controlling German politics for three decades bequeathed a legacy of branding political opponents as 'enemies of the Reich'. The list went beyond Catholics and Social Democrats and Radical Liberals to include those deemed unworthy of membership of the German nation, Poles, Guelphs and Jews. This dualism between 'friends' and 'enemies' both 'internal' and 'external' also had a profound effect on political ideas. Max Weber's reflections gave rise to the concept of 'negative integration' where such scapegoating of enemies played a key role in welding together domestic consensus. A generation later Carl Schmitt reinvented the same dualism when he wrote that the first principle of politics was the division between friend and foe.

In Bismarck's day the most direct and hostile response to this sort of politics came from critics of militarism. They parodied Bismarck's language and turned it against him. Wilhelm II's warnings to recruits to the guard regiments that they might have to shoot down their own parents and siblings at his order were tirelessly repeated by Social Democratic publicists. By the turn of the century, they had begun to revel in their notoriety as the 'enemy within', a bogey against which only those completely out of touch with the increasingly accepted norms of a civilised, law governed society could wish to unsheath real swords and bayonets. With some justice these critics regarded German politics as standing midway between Eastern and Western Europe. In tsarist Russia, repression was too real to lampoon it in this way. Absolutist government remained unreformed and no civil society had developed around its skirts in which such issues could be aired. In Russia it was simply not possible to hold the sort of public campaign against 'Prussianism' and the royal standing army in which the idea of 'militarism' had emerged in Germany in the 1860s. In France and Britain, democratic rights had already been won, even if the Boulanger and Dreyfus affairs in France made that victory appear precarious. In Germany, by contrast, the question of militarism continued to occupy prime time in opposition politics because of the uneasy balance between a highly pluralistic civil society and a still authoritarian state. The existence of such civic freedoms encouraged further criticism of the incomplete democratisation of the state. The frequent rumours of a *Staatsstreich* spurred Social Democrats not to take their new found liberties for granted. Situated mid-way between absolutism and parliamentary democracy, Central Europe described a political and intellectual as well as a physical geography.

The German economy also had particular contours. Having industrialised later, faster and apparently more successfully than France and even Britain, Germany had also done so at time when capital goods had replaced textiles as the most important growth sector. The coal and steel magnates made enormous fortunes in the late nineteenth century. Like their US counterparts they also formed trusts and cartels and employed political lobbyists. But here the similarity ended. The Reichstag passed no anti-trust laws along the lines of US legislation. On the contrary, barons of heavy industry were rewarded in the honours system and rose to positions of great prominence in German public life. The leading armament manufacturers already had a high political profile prior to the naval race with Britain. This particularly naked identification of big capital with armament and the authoritarian state no doubt assisted Social Democrats keen to transform the 1913 Krupp scandal into a full-scale investigation of the military–industrial complex. This was an investigation which would soon include Vickers and Armstrong in Britain.

In this movement of ideas and motifs the moral indictment of militarism necessarily also changed. Moral reproof concentrated less on the anti-democratic aspirations of the German ruling elite and more on its 'lust for world power'. War had upstaged the absolutist state as the locus of the problem. Great power conflict, the arms race and the militarisation of civil society were all analysed to show that this new militarism had deep sub-structures which had to be thoroughly rooted out before the threat of war would abate. International disarmament and arbitration above all – but also the nationalisation of the arms industry, mass re-education and socialism – were canvassed as solutions.

The rise of the radical Right at home forced Social Democracy on to the defensive. In the 1890s Social Democrats had optimistically equated mass politics with humanitarian and socialist values. Now they had to explain why associational rights and universal suffrage did not automatically benefit the Left, but had led instead to an explosion of aggressively nationalist sentiment. Just as Liberals and Radicals in Britain struggled to make sense of the 'jingoism' and 'herd instincts' unleashed by the Boer War, so in Germany the new vocabulary of psychology was enlisted to explain such a 'mass psychosis' in which citizens willingly turned themselves into soldiers and subjects. But for all this, the enlightenment expectation that education and exposure to rational arguments would lead their fellow citizens away from war fever persisted until the outbreak of the first world war itself. Such optimism about the progressive thrust of European 'civilisation', consigning war and violence to a museum of horrors chronicling a barbarous past, underwrote much of the pacifist expectations to which liberals, radicals and socialists clung throughout Western and Central Europe. In this Lenin was at one with Lytton Strachey, German Marxists with the clergy at Basle.

The horror of the first world war itself and the rise of fascism in the 1920s provoked a tremendous counter-reaction from pacifists and anti-militarists in the inter-war years. But theirs was no longer an innocent Edwardian or Wilhelmine generation. Their wartime experience and its recapitulation and commemoration were more searing than any of the verbal prophecies – however prescient – which had been cast beforehand. The self-confident – in retrospect often complacent – optimism had been tempered. The triumphant progress of universal reason could not be taken for granted. The darker secrets of the human psyche would attract redoubled attention. Wilhelm Reich and Elias Canetti could not have written about crowds and militarism the way they did before 1914.

Militarism may have been a particularly polemical and pejorative term but conventions also governed its use. Not till 1914 did the 'militarists' themselves adopt the word and rework it into a positive, national virtue. Its monopoly until then by rationalist critics has conditioned the meaning of militarism down to the present. It also introduces a certain false naivety into their tracts. The critics purported to describe or explain what they wished to condemn wholesale. The difficulty of fashioning theories which explain the real political world out of ones created to justify an ideal one is a general problem. It is there in the origins of virtually any theory about the modern state, or civil society. But militarism is a particularly difficult term. Liberal political theory has tended to marginalise coercive force and focus on consensus. On the one hand, militarism appears at once too broad a concept and too one-sided to serve as an analytical category itself, in the way that other evaluative terms such as the military, the arms race, militarisation or even militaristic ideology might do. On the other hand, just because the idea of militarism is bound up with the illegitimate use of force it is resistant to being limited to what Radicals would have claimed was only one aspect of a greater whole.

But in fact just such a movement in the meaning of militarism took place. As the pacifist indictment of bellicose foreign policies and mass movements grew in the 1910s, so the old anti-militarist critique of domestic government shrank. The broad fusillades against the 'garrison state' which harked back to Rousseau, Kant and Montesquieu were displaced by a new technical and more narrowly economic language. Fichte's phrase about the army forming a 'state within a state' was upstaged by questions about the financial interests of the weapons producers, the army and the navy. In their quest for the widest possible pacifist support, Social Democratic leaders also deliberately abandoned their identification of anti-militarism with the proletarian class struggle. The arms race, colonialism and war served some capitalist interests but no longer all. The rhetoric of class became less important and appeals to humanity more so.

This turning away from orthodox Marxist concerns was nowhere more evident than in the matter of prediction. Teleological certainty gave way to uncertainty and anxious choices. It was self-evident to Kautsky in the 1890s that the modern state would leave coercion behind with the rest of its absolutist past as it embarked on its true destiny, to plan and co-ordinate the socialist economy. His Marxist theory of history with its inexorable sequence of stages of development provided a ready frame on which to hang such a picture of the 'state of the future'. By the time Karl Liebknecht depicted militarism as a 'supreme Machiavellianism' in 1907, the certainty was gone. Humanity was left with neo-Kantian ethics to choose its path as best it could. This drift away from belief in historical guarantees about the future beset even that bastion of Marxist theory, economics. Where once armament had appeared as a minor detail in a story about the progress of capitalism towards its final economic collapse, by 1913 the question of crisis had become irrelevant and it was armament itself which had become central. Such pessimism had intellectual dividends. The effects of armament on growth, employment and income distribution could only be addressed seriously once it had been separated from the broad sweep of the theory of history. The idea of militarism had been set in much the same contours as it still holds. The enlightenment preoccupations which had originally breathed meaning into the term had been displaced.

But what does this intellectual and programmatic journey tell us about the German labour movement itself? Does the erosion of radical democratic anti-militarism simply confirm the oft-attested drift towards reformism within the party? Two moments stand out in relief. One is the Erfurt Programme of 1891, the moment when Social Democracy officially adopted Marxist principles and embarked on a period of intellectual and political hegemony over the international labour movement which lasted for the next two decades. The other moment is the vote for war credits on 4 August 1914, the symbol of socialist internationalism betrayed if not entirely destroyed; at any rate the end of the SPD's ideological ascendancy.

Engels and Kautsky depicted the Erfurt Programme as the replacement of a series of earlier 'botched' programmes with clear and coherent Marxist principles; however much later scholars have themselves cast doubt on the purity of both figures' reception of Marx's ideas, this schematic comparison between the Erfurt Programme and its predecessors has usually passed unquestioned. Instead, writers have drawn attention to the putative conflict between the first part of the programme, an uncompromising statement of the Marxist theory of history and the second 'practical' part of the programme. The neat division supposedly demonstrates that the SPD was committed to revolution in theory but reformism in practice, a point further underlined by the fact that the first part was written by Kautsky, the *doyen* of orthodox Marxism, and the second by Bernstein, the future progenitor of revisionism. It is true that the two parts are very different. The second part does not represent the party's reformist future but rather its radical past. The old radical demand for a 'free people's state' – to which Marx had so strongly objected in the 1875 Gotha programme – was carried over into the 1891 programme in a disaggregated fashion: demands for representative government; equal suffrage in the federal states; direct and progressive taxation and the citizens' militia. It was only in the late 1900s that it would start to matter that these demands had been listed separately. Only when tax reform became feasible at a time when equal suffrage in Prussia seemed further off than ever did it become apparent that these demands could be separated entirely. In the 1890s, it was undoubtedly the radical democratic part of Social Democracy's programme which the government found most subversive; small wonder, for it presented a direct frontal challenge to the very foundation of the Imperial state.

During the 1880s and 1890s, Social Democratic leaders gradually realised that any democratic transformation of German politics would be slow and hard won. By adopting Marxism, the party leadership deepened its critique of German society but also backed away from direct confrontation with the authorities. Marxism helped to explain to Social Democrats why they should not despair that their political programme would not be fulfilled quickly. By shifting the accent from the state to social class, from politics to economics and sociology, the new theoreticians justified a long-run strategy of winning social support, creating, educating and morally involving a mass 'proletarian' membership while they waited for the economic crisis to mature. The earlier polarity between the garrison state with its standing army and the 'free people's state' with its active and armed citizenry was not discarded. Instead, it was toned down and from the turn of the century increasingly displaced from an object of agitation to a subject of propaganda. The tension in the Erfurt Programme was between this old democratic radicalism and the new Marxism. To antedate reformism to 1891 is symptomatic of a historiography which has focused too heavily on the search for a linear progression from a revolutionary 'golden age' to the realism of 1914.

The oft-noted 'dual loyalty' of the SPD to the Socialist International and the German nation was decided definitively on 4 August in favour of the latter. Convention dictates that accounts of this decision contrast it with the earlier internationalism of the labour movement. Most of the competing explanations of the slide from the internationalist ideals of the early congresses of the International to the nationalist realism of 1914 stress some measure of gradual decline. Whether the causal weight is placed on the 'embourgeoisement of the proletariat', the rise of reformism in the trade unions and SPD, or their 'negative integration' into the structure of the Reich this stress on the gradual erosion of an internationalist commitment remains a common denominator. The trajectory turns out, however, to be illusory. The SPD had no earlier pacifist commitments. On the contrary, throughout the 1890s when other groups in the International raised pacifist demands German Social Democrats peremptorily dismissed their proposals as wishful thinking which could only end in disaster. The SPD was strongly realist long before it flirted with pacifism.

Social democratic policies became more internationalist, not less so. The pacifist campaign it mounted from 1908 to 1914 was an entirely new departure, which in its turn provided much of the protocol of mass protests for the inter-war years down to the printed resolutions and red-armband-wearing stewards. But the pacifist policy itself was not based on a fundamental conscientious objection. The party retained all its earlier qualifications about the duty of nations to defend themselves. Its opposition politics had always been circumscribed by its attitude to the German nation. In its version of a non-aggressive nationalism, the liberal democratic spectrum of politically 'advanced' and 'backward' countries merged with a social Darwinist ladder of the relative economic and cultural progress of nations. Both confirmed Social Democratic prejudices about the threat Russian 'barbarism' posed to German 'culture'. In contrast, the party leaders decried every conflict with 'advanced' Britain and France as caused by reactionary and aggressive German policies; there was nothing to defend the German nation against here. But the knout of tsarist autocracy was feared as much as the 'dark instincts' of the unenlightened Russian peasant. The SPD had never ceased to believe in the so-called right of the higher – in this case the German – culture to defend itself. In the years immediately prior to the first world war, the party had hoped to forestall such a necessity but it had not foresworn it.

Within these limits – ultimately crucial as they turned out to be – Social

Democracy became more idealistic and more internationalist than it had been, not less so, in the years leading up to the first world war. What these cases illustrate is that the old focus on topics like reform versus revolution imposes an abstract yardstick on political behaviour. It turns the spotlight entirely on political debates internal to Marxism, and leaves the wider context in darkness. At best it prompts close comparative study of the attitudes of Social Democratic politicians with those of the social constituents they claimed to represent. This fragmented view of Wilhelmine politics finds its counterpart in studies of the government and other parties which leave Social Democracy out of the equation. But Social Democracy acted within an increasingly established party system and an increasingly pluralistic civil society. The SPD may have been excluded from power, but even this was a political objective which had to be continually secured rather than a natural state of affairs.

If we are to understand how the Wilhelmine polity really fitted together, it is not enough to chart Social Democracy's collision with and stand off from the state, vitally important as this is. We also need to know how Social Democracy competed with the other parties and how they manoeuvred around it. Why could only some flimsy bridges be built between them, such as secularism in the South or tax reform in 1913? Why did imperialism pose such an insuperable ideological obstacle to co-operation between Left Liberals and Social Democrats? Whilst the choices were specific to the Wilhelmine context, our understanding of the political environment within which they were made has been clouded by the metaphors of stable two- and three-party systems developed in Britain and the USA. A better analogy for the complexities of Wilhelmine party politics is Italy during the cold war, with its shifting coalitions of parties oriented towards the continuous isolation of the Italian Communist Party. The Bismarckian cartel of National Liberals and agrarian Conservatives collapsed under the pressure of mass politics in the 1890s. The Centre and Left Liberals were then able to exercise a leverage they might not have been able to acquire had Social Democracy not been cast in such a subversive role. In Germany it was the tension between a still authoritarian if legalistic state and a complex multi-party system which provides the backdrop to these struggles over popular identity, political values and electoral support. The idea of militarism was so central because it addressed both the relation of the German state to civil society and the increasing polarisation of that civil society into rhetorical extremes.

Just because militarism was constructed out of a medley of intellectual traditions and political preoccupations does not mean that it did not describe realities. The indirect taxes, abuse of conscripts, lack of parliamentary responsibility, threats of a *Staatsstreich*, social cachet of reserve officers, the arms race and the threat of world war were all real enough. But that they should be linked together in the way they were was not predetermined. It was a striking and imaginative response. That response is also notoriously absent from many accounts of Wilhelmine politics. Imperial Germany was a country in which hundreds of thousands signed up for military associations *and* hundreds of thousands demonstrated for peace. Civil society was sophisticated, pluralist and deeply divided. To seek out only the thread of militarist continuity from Frederician absolutism to Nazism not only violates the origins of German 'militarism'; it also ferociously straitjackets modern German history. The real peculiarities of that history are the abrupt discontinuities – of which anti-militarism is one – between its pasts and futures.

Notes

INTRODUCTION

1 W. Voigt, *Wie ich Hauptmann von Köpenick wurde: Mein Lebensbild*, Leipzig and Berlin, 1909, p. 108. For all the other details described here: *ibid.*, pp. 107–27.

2 *Vorwärts*, 26 October 1906.

3 The police refused him residence permits because he was an ex-convict, and they refused him a passport – which he would have needed to emigrate to Prague or Vienna – because he was not a resident. Despite having work and lodgings, he was expelled from Rawitch, Posen, Tilsit (his birthplace), Wismar, Rixdorf and Berlin (twice). But passports, which he had aimed to steal at the Köpenick *Rathaus*, were issued not by the *Polizeisekretariat* but by the *Landratsamt*, and there wasn't one at Köpenick. Voigt, *Wie ich Hauptmann von Köpenick wurde*, pp. 88–94 and 116–17.

4 A. Mitchell, *Victors and Vanquished: The German Influence on Army and Church in France after 1870*, Chapel Hill, 1984.

5 For examples including the references to the *Times* and to French opinion see *Vorwärts*, 18, 19, 20, 21, 23 and 28 October 1906.

6 See W. Schröder, *Das persönliche Regiment: Reden und sonstige öffentliche Äusserungen Wilhelms II*, Munich, 1907.

7 *Sten. Ber. RT*, 12th Leg. Per., 2nd Sess., pp. 897 ff. See also D. Fricke, 'Zur Rolle des Militarismus nach Innen in Deutschland vor dem 1. Weltkrieg', *Zeitschrift für Geschichtswissenschaft*, 6 (1958), p. 1309.

8 M. Kitchen, *The German Officer Corps, 1890–1914*, Oxford, 1968, p. 203.

9 F. Mehring, 'Das zweite Jena', *NZ*, 25.1 (1906), pp. 81–4.

10 C. Zuckmayer, *Der Hauptmann von Köpenick: Ein deutsches Märchen in drei Akten*, H. F. Garten, ed., London, 1960.

11 F. von Papen, *Der Wahrheit eine Gasse*, Munich, 1952, p. 218.

12 H.-U. Wehler, *The German Empire, 1871–1918*, Leamington Spa, 1985, p. 156, for the example of Scholz; I. V. Hull, *The Entourage of Kaiser Wilhelm II, 1888–1918*, Cambridge, 1982; on the role of Tirpitz, V. R. Berghahn, *Der Tirpitz-Plan: Genesis und Verfall einer innenpolitischen Krisenstrategie unter Wilhelm II*, Dusseldorf, 1971; W. J. Mommsen, 'Das Kaiserreich als System umgangener Entscheidungen', in H. Berding, K. Düwell *et al.*, eds., *Vom Staat des Ancien Regime zum modernen Staat*, Munich, 1978; D. Blackbourn and G. Eley, *Peculiarities of German History: Bourgeois Society and Politics in*

Nineteenth-Century Germany, Oxford, 1984, pp. 253–4, also endorse this view whatever their other criticisms of Wehler.

13 See V. R. Berghahn, *Militarism: The History of an International Debate, 1861–1979*, Leamington Spa, 1981, p. 10; W. Conze, R. Stumpf and M. Geyer, 'Militarismus', in O. Brunner, W. Conze and R. Koselleck, eds., *Geschichtliche Grundbegriffe*, 4 (Stuttgart), 1978, pp. 1–47.

14 See A. J. P. Taylor, *The Trouble Makers: Dissent over Foreign Policy, 1792–1939*, London, 1969, p. 47; M. Ceadel, *Thinking about War and Peace*, Oxford, 1987; S. Hayhurst, 'In Pursuit of Peace: Bertrand Russell's Political Ideals and the Problem of War', unpublished PhD thesis, University of Cambridge, 1990, pp. 75 ff.

15 C. Schmitt, *The Concept of the Political*, New Brunswick, 1976.

16 H. Spencer, *Principles of Sociology*, 1, London, 1885, pp. 544–63.

17 D. Senghaas, *Rüstung und Militarismus*, Frankfurt, 1972, pp. 23–7.

18 *Kant's Political Writings*, H. Reiss, ed. and intr., Cambridge, 1970; A. and W. Dietze, eds., *Ewiger Friede: Dokumente einer deutschen Diskussion um 1800*, Leipzig, 1989.

19 In Britain, the Peace Society and radicalism were strongly entwined. See the long-running activities of Henry Richard: H. Richard, *Defensive War: Extracted from a Lecture Delivered at the Hall of Commerce, Threadneedle St. London, 6th February 1845*, London, 1846; *Report of the Proceedings of the Third General Peace Congress Held in Frankfurt*, London, 1851; *On Standing Armies and their Influence on the Industrial, Commercial and Moral Interests of Nations*, London, 1868; *International Arbitration*, London, 1873. Also see H. Whitfield, *War and Peace: Their Axioms and their Fallacies and the International Means of Securing Peace and Plenty in the Future*, London, 1855; for Richard Cobden, *The Political Writings*, 2 vols., London, 1867. On the German Peace Society, see R. Chickering, *Imperial Germany and a World without War: The Peace Movement and German Society, 1892–1914*, Princeton, 1975.

20 For the resolutions of the Socialist International, see C. Grünberg, *Die Internationale und der Weltkrieg: Materialen*, Leipzig, 1916, pp. 7–13.

21 M. Mann, 'Capitalism and Militarism', M. Shaw, ed., *War, State and Society*, London, 1984; H. A. Kissinger, *A World Restored: Metternich, Castlereagh and the Problems of Peace, 1812–22*, London, 1957; and *American Foreign Policy*, New York, 1977.

22 O. Hintze, *The Historical Essays of Otto Hintze*, F. Gilbert, ed., New York, 1975, p. 181.

23 C. von Clausewitz, *On War*, M. Howard and P. Paret, eds., Princeton, 1976, p. 607.

24 Hintze, *Historical Essays*; F. Meinecke, *Die Idee der Staatsräson* (new ed.), Munich, 1963; G. Ritter, *Staatskunst und Kriegshandwerk*, 1, Munich, 1954; M. Stürmer, *Das ruhelose Reich: Deutschland, 1866–1918*, Berlin, 1983; A. Hillgruber, *Zweierlei Untergang*, Berlin, 1986.

25 Ritter, *Staatskunst*, p. 13.

26 M. Geyer in W. Conze, R. Stumpf and M. Geyer, 'Militarismus', pp. 41–6.

27 For the nineteenth century German side of the story, see chapter 1 below. On Machiavelli and the Italian humanists, see Q. R. D. Skinner, *The Foundations*

of Modern Political Thought, 2 vols., Cambridge, 1. For the English and Scottish debates from Harrington's *Oceania* to the debate on William III's standing army, see L. Schwoerer, *No Standing Armies! The Antiarmy Ideology in Seventeenth-Century England*, Baltimore, 1974, and J. Robertson, *The Scottish Enlightenment and the Militia Issue*, Edinburgh, 1985. On the French and German Enlightenment, see Berghahn, *Militarism* and Conze, Stumpf and Geyer, 'Militarismus', as well as A. and W. Dietze, *Ewiger Friede*. For Spinoza's endorsement of the militia in his *Tractatus Politicus*, see E. O. G. Haitsma Mulier, *The Myth of Venice and Dutch Republican Thought in the Seventeenth Century*, Assen, 1980.

28 In contradistinction, the 'old' Liberal grandees were content to leave the army under the royal prerogative, while radical democrats demanded the full militia programme. Ritter, *Staatskunst*, 1.

29 A. J. P. Taylor, *The Course of German History*, London, 1945; G. Barraclough, *The Origins of Modern Germany*, Oxford, 1946.

30 Of particular note was the work of Dieter Fricke, 'Zur Rolle des Militarismus nach innen in Deutschland vor dem ersten Weltkrieg', *Zeitschrift für Geschichtswissenschaft*, 6 (1958), pp. 1298–310; 'Zum Bündnis des preussisch-deutschen Militarismus mit dem Klerus gegen die Sozialistische Arbeiterbewegung am Ende des 19. Jahrhunderts', *Zeitschrift für Geschichtswissenschaft*, 8.2 (1960), pp. 1378–95; 'Die Sozialistischen Monatshefte und die imperialistische Konzeption eines Kontinentaleuropa (1905–1918)', *Zeitschrift für Geschichtswissenschaft*, 23.1 (1975), pp. 528–37.

31 W. Bartel, *Die Linken in der deutschen Sozialdemokratie im Kampfe gegen Militarismus und Krieg*, Berlin, 1958; W. Wittwer, *Streit um die Schicksalfragen: Die deutsche Sozialdemokratie zu Krieg und Vaterlandsverteidigung, 1907–1914*, Berlin, 1967; Wohlgemuth, *Burgkrieg, nicht Burgfriede! Der Kampf Karl Liebknechts, Rosa Luxemburgs und ihrer Anhänger um die Rettung der deutschen Nation in den Jahren 1914–1916*, Berlin, 1963; *Karl Liebknecht: Eine Biographie*, Berlin, 1973; O. Öckel, *Volkswehr gegen Militarismus: Zur Militärfrage in der proletarischen Militärpolitik in Deutschland von der Mitte des 19. Jahrhunderts bis zum ersten Weltkrieg*, Berlin, 1962.

32 The best antidote to this literature are J. P. Nettl's biography of Rosa Luxemburg, which shows how unorthodox and original a Marxist she was, and Helmut Trotnow's of Karl Liebknecht, which demonstrates that he was neither a Marxist nor for most of the pre-1914 period in the same faction as Luxemburg: J. P. Nettl, *Rosa Luxemburg*, 2 vols., London, 1966; H. Trotnow, *Karl Liebknecht, 1871–1919: A Political Biography*, Hamden, Connecticut, 1984.

33 Wehler, *The German Empire*; Berghahn, *Der Tirpitzplan*; H.-J. Puhle, *Agrarische Interessenpolitik und preussischer Konservatismus im wilhelminischen Reich*, Hanover, 1966. Eckart Kehr has been widely accredited with first stating this interpretation in the inter-war period: *Economic Interest, Militarism and Foreign Policy*, G. Craig, ed., Berkeley, 1977. For an introduction to the Fischer controversy over German war aims in 1914, see H. W. Koch, ed., *The Origins of the First World War*, London, 1972, and W. Jäger, *Historische Forschung und politische Kultur in Deutschland: Die Debatte 1914–1980 über den Ausbruch des ersten Weltkrieges*, Göttingen, 1984.

34 For an interesting collection, see *Deutscher Sonderweg – Mythos oder Realität?*, Munich and Vienna, 1982; for an overview, C. S. Maier, *The Unmasterable Past: History, Holocaust and German National Identity*, Cambridge, Mass., 1988.

35 R. J. Evans, *Rethinking German History*, London, 1987.

36 Eley and Blackbourn, *Peculiarities of German History*.

37 As Kurt Sontheimer remarked, 'The thesis of a *Sonderweg*, even if it is not always called that, is essentially a component part of a new political consciousness which must be directed towards the readmission of Germany into the circle of civilised, liberal and peace-loving nations.' *Deutscher Sonderweg*, p. 31.

38 G. W. F. Hegel, *The Philosophy of History*, C. Friedrich, intr., New York, 1956, pp. 438–57. For a liberal defence of Hegel's view, see C. Taylor, *Hegel*, Cambridge, 1975, pp. 449–61.

39 Of seminal importance among British historians was G. Stedman Jones, *Languages of Class*, London, 1983; for a discussion of German historiography, see the special issue of *Central European History*, 3/4 (1989), especially Jane Caplan, 'Postmodernism, Poststructuralism and Deconstruction: Notes for Historians', *ibid.*, pp. 260–78.

40 As J. Lawrence and M. Taylor argue in their 'Poverty of Protest: Gareth Stedman Jones and the Politics of Language – A Reply', *Social History*, 187 (1993), pp. 1–15, social historians have tended to concentrate on the fragmentation and heterogeneity of the working class rather than on what E. P. Thompson called the common 'class experience'; E. P. Thompson, *The Making of the English Working Class*, New York, 1963, pp. 9–10.

41 One of the most comparative and impressive attempts in this direction is I. Katznelson and A. Zollberg, eds., *Working Class Formation: Nineteenth-Century Patterns in Western Europe and the United States*, Princeton, 1986; for the new direction among Russian historians see D. Koenker, W. G. Rosenberg and R. G. Suny, eds., *Party, State and Society in the Russian Civil War*, Bloomington, 1989; on Tory constructions of working class identity in Victorian Britain, J. Lawrence, 'Class and Gender in the Making of Urban Toryism, 1880–1914', *English Historical Review* 428 (1993), pp. 629–52.

42 See chapter 3 below.

43 L. Quidde, *Caligula: Schriften über Militarismus und Pazifismus*, H.-U. Wehler, ed. and intr., Frankfurt, 1977.

44 On Kautsky, see chapter 3 below; since Kautsky's writings on German militarism are not well known, Eley himself claimed he was influenced by Gramsci; G. Eley, *From Unification to Nazism: Reinterpreting the German Past*, Boston, 1986, pp. 12 and 93; on the parallels between Kautsky's and Gramsci's political ideas, see M. Salvadori, *Karl Kautsky and the Socialist Revolution, 1880–1938*, London, 1979, p. 13.

45 G. Eley, *Reshaping the German Right: Radical Nationalism and Political Change after Bismarck*, New Haven, 1980.

46 M. John, *Politics and the Law in Late Nineteenth-Century Germany: The Origins of the Civil Code*, Oxford, 1989; J. J. Sheehan, *German Liberalism in the Nineteenth Century*, Chicago, 1978.

47 A. Hall, *Scandal, Sensation and Social Democracy: The SPD Press and Wilhelmine Germany, 1890–1914*, Cambridge, 1977.

48 In tracing the development of Kautsky's thought in chapter 3, I have not stopped at 1900, and so the last chapter of part I prefigures some of the issues dealt with in part II.

1 DEMOCRACY AND CHEAP GOVERNMENT

1 From the late 1850s on, Marx and Engels produced a stream of articles and pamphlets charting the arms race between the European powers, and it was this process that Engels described as 'militarism' in 1874: 'Eine polnische Proklamation', *Werke*, 39 vols., Berlin, 1962–8, 18, p. 522.

2 *Littré*, vol. 2 and *Heyse* lexica: W. Conze, R. Stumpf and M. Geyer, 'Militarismus', pp. 21 and 26.

3 In his reply Bebel at one point outraged the French by declaring that they owed their republic solely to 'your enemy Bismarck who dragged Napoleon III to Wilhelmshöhe after Metz and Sedan'. J. Braunthal, *History of the International, 1864–1914*, London, 1966, pp. 279–83.

4 Even in 1848, the Liberal majority in the Frankfurt Parliament rejected the militia demand; R. Höhn, *Verfassungskampf und Heereseid: Der Kampf des Bürgertums um das Heer 1815–1850*, Leipzig, 1938, pp. 131ff.

5 G. A. Ritter, *Staatskunst*, 1.

6 Geyer, in Conze, Stumpf and Geyer, 'Militarismus', pp. 26–7.

7 See Jacob Vennedy, *Der Südbund*, Mannheim, 1867 and J. E. Jörg, 'Der Anfang vom Ende' (1867, both in Geyer: Conze, Stumpf and Geyer, 'Militarismus', p. 28).

8 Löwenthal's *Der Militarismus als Ursache der Massenverarmung in Europa und die europäische Union als Mittel zur Überfüssigmachung der stehenden Heere*, Pottschappel, 1870, was the first pamphlet to carry the word in its title: Geyer: Conze, Stumpf and Geyer, 'Militarismus', pp. 26–7.

9 S. Na'aman, *Ferdinand Lassalle: Eine neue politische Biographie*, Hanover, 1970. The last gasp of the Lassallean wing of the movement came in 1885 when it wished to accede to Bismarck's proposal to subsidise steamship lines in the hope that it would create jobs: H.-C. Schröder, *Sozialismus und Imperialismus: Die Auseinandersetzungen der deutschen Sozialdemokratie mit dem Imperialismusproblem und der 'Weltpolitik' vor 1914*, Hanover, 1968, chapter 3; V. Lidtke, *The Outlawed Party: Social Democracy in Germany, 1878–1890*, Princeton, 1964.

10 R. P. Morgan, *The German Social Democrats and the First International, 1864–1872*, Cambridge, 1965; pp. 18ff.

11 Eisenach Programme, *Programmatische Dokumente der deutschen Sozialdemokratie*, D. Dowe and K. Klotzbach, eds. and intr., Bonn/Berlin, 1984, p. 175. On the trade unions, see Ulrich Engelhardt, '*Nur vereinigt sind wir stark*': *Die Anfänge der deutschen Gewerkschaftsbewegung*, 2 vols, Stuttgart, 1977.

12 W. Liebknecht, speech to the North German Assembly, 17 October 1867, *Gegen Militarismus und Eroberungskrieg: Aus Schriften und Reden*, Berlin, 1986, p. 21.

13 G. Mayer, *Friedrich Engels: Eine Biographie*, 2 vols., Frankfurt, 1975, 2, chapters 4–6.

14 F. Engels, 'The Prussian Military Question and the German Workers' Party', in K. Marx and F. Engels, *Collected Works*, London, 1985, 20, p. 67.

15 Engels, 'Sozialismus in Deutschland', in K. Marx and F. Engels, *Werke*, 1982, 22, p. 251; Engels, 'Einleitung zu Karl Marx' "Klassenkämpfe in Frankreich 1848 bis 1850"', in *ibid.*, pp. 524–5; Mayer, *Engels*, pp. 496–9; M. Berger, *Engels, Armies and Revolution: The Revolutionary Tactics of Classical Marxism*, Hamden, Connecticut, 1977, pp. 154–70, makes Engels' views appear even more deterministic than they probably were.

16 On Rotteck, Sheehan, *German Liberalism in the Nineteenth Century*, p. 8; Conze, Stumpf and Geyer, 'Militarismus', pp. 16–18.

17 J.-J. Rousseau, 'Considerations on the Government of Poland', *Political Writings*, F. Watkins, ed., London, 1953; see Conze, Stumpf and Geyer, 'Militarismus', pp. 8–10. J. N. Shklar, *Men and Citizens: A Study of Rousseau's Social Theory*, Cambridge, 1969.

18 *Kant's Political Writings*, ed. Reiss; A. and W. Dietze, *Ewiger Friede*.

19 J. G. Fichte, *Beitrag zur Berichtigung der Urtheile des Publikums über die französische Revolution*, Zurich, 1848; see F. H. Hinsley, *Power and the Pursuit of Peace*, Cambridge, 1963, chapter 1.

20 'If you want peace prepare for war'; Montesquieu, *The Spirit of the Laws*, A. Cohler *et al.*, eds., Cambridge, 1989, pp. 224–5.

21 See introduction, n. 19.

22 Conze, Stumpf and Geyer, 'Militarismus', pp. 8–25.

23 J. Holms, *Sound Military Reform: Are We to Obtain it?*, London, 1872; *The British Army in 1875 With Suggestions on its Administration and Organisation*, London, 1876; and see introduction, n. 19. For the perpetuation of Cobdenite ideas after the turn of the century by J. A. Hobson, see P. J. Cain, 'J. A. Hobson, Cobdenism and the Radical Theory of Economic Imperialism, 1898–1914', *Economic History Review*, 31 (1978), pp. 565–84, and also 'Capitalism, Internationalism and Imperialism in the Thought of Richard Cobden', *British Journal of International Studies*, 5. 3 (1979), pp. 229–47.

24 Marx's most prescient observation was to suggest to Engels that armies had precipitated a series of economic developments, ranging from the division of labour to cash salaries and the use of machinery. But neither thinker followed this idea up: Marx to Engels, 25 September 1857, in K. Marx and F. Engels, *Collected Works*, 40, p. 186.

25 C. von Clausewitz, *On War*, pp. 365–72 and 469–79.

26 Conze, Stumpf and Geyer, 'Militarismus', p. 24.

27 A. Bebel, *Nicht stehendes Heer sondern Volkswehr*, Stuttgart, 1898.

28 Conze, Stumpf and Geyer, 'Militarismus', p. 25.

29 H.-U. Wehler, *The German Empire, 1871–1918*, pp. 90–4; Sheehan, *German Liberalism*.

30 M. H. Fassbender-Ilge, *Liberalismus, Wissenschaft, Realpolitik: Untersuchung des 'Deutschen Staats-Wörterbuchs' von J. Caspar Bluntschli und Karl Brater als Beitrag zur Liberalismusgeschichte zwischen 48er Revolution und Reichsgründung*, Frankfurt, 1981; M. John, *Politics and the Law in late Nineteenth-Century Germany; Blackbourn and Eley, *Peculiarities of German History*.

31 This commemorated the so-called 'Battle of the Nations' at which Napoleon
    was defeated in 1813: in Wilhelmine iconography its significance was
    tantamount to Waterloo and Trafalgar rolled into one for a Victorian audience.
    E. J. Hobsbawm, 'Mass-Producing Traditions: Europe, 1870–1914', in *The
    Invention of Tradition*, E. J. Hobsbawm and T. Ranger, eds., Cambridge, 1983,
    pp. 263–307; G. L. Mosse, *The Nationalization of the Masses: Political
    Symbolism and Mass Movements from the Napoleonic Wars Through the Third
    Reich*, New York, 1975.

32 W. Conze and D. Groh, *Die Arbeiterbewegung in der nationalen Bewegung*,
    Stuttgart, 1966, p. 44.

33 Treitschke, 'Parteien und Fraktionen', 1871, cited by Conze, Stumpf and
    Geyer, 'Militarismus', p. 26; see also Gustav Tuch, *Der erweiterte deutsche
    Militärstaat in seiner sozialen Bedeutung*, Leipzig, 1886.

34 Colmar von der Goltz, *The Nation in Arms: A Treatise on Modern Military
    Systems and the Conduct of War*, London, 1906.

35 See the draft programme of the Centre Party of 1870, as well as the Jesuit Georg
    Michael Pachtler's 1876 diatribe, *Der europäische Militarismus*, Conze, Stumpf
    and Geyer, 'Militarismus', pp. 26–9.

36 Philipp Wasserburg, *Gedankenspähne über den Militarismus*, Mainz, 1874, in
    Conze, Stumpf and Geyer, 'Militarismus', p. 29.

37 Kehr, *Economic Interest, Militarism and Foreign Policy*; Wehler, *The German
    Empire*.

38 G. Mayer, 'Die Trennung der proletarischen von der bürgerlichen Demokratie
    in Deutschland (1863–1870)', *Archiv für die Geschichte des Sozialismus und der
    Arbeiterbewegung*, 2 (1912), pp. 1–67.

39 A. Gerschenkron, *Bread and Democracy in Germany*, Los Angeles, 1943.

40 R. J. Evans, *Death in Hamburg: Society and Politics in the Cholera Years,
    1830–1910*, Oxford, 1987; Sheehan, *German Liberalism*; J. Retallack, '"What
    is to be done?": The Red Specter, Franchise Question and the Crisis of
    Conservative Hegemony in Saxony, 1896–1909', *Central European History*, 23.
    4 (1990), pp. 271–312.

41 Berghahn, *Der Tirpitz-Plan*.

42 R. Fletcher, *Revisionism and Empire: Socialist Imperialism in Germany
    1897–1914*, London, 1984; R. Jacoby, 'The Politics of Crisis Theory: Toward
    the Critique of Automatic Marxism II', *Telos*, 23 (1975), pp. 3–52.

43 A. Rosenberg, *Imperial Germany*, London, 1931, p. 18; D. Blackbourn, *Class,
    Religion and Local Politics in Wilhelmine Germany: The Centre Party in
    Württemberg before 1914*, London, 1980, chapter 1.

44 Blackbourn, *Class, Religion and Local Politics*, p. 26.

45 D. Groh, *Negative Integration und revolutionärer Attentismus: Die deutsche
    Sozialdemokratie am Vorabend des ersten Weltkrieges*, Frankfurt, 1973, pp.
    282ff.; R. J. Geary, *European Labour Protest, 1848–1919*, London, 1981, pp. 77
    and 98.

46 In 1909–10, the Free Trade Unions grew from 57,500 to 74,500 members, the
    liberal Hirsch-Duncker unions from 2,000 to 10,000 members and the Christian
    Trade Unions from 6,000 to 7,000: Blackbourn, *Class, Religion and Local
    Politics*, p. 191.

47 Puhle, *Agrarische Interessenpolitik*.
48 Blackbourn, *Class, Religion and Local Politics*, pp. 174ff and 234–5.
49 G. Eley, '*Sammlungspolitik*, Social Imperialism and the Navy Law of 1898', in *From Unification to Nazism: Reinterpreting the German Past*, pp. 110–53.
50 Even Max Weber was unable to have this academic bar lifted in the case of his pupil Robert Michels: W. J. Mommsen, *Max Weber and German Politics*, Chicago, 1984, pp. 112–13.
51 Eley, '*Sammlungspolitik*'; V. R. Berghahn, *Germany and the Approach of War in 1914*, London, 1973, pp. 34–57 for a different view.
52 The Centre deputies who staged back-bench revolts against the 1897–8 and 1899–1900 Naval Laws and the 1899 Army Law predictably came from non-Prussian areas: Hesse, Baden, Southern Württemberg, Bavaria and the Palatinate. Erzberger continued this back-bench tradition by co-ordinating criticisms of colonial policy in 1904 and 1907 against the wishes of the Centre leadership. G. Eley, 'Army, State and Civil Society: Revisiting the Problem of German Militarism', in *From Unification to Nazism*, pp. 91–2; I. Farr, 'Populism in the Countryside: The Peasant Leagues in Bavaria in the 1890's', in Evans, ed., *Society and Politics in Wilhelmine Germany*, pp. 136–59.
53 B. Heckart, *From Bassermann to Bebel*, New Haven, 1974.
54 E. Engelberg, *Revolutionäre Politik und rote Feldpost 1878–1890*, Berlin, 1959; Lidtke, *The Outlawed Party*.
55 For the difficulties this posed in Catholic-dominated Dusseldorf, see M. Nolan, *Social Democracy and Society: Working-Class Radicalism in Dusseldorf, 1890–1920*, Cambridge, 1981, pp. 25–30.
56 Lidtke, *The Outlawed Party*; Salvadori, *Karl Kautsky and the Socialist Revolution, 1880–1938*; G. Mayer, *Friedrich Engels*, 2.
57 W. H. Maehl, *August Bebel: Shadow Emperor of the German Workers*, Philadelphia, 1980.
58 J. Joll, *The Second International, 1889–1914*, London, 1955; Braunthal, *The History of the International*; G. D. H. Cole, *The Second International, 1889–1914*, 2 vols., London, 1956; G. Haupt, *La Deuxième Internationale, 1889–1914: Etude critique des sources: Essai bibliographique*, The Hague, 1964.
59 E. Matthias, 'Kautsky und der Kautskyanismus', *Markismusstudien*, 2 (1957), pp. 151–97; and the critique by H.-J. Steinberg, *Sozialismus und deutsche Sozialdemokratie: Zur Ideologie der Partei vor dem 1. Weltkrieg*, Bonn, 1979; see also C. Schorske, *German Social Democracy, 1905–1917: The Development of the Great Schism*, Cambridge, Mass., 1955.
60 See p. 36 below.
61 Lidtke, *The Outlawed Party*.
62 'Training of all to bear arms. The armed people in place of the standing army. Decisions over war and peace by the people's representatives. Submission of all international disputes to arbitration.' *Programmatishe Dokumente*, p. 191.
63 W. Schröder, *Handbuch der sozialdemokratischen Parteitage von 1863 bis 1909*, Munich, 1910, pp. 311 and 312–13.
64 Bebel, *Nicht stehendes Heer sondern Volkswehr*; Gaston Moch, *L'Armée d'une démocratie*, Paris, 1900, and *La Réforme militaire: Vive la milice!*, Paris, 1900; and Jean Jaurès' monumental *L'Organisation socialiste de la France: L'armée nouvelle*, Paris, 1911.

65 ZK der SED, ed., *Geschichte der deutschen Arbeiterbewegung*, 1, Berlin, 1966, p. 440.

66 E. Bernstein, *Cromwell and Communism*, London, 1980, pp. 193 and 207.

67 The German word *Staatsstreich* is not really the equivalent of the French *coup d'état*, because whereas the latter is derived from Bonapartist usage to mean the overthrow of a government by the military, the former carries neo-absolutist connotations, of the reversal of reform by the monarch: see M. Stürmer, 'Staatsstreichgedanken im Bismarckreich', *Historische Zeitschrift*, 209 (1969), pp. 566–615.

68 E. Zechlin, *Staatsstreichpläne Bismarcks und Wilhelms II 1890–1894*, Stuttgart, 1929; W. Pöls, *Sozialistenfrage und Revolutionsfurcht in ihrem Zusammenhang mit den angeblichen Staatsstreichplänen Bismarcks*, Lübeck, 1960.

69 Stürmer, 'Staatsstreichgedanken', p. 567.

70 J. C. G. Röhl, *Germany without Bismarck: The Crisis of Government in the Second Reich, 1890–1900*, Berkeley, 1967, pp. 246–51.

71 Kitchen, *The German Officer Corps, 1890–1914*, chapter 6.

72 Wilhelm II at the swearing in of recruits to the Guards' Regiment, 23 November 1891: Schröder, *Das persönliche Regiment*, p. 12.

73 For the case of Albert Langen, the editor of the Munich-based Left Liberal satirical journal *Simplicissimus*, see H. Albret and A. Keel, *Die Majestätsbeleidigungsaffäre des 'Simplicissimus'-Verlegers Albert Langen*, Frankfurt, 1985.

74 Hermann Molkenbuhr for example was fined 300 Marks for insulting the entire officer corps in 1900. For this and other cases, see Hall, *Scandal, Sensation and Social Democracy*, pp. 96–8 and 128–9. On Liebknecht's trial see Trotnow, *Karl Liebknecht*; and on Luxemburg's see *Rosa Luxemburg im Kampf gegen den deutschen Militarismus: Prozessberichte und Materialen aus den Jahren 1913 bis 1915: Mit einem Anhang*, Berlin, 1960.

75 Maehl, *August Bebel*.

76 Schröder, *Das persönliche Regiment*. No doubt it was also significant that it was printed in Munich and not Berlin.

77 Wehler, *The German Empire*, pp. 157–8; Kitchen, *The German Officer Corps*, p. 147.

78 K. Kautsky, 'Demokratische und reaktionäre Abrüstung', *NZ*, 16.2 (1898), p. 743.

79 C. von Massow, *Reform oder Revolution?*, Berlin, 1894; F. Engels, 'Sozialismus in Deutschland', in K. Marx and F. Engels, *Werke*, 22, p. 251.

80 F. von Bernhardi, *Germany and the Next War*, London, 1914, p. 243.

81 I am grateful to J. M. Winter, Pembroke College, Cambridge, for showing me how much higher casualty rates were among peasants than Berlin and Hamburg workers in the early months of the first world war: see J. M. Winter and J. L. Robert, eds., *Paris, London, Berlin: Capital Cities at War, 1914–1919*, chapter 3 (forthcoming).

82 Bebel, 11 December 1897, cited in Maehl, *August Bebel*, p, 297.

83 For example, Wilhelm Liebknecht told the Reichstag on 30 November 1893, 'The social democratic outlook, the outlook of the people, accompanies every recruit into the army, and the more recruits there are, the more the social democratic outlook is there. That is why there is no need for social democratic

propaganda in the barracks.' A. Bebel and W. Liebknecht, *Gegen den Militarismus und die neuen Steuern*, Berlin, 1893, p. 49.

84 Thus Bebel to Engels, 'Social Democratic literature is circulating in the army to a greater extent than one could have imagined; people know of course how to keep it hidden' (8 June 1893). A. Bebel, *August Bebels Briefwechsel mit Friedrich Engels*, W. Blumenberg, ed., The Hague, 1965, p. 688.

85 His case was raised by Karl Frohme in the Reichstag and in *Vorwärts* in 1897: see Hall, *Scandal, Sensation and Social Democracy*, p. 129.

86 Groh, *Negative Integration*, p. 38.

87 Maj-Gen. Keim in the 1905 *Jahrbücher für die deutsche Armee und Marine*, cited in Kitchen, *The German Officer Corps*, p. 149.

88 Minister of Interior to Police President of Berlin, 3 April 1907, Brandenburgisches Landeshauptsarchiv, Rep. 30 Berlin C, Nr. 15905, Bl. 40.

89 Prussian Ministers of Interior and War, administrative circular, 11 February 1914, Brandenburgisches Landeshauptsarchiv, Rep. 30 Berlin C, Nr. 15905, Bl. 63.

90 Kitchen, *The German Officer Corps*.

91 J. P. Nettl, 'The German Social Democratic Party as Political Model', *Past and Present*, 30 (1965), pp. 65–95.

92 K. Demeter, *Das deutsche Offizierkorps in Gesellschaft und Staat 1650–1945*, Frankfurt, 1962; Eley, 'Army, State and Civil Society', p. 98.

93 Hall, *Scandal, Sensation and Social Democracy*, pp. 118–19; Blackbourn, *Class, Religion and Local Politics*, p. 167.

94 H. John, *Das Reserveoffizierkorps im deutschen Kaiserreich, 1890–1914*, Frankfurt, 1981.

95 E. O. Volkmann, *Der Marxismus und das deutsche Heer im Weltkriege*, Berlin, 1925, p. 49.

96 A. T. Allen, *Satire and Society in Wilhelmine Germany: Kladderadatsch and Simplicissimus, 1890–1914*, Lexington, Kentucky, 1984.

97 Assaults carried out by soldiers of the same rank, the so-called *Kameradenmisshandlungen*, did not count as breaches of the military code even when they had been ordered by an NCO, because they did not involve any direct abuse of power. Floggings were often dismissed as being legitimate disciplinary measures. H. Wiedner, 'Soldatenmisshandlungen im wilhelminischen Reich (1890–1914)', *Archiv für Sozialgeschichte*, 22 (1982), pp. 159–99.

98 Kitchen, *The German Officer Corps*, p.182.

99 Fricke, 'Zum Bündnis des preussisch-deutschen Militarismus', p. 1380.

100 E. Goldbeck, *Henker Drill: Schülerselbstmord, Soldatenselbstmorde*, Berlin, 1908.

101 Fricke, 'Zur Rolle des Militarismus', *Zeitschrift* p. 1306.

102 *Vorwärts*, 25 September 1906 for example, and see Hall, *Scandal, Sensation and Social Democracy*, pp. 125–30.

103 V. Buhr, *Der Sozialismus in der deutschen Armee: Selbst-Erlebtes*, Berlin, 1893; R. Krafft, *Kasernenelend: Offene Kritik der Verhältnisse unserer Unteroffiziere und Soldaten*, Stuttgart, 1895; F. Kuhnert, *Die heilige Vehme des Militarismus nach kriegsgerichtlichen Erkenntnissen*, Nuremberg, 1893, and 'Die Opfer der Kaserne', *NZ*, 22.1 (1904), pp. 773–5.

104 A. Bebel, *Der Sozialdemokratie im deutschen Reichstag: Die parlamentarische*

Tätigkeit des Deutschen Reichtages und der Landtage und die Sozialdemokratie, Berlin, 1909, p. 38ff. For incidents in the early 1890s, see Georg von Vollmar's collection, F. 3297, I, Vollmar NL, IISH/AdSD.

105 E. Weber, *Peasants into Frenchmen: The Modernisation of Rural France, 1870–1914*, London, 1979.

106 Bebel to unknown, 2 March 1900, F 2, Verschiedene Originalbriefe und Dokumente, AdSD; R. Krafft, 'Gedanken zu einer Reform des Militärstrafrechts', *NZ*, 18.2 (1900), pp. 114–17. *Handbuch für sozialdemokratische Wähler. Der Reichstag 1893–98*, ed. Executive of the German Social Democratic Party, Berlin, 1898, pp. 362–4.

107 See Hull, *The Entourage of Kaiser Wilhelm II, 1888–1918*, pp. 215–25.

108 Constructing accurate statistics of the extent of maltreatment is a difficult task. Fearful of any publicity that might assist the 'unpatriotic' parties, military tribunals in Prussia heard cases *in camera*, and soldiers could be punished for bringing false charges. Conscripts and even reservists could also be tried before military tribunals for charges brought against them while in civil life. Furthermore, the rate of convictions was so low and the sentences handed down by the military courts so lenient that there were strong disincentives to bringing cases in addition to the obvious fears associated with accusing a superior officer. In fact, most of those brought to justice appear to have been extreme offenders, who were not infrequently found guilty on more than a thousand counts, thereby also making a nonsense of the official statistics: for example, one captain found guilty in 1910 had committed 1,389 offences between 1908 and 1910, while the official total for the entire army and navy for 1910 was only 505. H. Wiedner, 'Soldatenmisshandlungen'.

109 Thus Georg von Vollmar raised awkward cases in the Bavarian Landtag, in 1903–4: F 3298, I, Vollmar NL, IISH/AdSD; and Bebel in the Reichstag, 24 April 1907, *Sten. Ber. RT*, pp. 1062–4.

110 *Germania*, 1903; cited in Hall, *Scandal, Sensation and Social Democracy*, p. 127.

111 *Rosa Luxemburg im Kampf gegen den deutschen Militarismus*.

112 Lidtke, *The Outlawed Party*, pp. 292–5.

113 Kitchen, *The German Officer Corps*, pp. 90–1.

114 K. Saul, *Staat, Industrie und Arbeiterbewegung. Zur Innen- und Sozialpolitik des Wilhelminischen Deutschlands, 1903–1914*, Dusseldorf, 1974.

115 For some interesting reflections on the character of the Prussian police see Evans, *Rethinking German History* pp. 156–65.

116 See the regional study of women workers in the *Nord* by P. Hilden, *Working Women and Socialist Politics in France, 1880–1914: A Regional Study*, Oxford, 1986, pp. 141–60.

117 The idea of what we might call 'special forces' was proposed in 1890 and 1894: Kitchen, *The German Officer Corps*, pp. 163–4; on the Mansfeld strike, see Fricke, 'Zur Rolle des Militarismus nach innen', p. 1308.

118 Fricke, 'Zur Rolle des Militarismus nach innen', p. 1299 and Hall, *Scandal, Sensation and Social Democracy*, pp. 133–6.

119 For example, the grenadier who shot a drunk mechanic in Berlin while on guard duty in 1892 was granted a private audience by Wilhelm and promoted. Schröder, *Das persönliche Regiment*, p. 18.

120 The vote of no confidence was 293 to 54: D. Schoenbaum, *Zabern 1913: Consensus Politics in Imperial Germany*, London, 1982. For Social Democratic responses see also Hermann Molkenbuhr, Diary, 2, 30 November 1913, Molkenbuhr NL, AdSD, and notes for a speech on the same issue, F 4, (Rede-Dispositionen), 2, Molkenbuhr NL, AdSD; Carl Severing, F 3, 95 (The Zabern Affair before the Reichstag), Severing NL, AdSD.

121 Not surprisingly, Bebel focused entirely on the democratic arguments in 1869 when he participated in a debate on the military budget for the first time: Bebel, speech to the North German Assembly, 24 April 1869, in A. Bebel, *Ausgewählte Reden und Schriften*, 1, Berlin, 1983, pp. 47–9.

122 Bebel and Liebknecht, 'Gegen den Militarismus und die neuen Steuern'.

123 Bebel NL 22/71, Bl. 1–8, ZPA, Institut für die Geschichte der Arbeiterbewegung.

124 Bebel and Liebknecht, 'Gegen den Militarismus und die neuen Steuern', pp. 51–52.

125 *Ibid.*, p. 47; Bebel, *Nicht stehendes Heer sondern Volkswehr*, p. 59; Engels to the organising committee of the international festival in Paris, 13 February 1887, Marx and Engels, *Werke*, 21, p. 345.

126 R. Wistrich, 'The SPD and Antisemitism in the 1890s', *European Studies Review*, 7 (1977), pp. 177–97.

127 Bebel and Liebknecht, 'Gegen den Militarismus und die neuen Steuern', pp. 29, 53 and 56.

128 For example, for the period 1893–8, the different taxes and tariffs on corn, meat, wool, butter, margarine, herring, wood, iron, petroleum, salt, tobacco, wine, beer, mulled wine and sugar were all described to the party's electors (*Handbuch ... 1898*, pp. 249–312). Many of the same items had further duties levied on them by the 1903 election (see *Handbuch für sozialdemokratische Wähler. Der Reichstag 1898–1903*, ed. Executive of the German Social Democratic Party, Berlin, 1903, pp. 90–141, 162–95). By the 1907 elections taxation had been overshadowed by colonialism and therefore received less coverage: *Handbuch für sozialdemokratische Wähler anlässich der Reichstagsauflösung 1906*, ed. Executive of the German Social Democratic Party, Berlin, 1907, pp. 42–60.

129 *Handbuch... 1903*, pp. 31–3. For a detailed analysis of naval expenditure in response to the introduction of the first Navy Laws, see the *Handbuch... 1898*, pp. 200–7 and 216–25.

130 Like all SPD proposals, the income tax demand was costed. What is remarkable in retrospect is how low the recommended tax rates were. The highest band did not exceed 4%. It can perhaps be explained because Bebel was basing his estimates on the rates already levied in the state of Saxony and no advocate of cheap government could be seen to be arguing for higher levels of taxation. Bebel, *Nicht stehendes Heer sondern Volkswehr*, p. 28.

131 Nolan, *Social Democracy and Society*, pp. 74–5.

132 Berghahn, *Germany and the Approach of War*.

133 K. Kautsky, 'Was nun?', *NZ*, 21.2 (1903), pp. 390–8.

134 Ignaz Auer, speech to Reichstag, 1895, cited in Hall, *Scandal, Sensation and Social Democracy*, p. 127; see also Engels, 'Einleitung zu Marx' "Klassenkämpfe in Frankreich"'.

135 Schorske, *German Social Democracy*; G. Roth, *The Social Democrats in Imperial Germany: A Study in Working Class Isolation and National Integration*, Totawa, 1963; H. Grebing, *The History of the German Labour Movement: A Survey*, London, 1969; R. J. Geary, 'The German Labour Movement, 1848–1919', *European Studies Review*, 6.3 (1976), pp. 297–330, and *European Labour Protest, 1848–1919*.
136 S. Suval, *Electoral Politics in Wilhelmine Germany*, Chapel Hill, 1985.
137 Hall, *Scandal, Sensation and Social Democracy*, p. 118.
138 *Ibid.*
139 This was the central theme of Bebel's rejection of revisionism and lengthy attacks on Bernstein's ideas at the party congresses of the early 1900s: see Maehl, *August Bebel*, chapter 16.
140 Engels, 'Ludwig Feuerbach und der Ausgang der klassischen deutschen Philosophie', in Marx and Engels, *Werke*, 21, p. 307.

2 SOCIAL DEMOCRACY AND THE FATHERLAND

 1 S. Miller, *Burgfrieden und Klassenkampf: Die deutsche Sozialdemokratie im ersten Weltkrieg*, Dusseldorf, 1974, pp. 62–3; K. R. Calkins, *Hugo Haase: Democrat and Revolutionary*, Durham, North Carolina, 1979, for the characterisation of Haase.
 2 D. Groh, 'The "Unpatriotic Socialists" and the State', *Journal of Contemporary History*, 1.4 (1966), pp. 151–77; see also his *Negative Integration*.
 3 K. Radek, (manuscript), 'Militärische Jugenderziehung im Lichte der deutschen Heeresgeschichte', F. 149, Henke NL, AdSD; F. Mehring, 'Die Sozialdemokratie in der Armee und die Wehrvorlage', *NZ*, 31.2 (1913), pp. 259–62.
 4 Bebel, *Nicht stehendes Heer sondern Volkswehr*, pp. 72–3.
 5 Thus Wilhelm Liebknecht in his speech to the Nurenberg Vereinstag, 7 September 1868, Liebknecht, *Gegen Militarismus und Eroberungskrieg*, pp. 27–33.
 6 Bebel and Liebknecht, *Gegen den Militarismus und die neuen Steuern*, Berlin, 1893.
 7 Motteler to Kautsky, 4–6 September 1900, Karl Kautsky, NL 55/20, Bl. 101–04, ZPA, Institut für die Geschichte der Arbeiterbewegung.
 8 As Engels put it forcefully to Mehring on Bastille Day 1893, 'In studying German history – the story of a continuous state of wretchedness – I have always found that only a comparison with the corresponding periods French periods gives a correct idea of proportions, because what happens there is the direct opposite of what happens in our country.' Marx and Engels, *Werke*, 39, p. 99. See also B. W. Bouvier, *Französische Revolution und deutsche Arbeiterbewegung: Die Rezeption des revolutionären Frankreich in der deutschen sozialistischen Arbeiterbewegung von den 1830er Jahren bis 1905*, Bonn, 1982.
 9 They also do not appear to have been aware of Clausewitz's justification of militias. See introduction and chapter 1.
10 Engels, 'Letter to the organising committee of the international festival in Paris', *Der Sozialdemokrat*, 11 March 1887, Marx and Engels, *Werke*, 21, p. 345.

11 Bebel and Liebknecht, *Gegen den Militarismus und die neuen Steuern*, pp. 7–10 and 39.

12 Thus Bebel, *Nicht stehendes Heer sondern Volkswehr*, p. 48, drew on an 1890 tract *Videant Consules* to show that parade drill was useless, and on Colmar von der Goltz to back up the assertion that Germany would need a Gambetta if ever its armies were defeated (p. 72). See also the *Handbuch ... 1903*, pp. 20–1; Bebel, 5 December 1904, *Sten. Ber. RT.*, p. 3361.

13 Karl Liebknecht, *Militarism and Anti-Militarism with Special Regard to the International Young Socialist Movement*, Cambridge, 1973, p. 35.

14 Bebel, *Nicht stehendes Heer sondern Volkswehr*, pp. 46ff.; *Handbuch ... 1903*, pp. 20–1; Bebel, 5 December 1904, *Sten. Ber. RT.*, p. 3361. The German army adopted field grey in the wake of the British change to khaki during the Boer war, but educational criteria were not applied to officer selection until the first world war: W. Deist, 'Zur Geschichte des preussischen Offizierkorps 1888–1918', in H. H. Hoffmann, ed., *Das deutsche Offizierkorps 1888–1918*, Boppard, 1980, p. 40.

15 Moch, *L'Armée d'une démocratie*, and his pamphlet *La Réforme militaire: Vive la milice!*, which Bebel enthusiastically reviewed: 'Stehendes Heer und Überproduktion', *NZ*, 17.2 (1899), pp. 50–6; see the *Handbuch ... 1903*, p. 20, and Liebknecht, *Militarism and Anti-Militarism*, p. 24.

16 J. Jaurès, *L'Armée nouvelle*, Paris, 1911.

17 I. Deutscher, *The Prophet Armed: Trotsky, 1879–1921*, Oxford, 1954, pp. 477–80.

18 E. Bernstein, *Die Voraussetzungen des Sozialismus und die Aufgaben der Sozialdemokratie*, Stuttgart, 1899, pp. 201–4. Schippel embarrassed the SPD leadership by resurrecting Engels' poor opinion of militias, which he had only abandoned in the late 1880s: 'War Friedrich Engels milizgläubich?', *Sozialistische Monatshefte*, 2 (1898), pp. 495–8; 'Friedrich Engels und das Milizsystem', *NZ*, 17.1 (1899), pp. 580–8; 613–17; 'Siehe da: das stehende Milizheer', *NZ*, 17.1 (1899), pp. 780–6.

19 R. Luxemburg, *Selected Political Writings*, D. Howard, ed., New York, 1971, p. 140. K. Kautsky, 'Friedrich Engels und das Milizsystem', *NZ*, 17.1 (1898), pp. 335–42; 'Schippel und der Militarismus', *NZ*, 17.1 (1899), pp. 618–26; 644–54; 686–91; 'Siegfried der Harmlose', *NZ*, 17.1 (1899), pp. 787–91.

20 Liebknecht, *Militarism and Anti-Militarism*, pp. 25 and 63–5.

21 August Bebel, Bebel NL 22/71, Bl. 1–8, ZPA, Institut für die Geschichte der Arbeiterbewegung.

22 Von der Goltz, *The Nation in Arms*; Bernhardi, *Germany and the Next War*.

23 Cited in Mommsen, *Max Weber and German Politics*, p. 25.

24 Even at the end of his life, Bebel confessed in Vienna during the 60th birthday celebrations for Victor Adler that 'It was one of the saddest days of my life, when in 1866 it was announced that Austria had been expelled from the German Federation; and it would be one of the finest moments of my life, if the day should come when Austria and Germany might again be united. You, Austrian party comrades, are of the same flesh and blood as we are.' 24 June 1912, V. Adler, *Briefwechsel mit August Bebel und Karl Kautsky*, F. Adler, ed., Vienna, 1954, pp. 547–8.

25 Motteler, 20 April 1874, *Sten. Ber. RT.*, p. 961.
26 See H.-U. Wehler, *Sozialdemokratie und Nationalstaat*, Würzburg, 1962.
27 W. Jung, *August Bebel: Deutscher Patriot und internationaler Sozialist*, Pfaffenweiler, 1988, p. 103: Bebel, 12 January 1892, *Sten. Ber. RT.*, p. 3581; 17 November 1896, *Sten. Ber. RT.*, p. 3310.
28 Jung, *August Bebel*, p. 107.
29 The first statement of this position was in the Reichstag, 2 March 1880, which Bebel then defended in an article in *Der Sozialdemokrat*, 10 April 1880, in A. Bebel, *Ausgewählte Reden und Schriften*, 2.1, Berlin, 1978, pp. 91–6. See Maehl, *August Bebel*, p. 201. A typical example of Bebel's rhetoric is this example, when he addressed the Reichstag in 1904:

> Gentlemen, in future you cannot fight a victorious war *without us*. If you win [a war], you will win with us, not against us ... I say further: we have the greatest interest if we are forced into a war – I assume that German policy is itself too cautious to provide any grounds for causing a war – but if the war should be a war of aggression [against Germany], a war in which the existence of Germany was at stake, then, I give you my word, every last man of us, even the oldest, is ready to shoulder arms and defend our German soil, not for your but for our sake, and if necessary in spite of you. We would live and fight on this soil to preserve this Fatherland, our homeland, which is at least as much if not more our Fatherland than yours, so that it is a joy even for the lowest among us to live here. We will fight to the last breath against any attempt to take a piece of our Fatherland away.

   7 March 1904, *Sten. Ber. RT.*, p. 1588. See also H. Bartel, 'August Bebels Stellung zur Vaterlandsverteidigung', *Beiträge zur Geschichte der deutschen Arbeiterbewegung*, 5 (1963), pp. 846–60, for an attempt to give this defence of the Fatherland a Leninist gloss.
30 Roth, *The Social Democrats in Imperial Germany*; Groh, *Negative Integration*.
31 Jung, *August Bebel*, p. 107: article in *Der Sozialdemokrat*, 10 April 1880, in Bebel, *Ausgewählte Reden und Schriften*, 2, pp. 91–2.
32 See Jung, *August Bebel*, pp. 103–15.
33 Schröder, *Sozialismus und Imperialismus*, pp. 144–9 and 172–3.
34 K. Kautsky, 'Die moderne Nationalität', *NZ*, 5 (1887), pp. 392–405; 442–51; 'Nationalität und Internationalität', *NZ*, 1908, Ergänzungsheft, 1; *Congrès international socialiste des travailleurs et des chambres syndicales ouvriers Londres 26 juillet-2 août 1896*, M. Winock, intr., Geneva, 1980.
35 R. Chickering, *We Men Who Feel Most German: A Cultural Study of the Pan-German League, 1886–1914*, London, 1984; Eley, *Reshaping the German Right*; M. S. Coetzee, *The Army League: Popular Nationalism in Wilhelmine Germany*, Oxford, 1990; E. Cahm, 'Socialism and the Nationalist Movement in France at the time of the Dreyfus affair', in E. Cahm and V. Fisera, eds., *Socialism and Nationalism in Contemporary Europe (1848–1945)*, 2, Nottingham, 1979, pp. 48–64.
36 M. Drachkovitch, *Les Socialistes allemands et français et la problème de la guerre, 1870–1914*, Geneva, 1953.
37 *Ibid.*, and H. Goldberg, *The Life of Jean Jaurès*, Madison, 1962.
38 Drachkovitch, *Les Socialismes français et allemand*, p. 122; Jung, *August Bebel*, pp. 155–60 and 222–26.

39 See Braunthal, *History of the International*, pp. 278–84, on the 1904 Amsterdam Congress.

40 Hegel, *The Philosophy of History*, pp. 103–4.

41 See Engels, 'The Magyar Struggle' and 'Democratic Pan-Slavism', in Marx and Engels, *Collected Works*, 8, pp. 227–38 and 362–78; 'Revolution and Counter-Revolution in Germany', in *ibid.*, 11, pp. 46–8; Mayer, *Friedrich Engels*, 1, pp. 324–9; R. Rosdolsky, 'Friedrich Engels und das Problem der "geschichtslosen" Völker', *Archiv für Sozialgeschichte*, 4 (1964), pp. 87–251; and Wehler, *Sozialdemokratie und Nationalstaat*, pp. 17–23, for some useful guidelines to understanding Marx's and Engels' perception of the national question. For their views on the Eastern Question during the Crimean conflict, see Mayer, *Friedrich Engels*, 2, pp. 42–60.

42 Conze and Groh, *Die Arbeiterbewegung in der nationalen Bewegung*.

43 D. Gasman, *The Scientific Origins of National Socialism: Ernst Haeckel and the German Monist League*, London, 1971; P. Weindling, *Health, Race and German Politics between National Unification and Nazism, 1870–1945*, Cambridge, 1989; B. A. Boyd, *Rudolf Virchow: The Scientist as Citizen*, New York, 1991.

44 Cited in G. Mergner, 'Solidarity with the "Savages": The Relationship of the German Social Democrats to African Resistance in the Former German Colonies around the Turn of the Century', *IISH Symposium: Internationalism in the Labour Movement before 1940*, Amsterdam (*mimeo*), 1985, p. 5.

45 Steinberg, *Sozialismus und deutsche Sozialdemokratie*, pp. 45–60.

46 Kautsky, 'Phäakentum', *Der Sozialdemokrat*, 6 July 1882, cited in Salvadori, *Karl Kautsky and the Socialist Revolution*, p. 24.

47 Fletcher, *Revisionism and Empire*; Schröder, *Sozialismus und Imperialismus*, pp. 183–98; Braunthal, *History of the International*, pp. 305–19.

48 Schorske, *German Social Democracy*; Groh, *Negative Integration*.

49 So even Rosa Luxemburg and Karl Liebknecht had both responded thus to the joint expedition of 1900 to put down the Boxer uprising in China: Schröder, *Sozialismus und Imperialismus*, p. 172.

50 See Fletcher, *Revisionism and Empire*, and especially the outspoken racism of Gustav Noske: H.-C. Schröder, *Gustav Noske und die Kolonialpolitik des deutschen Kaiserreichs*, Bonn, 1979.

51 Kautsky himself refused to draw from these Darwinist ideas the 'right of the higher culture': Schröder, *Sozialismus und Imperialismus*, p. 196.

52 See chapter 1 above. During the 1905 Russian Revolution, there were rumours that Wilhelm II would intervene to restore tsarist autocracy, and the SPD mounted a major campaign to prevent this.

53 Bebel, 13 June 1896, *Sten. Ber. RT.*, p. 2587; for a wealth of other quotations about Russia as the 'barbarian state', 'barbarian land', etc. see Jung, *August Bebel*, pp. 339–44.

54 Nolan, *Social Democracy and Society*; L. Abrams, *Workers' Culture in Imperial Germany: Leisure and Recreation in the Rhineland and Westphalia*, London, 1992, pp. 127–8.

55 R. J. Evans, *Proletarians and Politics: Socialism, Protest and the Working Class in Germany before the First World War*, Hemel Hempstead, 1990, pp. 173–82.

56 See the Bebel–Engels correspondence especially: *August Bebels Briefwechsel*

mit Friedrich Engels; Mayer, *Friedrich Engels*, 2, pp. 463–70 and 504–20; Maehl, *August Bebel*, pp. 201–11.

57 Wilhelm Liebknecht, speech to the North German Reichstag, Liebknecht, *Gegen Militarismus und Eroberungskrieg*, p. 51; Bebel, Speech to the Reichstag, 24 April 1871, *Ausgewählte Reden und Schriften*, 1, p. 144. Engels to Marx, 15 August 1870, Marx and Engels, *Werke*, 33, pp. 40–1; Marx to Engels, 17 August 1870, *ibid.*, p. 43; Marx to the Brunswick Committee of the SDAP, 1 September 1870, Marx and Engels, *Selected Correspondence*, Moscow, 1965, p. 246.

58 Bebel to Guesde, 17 April 1893, Guesde NL, 225/3, IISH.

59 Bebel, 'Deutschland, Russland und die orientalische Frage', *NZ*, 4 (1886), pp. 502–15, pp. 508 and 511; Engels, 'Die auswärtige Politik des russischen Zarentums', K. Marx and F. Engels, *Werke*, 22, p. 45.

60 Engels, 'Die auswärtige Politik des russischen Zarentums', Marx and Engels, *Werke*, 22, p. 13.

61 Bebel, 'Deutschland, Russland und die orientalische Frage'; Engels, 'Die auswärtige Politik', p. 45.

62 For details of the conservative David Urquhart's influence on Marx and Marx's collaboration with him in his campaign against Palmerston for allegedly being a secret agent of tsarism, see B. Nicolaievsky and O. Maenchen-Helfen, *Karl Marx: Man and Fighter*, Harmondsworth, 1976, pp. 245–7. For a historical evaluation of Marx's major Russophobic tract, 'Revelations of the Diplomatic History of the Eighteenth Century', see the editors' preface, to Marx and Engels, *Collected Works*, 15, pp. xix–xxiv.

63 A. J. P. Taylor, *The Struggle for the Mastery of Europe*, Oxford, 1954; Berghahn, *Germany and the Approach of War*.

64 Bebel, 'Deutschland, Russland und die orientalische Frage', p. 513.

65 Engels, 'Die auswärtige Politik', p. 43. Engels' willingness to set about learning Bulgarian at the age of 73 in order 'to follow the progress of socialism eastward and southward' was a touching reversal from his diatribes against 'historyless peoples' of 45 years earlier. Engels, letter to the editorial board of the Bulgarian symposium 'Social-Democrat', 9 June 1893, Marx and Engels, *Selected Correspondence*, p. 458.

66 See E. Bernstein, 'Die Briefe von Karl Marx über den Krimkrieg und die Orientfrage', *NZ*, 16.1 (1897), pp. 209–17, p. 212. Wilhelm Liebknecht stuck by Marx's and Engels' earlier Turkophile and Slavophobe views: W. Liebknecht, *Zur orientalischen Frage oder Soll Europa kosakisch werden? Ein Mahnwort an das deutsche Volk*, Leipzig, 1878, which he reissued in 1897. Julius Motteler still sided with Wilhelm Liebknecht: Motteler to Kautsky, 4–6 September 1900, Karl Kautsky NL 55/20, Bl. 106, ZPA, Institut für die Geschichte der Arbeiterbewegung. For Kautsky's and Bernstein's rebuttal of this older position, see Bernstein, 'Der Sieg der Türken und die Sozialdemokratie', *NZ*, 15.2 (1897), pp. 260–8 and 'Die Briefe von Karl Marx über den Krimkrieg'; Kautsky to Adler, 12 November 1896, Adler, *Briefwechsel mit August Bebel und Karl Kautsky*, p. 221. It was left to the revisionist Right to rediscover Marx's Crimean war journalism, in 1908 – in the new edition Eleanor Marx had brought out in 1897 – and trot out Marx's pro-Turkish sentiments to justify their endorsement of the government's aid to the new Turkish regime. But by

then any quotation would do in an ideological battle between different factions of the SPD Left, Centre and Right which had everything to do with the actualities of Wilhelmine politics and little with textual exegesis. For the revisionist case, see Max Schippel, 'Balkanwirren und Demokratie einst und heute', *Sozialistische Monatshefte*, 21 (1908), and for a Left refutation D. Riazanov, 'Marx, "Was soll aus der Türkei in Europa werden?"' *NZ*, 28.2 (1910), pp. 4–12.

67 This tenet remained a constant of Kautsky's criticism of other Marxist attempts to theorise about nationality, especially those of Rosa Luxemburg and Otto Bauer. See Kautsky, 'Die moderne Nationalität'; (against Luxemburg) 'Finis Poloniae?', *NZ*, 14.2 (1896), pp. 484–91; 513–25; and (against Bauer) 'Nationalität und Internationalität', *NZ*, 1908, Ergänzungsheft, 1. On this as so many other issues Lenin followed Kautsky closely: V. I. Lenin, 'The Rights of Nations to Self-Determination', *Collected Works*, 20, pp. 393–454.

68 Engels to Bernstein, 22/25 February 1882, *Eduard Bernsteins Briefwechsel mit Friedrich Engels*, H. Hirsch, ed., Assen, 1970, p. 80; 15 October 1885, *ibid.*, p. 327, 9 October 1886, *ibid.*, pp. 343–6, and 5 May 1887, pp. 254–5. On the International in 1912, G. Haupt, *Socialism and the Great War: The Collapse of the Second International*, Oxford, 1972, pp. 69–72.

69 Mayer, *Friedrich Engels*, 2, p. 514. On Jaurès, see Drachkovitch, *Les Socialismes français et allemands*, pp. 36–8 and 122–3.

70 Fletcher, *Revisionism and Empire*, pp. 172–8; see J. L. Hammond on the policy of the *Nation* in B. Russell, *The Autobiography of Bertrand Russell*, 2, London, 1968, p. 46.

71 Bebel, *Nicht stehendes Heer sondern Volkswehr*, pp. 28–9.

72 *Congrès international ouvrier socialiste tenu à Bruxelles du 16 au 23 août 1891*, intr. M. Winock, Geneva, 1976, p. 111; *Congrès international ouvrier socialiste tenu à Zurich du 6 au 12 août 1893*, intr. M. Winock, Geneva, 1977, p. 80; C. Bonnier to F. Engels, 21 October 1892, Engels NL, Correspondence I, L627, IISH, and October 1893, *ibid.*, L. 633.

73 *Congrès international ouvrier socialiste tenu à Bruxelles*, pp. 62–77.

74 Plekhanov, *Congrès international ouvrier socialiste tenu à Zurich*, pp. 227–9. His main opponent was the former Lutheran pastor, populariser of Marx and founder of Dutch Social Democracy, Ferdinand Domela Nieuwenhuis. He certainly hit the mark. 'This panic about Russia,' he declared, 'which Plekhanov has also expressed, is like frightening little children with an ogre. If Bebel describes the Russian nation as the bastion of cruelty and barbarism, then France could accuse Germany of the same, because France is a republic. But where would this lead if socialists make such accusations against other countries?' *Ibid.*

75 Joll, *The Second International*; Braunthal, *History of the International*.

76 See *Vpered*, 12 April (30 March old style) 1905; I am grateful to C. A. Merridale for drawing my attention to this material.

77 *Protokoll über die Verhandlungen des Parteitages der Sozialdemokratischen Partei Deutschlands. Abgehalten zu Essen vom 15. bis 21. September 1907*, Berlin, 1907, p. 255.

78 They also hoped that a German victory would destroy Bonapartism in France, and shift the centre of working-class politics to Germany, so increasing their

own influence over the European labour movement. See Marx to Engels, 17 August 1870, Marx and Engels, *Werke*, 33, p. 44; W. Wette, *Kriegstheorien deutscher Sozialisten*, Stuttgart, 1971, pp. 86–8.

79 Morgan, *The German Social Democrats and the First International*, pp. 208–11.
80 Grünberg, *Die Internationale und der Weltkrieg*, pp. 7–13.
81 Bebel, 9 November 1911, *Sten. Ber. R. T.*, p. 7730.
82 H. Bley, *Bebel und die Strategie der Kriegsverhütung 1904–1913: Eine Studie über Bebels Geheimkontakte mit der britischen Regierung und Edition der Dokumente*, Göttingen, 1975.
83 Schröder, *Sozialismus und Imperialismus*; H.-H. Paul, *Marx, Engels und die Imperialismustheorie der II. Internationale*, Hamburg, 1978.
84 Jäger, *Historische Forschung und politische Kultur in Deutschland*; Koch, *The Origins of the First World War*.
85 Schröder, *Sozialismus und Imperialismus*; Groh, *Negative Integration*.
86 Karl Liebknecht, cited in K. Mandelbaum, *Die Erörterungen innerhalb der deutschen Sozialdemokratie über das Problem des Imperialismus (1895–1914)*, Schweinfurt, 1926, p. 22; Groh, 'The "Unpatriotic Socialists" and the State', p. 164.
87 Engels, 'Kann Europa abrüsten?', Marx and Engels, *Werke*, 22, pp. 369–99. As Bebel wrote back to him, 'I can only regard the disarmament proposal as a means to demonstrate that we know of a feasible solution; I do not consider any of those who would have to implement it capable of doing so. It will be as unacceptable as our proposals to introduce the militia. For, one cannot treat militarism as if it was superficial, since it is a necessity to the state and the bourgeoisie. It is [also] necessary for business and as a sinecure for the sons of the nobility and the bourgeoisie.' Bebel to Engels, 28 February 1893, *August Bebels Briefwechsel mit Friedrich Engels*, p. 670.
88 Kautsky, 'Demokratische und reaktionäre Abrüstung', *NZ*, 16.2 (1898), pp. 740–6.
89 See chapter 6.
90 H. W. C. David, *The Political Thought of Heinrich von Treitschke*, London, 1910, pp. 29 and 107; Mommsen, *Max Weber and German Politics*, pp. 68–90.
91 Engels, 'The Foreign Policy of Russian Tsarism', Marx and Engels, *Werke*, 22, pp. 41–2; and Mayer, *Friedrich Engels*, 2, p. 505. On the numbers involved see Engels, 'Einleitung zu Sigismund Borkheims "Zur Errinerung für die deutschen Mordspatrioten. 1806–1807"', Marx and Engels, *Werke*, 21, p. 350; and 'Sozialismus in Deutschland', *ibid.*, 22, p. 256.
92 For Bebel's belief that the next war would be a world war as well as much longer and bloodier than any previous one, see Bebel, 'Der nächste Krieg in Zahlen', *NZ*, 1887, in *Ausgewählte Reden und Schriften*, 2.1, pp. 362–3 and speech to the Berlin voters, *Berliner Volksblatt*, 25 January 1890, where he also predicted that 'twelve to fourteen million' combatants would be involved on all sides. On the economic collapse that war would cause, see his article 'Deutschland, Russland und die orientalische Frage', p. 514; his parliamentary speeches: 30 November 1887, Bebel, *Ausgewählte Reden und Schriften*, 2.1, pp. 412–15; 16 December 1887, *Sten. Ber. RT.*, p. 300; 15 March 1889, *ibid.*, p. 931; 28 November 1891, *ibid.*, p. 3121; 13 February 1896, p. 940; 3 February 1893 in A. Bebel, *Schriften 1862–1913*, 1, C. Stephan, ed., Frankfurt, 1981, pp. 270–96.

93 Bebel's most famous speeches were at the 1907 Congress of the International: *Congrès socialiste international Stuttgart 6–24 août 1907*, intr. G. Haupt, Geneva, 1978, pp. 491–2; and in the immediate wake of the 1911 Morocco crisis: *Protokoll über die Verhandlungen des Parteitages der Sozialdemokratischen Partei Deutschlands. Abgehalten in Jena vom 10. bis 16. September 1911 sowie Bericht über die 6. Frauenkonferenz am 8. und 9. September 1911 in Jena*, Berlin, 1911, pp. 346ff. See Braunthal *History of the International*, pp. 335–6. See also Bebel to the Reichstag, 22 January 1903, *Sten. Ber. RT.*, p. 7471; 5 December 1904, p. 3364; 14 December 1905, p. 313. See also Bley, *August Bebel und die Strategie der Kriegsverhütung*.

94 Engels to Lafargue, 25 March 1889, Marx and Engels, *Werke*, 37, p. 171. In 1891 the French socialist Gabriel Deville wrote to Wilhelm Liebknecht warning him that Boulanger was trying to provoke an immediate war with Germany. G. Deville to W. Liebknecht, 5 March 1891, Liebknecht NL, D 122/31–32, IISH. Liebknecht and Vaillant also argued that war would disorganise the labour movement: *Congrès international ouvrier socialiste tenu à Bruxelles du 16 au 23 août 1891*, pp. 104–5.

95 W. Liebknecht to the National Council of the Parti Ouvrier, 15 March 1891, Liebknecht NL, D 208/3, IISH. The International formerly adopted this self-characterisation at the *Congrès international ouvrier socialiste tenu à Bruxelles du 16 au 23 août 1891*, p. 91. Bebel wrote to Guesde in preparation for the May Day celebrations of 1893, 'Against the anti-cultural efforts of the ruling classes and their governments, it is the sacred duty of the working class of both countries [France and Germany] to express the solidarity of the interests of both peoples most energetically and to declare that nothing can destroy their feelings of fraternity.' Bebel to Guesde, 17 April 1893, Guesde NL, 225/3, IISH.

96 M. Dommanget, *Histoire du premier mai*, Paris, 1953; A. von Saldern, *Vom Einwohner zum Bürger. Zur Emanzipation der städischen Unterschicht Göttingens 1890–1920*, Berlin, 1973, pp. 145–7; Mosse, *The Nationalisation of the Masses*, pp. 164–70; D. Dowe, 'The Workers' Choral Movement Before the First World War', *Journal of Contemporary History*, 13, no. 2 (1978), pp. 269–76.

97 See chapter 6.

98 Engels, 'Sozialismus in Deutschland'; for the dismay Bebel's Reichstag statements and Engels' article caused the French Left, see Charles Bonnier to J. Guesde, 27 February 1892, Guesde NL, 211/2, IISH.

99 Bebel to Nieuwenhuis, 30 December 1889, no. 140, *Ferdinand Domela Nieuwenhuis: Internationale Correspondentie*, ed., T. van Tyn and P. Wielsma, manuscript, IISH; Bebel to Victor Adler, 16 March 1896 and 28 July 1896, Adler, *Briefwechsel mit August Bebel und Karl Kautsky*, pp. 201 and 209.

100 The model for this sort of congress was only established in Stuttgart in 1907. As the Secretary of the International Socialist Bureau put it to Karl Kautsky, 'It is vital that we prepare for the next international congress at Stuttgart ... The disagreements of Amsterdam must not reappear.' C. Huysmans to Kautsky, 4 May 1906, Kautsky NL, D 13, 218, IISH.

101 Bonnier to Engels, 21 October 1892, Engels NL, Correspondence I, L 627, IISH.

102 As Bebel wrote, 'The International of the workers, which of all classes has been the only one so far to show how people can understand one another and work together irrespective of different origins, language or religion, must be broadened to become an International of the great popular majorities.' *Nicht stehendes Heer sondern Volkswehr*, p. 75.

103 J. Howorth, 'French Workers and German Workers: The Impossibility of Internationalism, 1900–1914', *European History Quarterly*, 15 (1985), pp. 71–97, p. 91, n. 22 on the role of Edouard Vaillant in defining the International Socialist Bureau as a co-ordinating rather than directing agency.

104 Schippel, 'Friedrich Engels und das Milizsystem', p. 588; David, *Protokoll Essen 1907*, pp. 247–8.

105 See K. Saul, 'Der Kampf um die Jugend zwischen Volksschule und Kaserne. Ein Beitrag zur "Jugendpflege" im Wilhelminischen Reich, 1890–1914', *Militärgeschichtliche Mitteilungen*, 1 (1971), pp. 97–143; H. Lemmermann, *Kriegserziehung im Kaiserreich*, 2 vols., Bremen, 1984.

106 Liebknecht, speech to the Prussian Chamber, 21 April 1910, *Gesammelte Reden und Schriften*, 3, Berlin, 1960, pp. 185–207, and speech to the Reichstag, 24 June 1913, *Gesammelte Reden und Schriften*, 6, pp. 346–7.

107 Bebel, 25 February 1905, *Sten. Ber. RT.*, p. 4791.

108 Bebel, *Nicht stehendes Heer sondern Volkswehr*, p. 26; *Handbuch...1898*, p. 211; *Handbuch...1903*, p. 41.

109 Berghahn, *Germany and the Approach of War*, pp. 165–74.

3 KARL KAUTSKY'S THEORY OF MILITARISM

1 R. J. Geary, *Karl Kautsky*, Manchester, 1987; G. Haupt, 'Un partito guida: l'influenza della socialdemocrazia tedesca nel Sudest europeo', *L'Internazionale socialista dalla Commune a Lenin*, Turin, 1978.

2 G. Lukacs, *History and Class Consciousness*, London, 1971; K. Korsch, *Marxism and Philosophy*, London, 1970; L. Colletti, 'Bernstein and the Marxism of the Second International', in *From Rousseau to Lenin*, London, 1972, pp. 45–108; Steinberg, *Sozialismus und deutsche Sozialdemokratie*; Salvadori, *Karl Kautsky and the Socialist Revolution*.

3 R. N. Hunt, *The Political Ideas of Marx and Engels*, 2, London, 1984.

4 Lidtke, *The Outlawed Party*; M. Nolan, 'Economic Crisis, State Policy, and Working Class Formation in Germany, 1870–1900', in Katznelson and Zollberg, eds., *Working Class Formation*, pp. 352–93.

5 K. Jarausch, *Students, Society and Politics in Imperial Germany: The Rise of Academic Illiberalism*, Princeton, 1982.

6 D. H. Müller, *Idealismus und Revolution: Zur Opposition der Jungen gegen den sozialdemokratischen Parteivorstand 1890 bis 1894*, Berlin, 1975.

7 A. Mitzmann, 'Personal Conflict and Ideological Options in Sombart and Weber', *Max Weber and his Contemporaries*, W. J. Mommsen and J. Osterhammel, eds., London, 1987, p. 100; see also R. H. Thomas, *Nietzsche in German Politics and Society, 1890–1918*, Manchester, 1983.

8 See chapter 1 above.

9 The *Anti-Dühring* was written between September 1876 and June 1878 and serialised, under Wilhelm Liebknecht's editorship of the Social Democratic

Vorwärts, between 3 September 1877 and 7 July 1878. Engels, 'Anti-Dühring', Marx and Engels, *Werke*, 20, p. 158.

10 Marx, 'The Eighteenth Brumaire of Louis Bonaparte', Marx and Engels, *Collected Works*, 11, p. 143 and 185–6; Marx, 'The Civil War in France', *Collected Works*, 22, p. 329; Engels, 1874 Preface to *The Peasant War in Germany*, Moscow, 1965, p. 13; J. M. Maguire, *Marx's Theory of Politics*, Cambridge, 1978, pp. 177–8.

11 Engels, 'Zur Wohnungsfrage', Marx and Engels, *Werke*, 18, pp. 258–9; and Engels to Marx, 11 June 1866, Marx and Engels, *ibid.*, 31, p. 227; 'Die Rolle der Gewalt in der Geschichte', Marx and Engels, *ibid.*, 21, pp. 452–56.

12 Wehler, *The German Empire*, pp. 55–62; and see introduction above.

13 Wette, *Kriegstheorien deutscher Sozialisten*.

14 Engels, 'Der Ursprung der Familie, des Privateigentums und des Staats', Marx and Engels, *Werke*, 21, pp. 164–6.

15 Engels, 'Die Rolle der Gewalt in der Geschichte'.

16 Marx, 'The Eighteenth Brumaire', p. 185.

17 R. Hilferding, *Finance Capital: A Study of the Latest Phase of Capitalist Development*, T. Bottomore, ed., London, 1981, pp. 336 and 346.

18 B. M. Goldstein, *Ludwig Quidde and the Struggle for Democratic Pacifism in Germany, 1914–1930*, unpublished PhD thesis, New York University, 1984, pp. 1 and 14.

19 Quidde, *Caligula*, p. 100. On Weber, see Mommsen, *Max Weber and German Politics*, pp. 94–100. The Kehr-Wehler school has been the one to inherit these terms.

20 Quidde, *Caligula*, p. 108.

21 *Ibid.*, p. 102.

22 Goldstein, *Ludwig Quidde*, pp. 22–34.

23 Quidde, *Caligula*, pp. 81–130; Berghahn, *Militarism*, p. 17.

24 *Ibid.*, pp. 28–31 and 48–50.

25 See chapter 1 above.

26 Engels, 'Der Ursprung der Familie', pp. 167–8; the classic interpretation of the SPD along these lines is A. Rosenberg, *Imperial Germany*, London, 1931, and *Democracy and Socialism*, London, 1939; on Kautsky's priority on democracy throughout his political life, see Salvadori, *Karl Kautsky and the Socialist Revolution*.

27 See Rosa Luxemburg, *Selected Political Writings*, p. 140.

28 K. Kautsky, *The Class Struggle*, New York, 1971, p. 105.

29 *Ibid.*, pp. 105–6.

30 *Ibid.*, p. 107.

31 *Ibid.*, p. 110.

32 *Ibid.*, pp. 107–8 and Kautsky, 'Krieg und Kapitalismus', *NZ*, 31.2 (1913), p. 439.

33 Kautsky, *The Class Struggle*, p. 108.

34 *Ibid.*, p. 109.

35 For Bukharin's views, which also greatly influenced Lenin by the time he came to write *State and Revolution*, see N. I. Bukharin, *Selected Writings on the State and the Transition to Socialism*, R. Day, ed. and intr., London, 1982, pp. 6–37.

36 Engels, 'Anti-Dühring', pp. 259–62.
37 Kautsky, 'Die chinesischen Eisenbahnen und das europaische Proletariat', *NZ*, 4, 1886, p. 516, and see R. J. Geary, 'Karl Kautsky and the Development of Marxism', unpublished PhD thesis, Cambridge, 1971, chapter 5. See also chapter 5 below.
38 Kautsky, *The Class Struggle*, p. 104.
39 See Kautsky, *Socialism and Colonial Policy: An Analysis*, Belfast, 1975; and chapter 5 below.
40 See Schröder, *Sozialismus und Imperialismus*, p. 165.
41 See P. M. Sweezy, *The Theory of Capitalist Development*, New York, 1970, pp. 158–69; G. Pugh, 'Economic Theory and Political Thought in German Social Democracy: An Essay on the "Rezeption" of Marx's Capital with Particular Reference to Kautsky, Parvus, Hilferding and Luxemburg', unpublished PhD thesis, University of Kent, 1983, pp. 348–63; and chapter 5 below.
42 Kautsky, 'Krieg und Kapitalismus', p. 444.
43 Cited by R. Höhn, *Sozialismus und Heer*, 1, Bad Harzburg, 1959, p. 8.
44 Kautsky, 'Der erweiterte deutsche Militärstaat', *NZ*, 5, 1887, p. 333 and 'Der erste Mai und der Militarismus', *NZ*, 11.2 (1893), pp. 100–1.
45 Kautsky, 'Kapitalismus und Militarismus', p. 195.
46 Kautsky, 'Der erste Mai und der Militarismus', p. 102.
47 Kautsky, 'Friedrich Engels und das Milizsystem', *NZ*, 17.1 (1898), p. 340 and 'Schippel und der Militarismus', *NZ*, 17.1 (1899), p. 651.
48 Kautsky, 'Moloch in Nöthen', *NZ*, 12.1 (1893), pp. 162–4.
49 Kautsky, 'Schippel und der Militarismus', *NZ*, 17.1 (1899), pp. 645 and 648–9.
50 Kautsky, 'Der erste Mai und der Militarismus', p. 101.
51 Engels was prone to make all-encompassing generalisations about the role of the state in assisting economic development: Engels to C. Schmidt, 27 October 1890, Marx and Engels, *Werke*, 37, pp. 490–1; and 'Anti-Dühring', pp. 169–70.
52 Kautsky, *The Social Revolution and On the Morrow of the Social Revolution*, London, 1909, pp. 7 and 38.
53 Hunt, *The Political Ideas of Marx and Engels*.

4 KARL LIEBKNECHT AND THE END OF DEMOCRATIC ANTI-MILITARISM

1 See Lenin to Kautsky, 10 October 1904, Kautsky NL, D15, 395, IISH, and 26 October 1904, D15, 396, seeking access to *Die neue Zeit*, which Kautsky refused: Kautsky to Lenin, Kautsky NL, C465, IISH; and again in 1911 Lenin attempted to gain Kautsky's patronage, this time as a correspondent for the *Mysl*: Lenin to Kautsky, 31 January 1911, Kautsky NL, D15, 397. Trotsky enjoyed a much closer relationship with Kautsky, partly because his attempts to unify the Bolshevik and Menshevik factions was in line with the views of Kautsky, Bebel and Victor Adler: see Trotsky to Kautsky, 1908–1912, Kautsky NL, D22, 159–180, IISH.
2 T. Willey, *Back to Kant: The Revival of Kantianism in German Social and Historical Thought, 1860–1914*, Detroit, 1978; K. Vorländer, *Kant und Marx*, Leipzig, 1911; both Hugo Haase and Otto Braun – later Prime Minister of

Prussia – were members of neo-Kantian reading circles in Königsberg: Calkins, *Hugo Haase*, p. 7.

3 See Geary, *Karl Kautsky*; Fletcher, *Revisionism and Empire*.

4 Nettl, *Rosa Luxemburg*, 2.

5 F. Eisner, *Kurt Eisner: Die Politik des libertären Sozialismus*, Frankfurt, 1979.

6 N. Leser, *Zwischen Reformismus und Bolschewismus: Der Austromarxismus als Theorie und Praxis*, Vienna, 1968; T. Bottomore and P. Goode, eds., *Austro-Marxism*, London, 1978.

7 Mommsen, *Max Weber and German Politics*.

8 Trotnow, *Karl Liebknecht*.

9 The final resolution against revisionism was so elastic that a string of prominent reformists, including Auer, Vollmar, Heine, Südekum, Legien and Quarck all voted with the party leadership: Salvadori, *Karl Kautsky and the Socialist Revolution*, p. 82.

10 Bebel to M. Quarck, 16 March 1906, Max Quarck NL, 35, AdSD.

11 Nolan, *Social Democracy and Society*, pp. 171–3.

12 See *Protokoll über die Verhandlungen des Parteitages der Sozialdemokratischen Partei Deutschlands. Abgehalten zu Jena vom 17. bis 23. September 1905*, Berlin, 1905, pp. 342–3. The first person to advocate political mass strikes within the SPD was Alexander Parvus-Helphand, and he had proposed them for precisely this sort of defensive action: Parvus, 'Staatsstreich und politischer Massenstreik', *NZ*, 14.2 (1896), pp. 199–206; 261–6; 304–11; 356–64; 389–95. On Luxemburg and the mass strike debate, see Nettl, *Rosa Luxemburg*, 1.

13 The SPD and its attorneys – including Liebknecht and Hugo Haase – were very involved in defending refugees from the counter-revolution: Calkins, *Hugo Haase*, pp. 9–10; Trotnow, *Karl Liebknecht*, pp. 101–12. The SPD press produced a wave of caricatures of Nicholas II surrounded by gallows and corpses under such titles as 'Christmas in Russia' or 'Peace'.

14 Saul, *Staat, Industrie und Arbeiterbewegung*.

15 See chapter 6 below on the peace movement, and on the suffrage campaign see Groh, *Negative Integration*, pp. 119–60.

16 Fricke, 'Zur Rolle des Militarismus nach innen', pp. 1298–1310; Kitchen, *The German Officer Corps*.

17 *Leipziger Volkszeitung*, 3 April 1906.

18 Fricke, 'Zur Rolle des Militarismus nach Innen', p. 1304.

19 *Vorwärts*, 28 September 1910; Fricke, 'Zur Rolle des Militarismus nach Innen', p. 1305. On such a traditional theme of domestic anti-militarism, even a right-wing SPD figure like Gustav Noske could wax radical and dedicate himself to struggle 'against this system with all our energy and strength until it is utterly vanquished'. *Ibid.*, p. 1307.

20 Bartel, *Die Linken in der deutschen Sozialdemokratie*, p. 68.

21 H. Bleiber, 'Die Moabit Unruhen 1910', *Zeitschrift für Geschichtswissenschaft*, 2, 1955, pp. 173–211.

22 Fricke, 'Zur Rolle des Militarismus nach Innen', p. 1309.

23 On Mansfeld, the SPD brought out a pamphlet, *Der Mansfelder Streik vor dem deutschen Reichstag*, Berlin, 1910: see Groh, *Negative Integration*, p. 126.

24 Bebel, 7 March 1904, *Sten. Ber. RT.*, pp. 1587–9.

25 Cited by Liebknecht, *Militarism and Anti-Militarism*, p. 132.

26 See chapter 1 above.
27 Thus Stadthagen, *Protokoll über die Verhandlungen des Parteitages der Sozialdemokratischen Partei Deutschlands. Abgehalten zu Essen vom 15. bis 21. September 1907*, Berlin, 1907, pp. 246 and 252.
28 Südekum, *Protokoll über die Verhandlungen des Parteitages der Sozialdemokratischen Partei Deutschlands. Abgehalten zu Bremen vom 18. bis 24. September 1904*, Berlin, 1904, p. 182.
29 Liebknecht, *Militarism and Anti-Militarism*, p. 53.
30 *Ibid.*, p. 134.
31 Richard Fischer, *Protokoll Bremen* 1904, p. 180 and Bebel, *Protokoll Jena* 1905, p. 284.
32 *Protokoll über die Verhandlungen des Parteitages der Sozialdemokratischen Partei Deutschlands. Abgehalten zu Mannheim vom 23. bis 29. September 1906 sowie Bericht über die 4. Frauenkonferenz am 22. und 23. September 1906 in Mannheim*, Berlin, 1906, p. 385.
33 Even the memoirs of Communist stalwarts collected by the East German regime are not very encouraging when it comes to the anti-militarist activities of the youth movement: see W. Koenen, Liebknecht NL, EA 0493, Bl. 182–83, ZPA, Institut für die Geschichte der Arbeiterbewegung.
34 It came out first in the *Mannheimer Volkstimme* and then the *Hamburger Echo*, 4 October 1906: Hall, *Scandal, Sensation and Social Democracy*, p. 122.
35 Trotnow, *Karl Liebknecht*, pp. 63–8; the SPD reaped propaganda value from the trial: F. Mehring, 'Der Prozess Liebknecht', *NZ*, 26.1 (1907), pp. 81–4.
36 U. Ratz, *Georg Ledebour 1850–1947: Weg und Wirken eines sozialistischen Politikers*, Berlin, 1969.
37 *Protokoll Bremen 1904*, p. 186. The argument was widely repeated: see, for example, Molkenbuhr, *Protokoll Mannheim 1906*, p. 385.
38 See Nettl, *Rosa Luxemburg*, 2, pp. 382–92.
39 Liebknecht, *Militarism and Anti-Militarism*, p. 17.
40 *Ibid.*, pp. 59–65.
41 *Ibid.*, pp. 65–6.
42 See chapter 1 above.
43 Liebknecht, *Militarism and Anti-Militarism*, pp. 34 and 38.
44 *Ibid.*, pp. 38 and 40.
45 *Ibid.*, p. 40.
46 *Ibid.*, p. 37.
47 Eley, *Reshaping the German Right*; Coetzee, *The Army League*; Berghahn, *Der Tirpitz-Plan*.
48 Bebel, 7 March 1904, *Sten. Ber. RT.*, pp. 1587–9.
49 Liebknecht, *Militarism and Anti-Militarism*, p. 32.
50 *Ibid.*
51 In Britain, J. A. Hobson had written in a similar vein about the 'herd instinct' in *Imperialism: A Study* (new edition), London, 1954, and in *The Psychology of Jingoism*, London, 1901.
52 Mosse, *The Nationalization of the Masses*, pp. 161–82.
53 Liebknecht, *Militarism and Anti-Militarism*, pp. 22 and 31.
54 *Ibid.*, pp. 134–5.
55 *Ibid.*, p. 23.

56 *Ibid.*, p. 78.

57 *Ibid.*, p. 10.

58 *Ibid.*, pp. 40–1.

59 *Ibid.*, p. 23.

60 As an instrument in the hands of the class in power to defeat its external enemies, Liebknecht concluded, a conscript army based on universal service, and, in a colonial era, a navy had become the normal forms of military organisation. He correctly predicted that even Britain and the USA would be forced to introduce conscription (*ibid.*, pp. 17–18). The argument that Russian industrialisation was stimulated by tsarism's fear of losing its military power in the aftermath of the Crimean war had become a familiar one: see, for example, Engels, 'Nachwort zu "Soziales aus Russland"', Marx and Engels, *Werke*, 22, p. 429.

61 Liebknecht, *Militarism and Anti-Militarism*, p. 23. Also 'Militarism undoubtedly possesses ... a plurality of aspects ... This flexibility, however, comes into play everywhere within the boundaries which are set by the goal which is absolutely essential to [capitalist] militarism, the protection of capitalism' (*ibid.*, p. 28).

62 *Ibid.*, p. 30.

63 Trotnow, *Karl Liebknecht*, p. 65.

64 See especially Liebknecht's correspondence with Kautsky: Liebknecht to Kautsky, 11 November 1907, 30 November 1907, 31 August 1908 and 2 September 1908, Kautsky NL, D15, 489–93, IISH; and from Kautsky to Liebknecht, 9 February 1908 and 5 September 1908, Bestand Karl Kautsky, NL 1/40, ZPA, Institut für die Geschichte der Arbeiterbewegung.

65 Trotnow, *Karl Liebknecht*, pp. 205–14.

66 K. Liebknecht, *Studien über die Bewegungsgesetze der sozialen Entwicklung*, 'Morris' (pseudonym for Rudolf Manasse) ed., Munich, 1922.

67 Bestand Karl Liebknecht, NL 1/25, Bl. 77–118, ZPA, Institut für die Geschichte der Arbeiterbewegung.

68 Liebknecht, *Studien*, pp. 252–60.

69 G. V. Plekhanov, *In Defence of Materialism: The Development of the Monist Theory of History*, London, 1947.

70 Liebknecht, *Studien*, p. 117, cited and translated by Trotnow, *Karl Liebknecht*, p. 210.

71 See Lenin's philosophical notebooks, *Collected Works*, 38, for the first steps towards the rediscovery of a critical Hegelian heritage; Korsch, *Marxism and Philosophy*; and Lukacs, *History and Class Consciousness*.

72 Liebknecht, *Studien*, p. 235. Liebknecht was also receptive to Freudian ideas which were circulating especially among the Austro-Marxists of the day: *ibid.*, p. 339.

73 *Ibid.*, p. 241. See also p. 237, for a similar distinction between different kinds of rule.

74 *Ibid.*, p. 236.

75 *Ibid.*, pp. 236–7.

76 *Ibid.*, p. 238.

77 *Ibid.*, p. 239.

78 *Ibid.*, pp. 14–15.

5 THE ECONOMICS OF ARMAMENT

1 Berghahn, *Germany and the Approach of War*; P. Witt, *Die Finanzpolitik des deutschen Reiches von 1903 bis 1913*, Lübeck, 1970.

2 See chapter 1 above.

3 For example, Bebel, 5 December 1904, *Sten. Ber. RT.*, pp. 3363–4, and Vollmar, 9 December 1904, *ibid.*, p. 3440.

4 *Protokoll über die Verhandlungen des Parteitages der Sozialdemokratischen Partei Deutschlands. Abgehalten zu Stuttgart vom 3. bis 8. Oktober 1898*, Berlin, 1898, pp. 138–42; *Protokoll über die Verhandlungen des Parteitages der Sozialdemokratischen Partei Deutschlands. Abgehalten zu Hannover vom 9. bis 14. Oktober 1899*, Berlin, 1899, p. 282. Bebel considered this proposal a far graver threat to the direction of the party than Bernstein's revision of Marxist theory: Bebel to Kautsky, 29 August 1903, *August Bebels Briefwechsel mit Karl Kautsky*, K. Kautsky Jr., ed., Assen, 1971, pp. 156–7.

5 Heckart, *From Bassermann to Bebel*.

6 One of the only forays into this field is M. Epkenhans, 'Grossindustrie und Schlachtflottenbau 1897–1914', *Militärgeschichtliche Mitteilungen*, 1 (1988), pp. 65–140.

7 Schippel, 'War Friedrich Engels milizgläubich?'; 'Friedrich Engels und das Milizsystem'; 'Siehe da: das stehende Milizheer'; Kautsky, 'Friedrich Engels und das Milizsystem'; 'Schippel und der Militarismus'; 'Siegfried der Harmlose', *ibid.*, pp. 787–91.

8 As Jacoby, 'The Politics of Crisis Theory: Toward the critique of automatic Marxism II', and Pugh, 'Economic Theory and Political Thought in German Social Democracy', show, Marxists at this time ignored Marx's theory of the falling rate of profit. See also Geary, 'Karl Kautsky and the Development of Marxism'.

9 J. London, *The Iron Heel*, London, 1974.

10 R. Luxemburg, *The Accumulation of Capital*, J. Robinson, intr., London, 1963; P. Baran and P. M. Sweezy, *Monopoly Capital*, London, 1968; Sweezy, *The Theory of Capitalist Development*.

11 Schippel, 'Friedrich Engels und das Milizsystem', pp. 616–17.

12 *Ibid.*

13 Maehl, *August Bebel*, chapter 16.

14 Kautsky, 'Schippel und der Militarismus', p. 654.

15 Luxemburg, *The Accumulation of Capital*, p. 282: Vorontsov also predated Schippel by a decade, having published his 'Militarism and Capitalism' in *Russian Thought*, in 1889: *ibid.*, pp. 459–60n.

16 Kautsky, *Socialism and Colonial Policy*, pp. 26–8.

17 *Ibid.*, p. 27.

18 E. Bernstein, 'Stehendes Heer und Überproduktion', *NZ*, 17.2 (1899), pp. 50–6.

19 *Ibid.*, p. 51; D. Ricardo, *On the Principles of Political Economy and Taxation*, P. Sraffa, ed., Cambridge, 1951, pp. 393–4.

20 Ricardo, *Principles of Political Economy*, p. 394. Kautsky also referred to this English experience of 1815: 'Schippel und der Militarismus', p. 654.

21 Bernstein, 'Stehendes Heer und Überproduktion', pp. 56–7.

22 Luxemburg, *Selected Political Writings*, pp. 135–58.
23 Luxemburg, *Accumulation of Capital*, p. 459.
24 *Ibid.*, p. 461.
25 For a good critique see R. Rowthorn, 'Rosa Luxemburg and the Political Economy of Militarism', in R. Rowthorn, *Capitalism, Conflict and Inflation*, London, 1980, pp. 258–60.
26 Luxemburg, *Accumulation of Capital*, pp. 466–7.
27 Luxemburg, *Selected Political Writings*, pp. 141–2.
28 *Ibid.*, pp. 141–2, and see Luxemburg, *Accumulation of Capital*, p. 459. Karl Liebknecht was to take up the effects of militarism on labour discipline in the arms sector in his *Militarism and Anti-Militarism*.
29 K. Marx, *Capital: A Critique of Political Economy*, 1 (new ed.), E. Mandel, ed., Harmondsworth, 1976, chapter 25; and *Capital: A Critique of Political Economy*, 2 (new ed.), E. Mandel, ed., Harmondsworth, 1978, chapter 21.
30 Sweezy, *The Theory of Capitalist Development*, pp. 158–69; on Hilferding see Pugh, 'Economic Theory and Political Thought', pp. 348–63; O. Bauer, 'Die Akkumulation des Kapitals', *NZ*, 31.1 (1913), pp. 831–8; 862–74.
31 See Eckstein's critique of Lensch, 'Imperialismus und Rüstungsbeschränkung', *NZ*, 30.2 (1912), pp. 911–12.
32 G. Eckstein, 'Militarismus und Volkswirtschaft', *NZ*, 31.2 (1913), pp. 119 and 123.
33 *Ibid.*, p. 124.
34 *Ibid.*
35 *Ibid.*, p. 171.
36 *Ibid.*, pp. 167–71; Luxemburg, *Accumulation of Capital*, p. 464n.
37 *Ibid.*, p. 166.
38 Bebel and Liebknecht, *Gegen den Militarismus und die neuen Steuern*, p. 29.
39 In 1913, one contributor to *Die neue Zeit* concluded that the increasing sums expended on the arms race would lead to an 'economic and financial collapse – a collapse which can only end in its [militarism's] destruction. So, militarism also carries "within itself the seed of its own destruction".' A. Mai, 'Wehrvorlage und Volkswirtschaft', *NZ*, 31.2 (1913), pp. 307–13, especially pp. 312–13.
40 PRO, FO 371/1648. The Foreign Office also noted the Bavarian Prime Minister's call for a halt in Germany's armament programme at this time on the grounds that the Reich could not bear the economic burden: PRO, FO 371/1654.
41 Eckstein, 'Militarismus und Volkswirtschaft', p. 168.
42 Eckstein, 'Imperialismus und Rüstungsbeschränkung', p. 913.
43 Hilferding, *Finance Capital*, pp. 259–63.
44 See Bernstein cited above, and Luxemburg, *Accumulation of Capital*, p. 459; on Kautsky, see Geary, 'Karl Kautsky and the Development of Marxism', chapter 5.
45 Eckstein, 'Militarismus und Volkswirtschaft', pp. 168–9.
46 The radical Left continued to insist on the traditional under-consumptionist position. This was the central point of Luxemburg's *Accumulation of Capital* and her interventions at the 1912 and 1913 party congresses: see Nettl, *Rosa*

Luxemburg, 2. Karl Radek and Paul Lensch also engaged in a heated debate with Kautsky on the question: P. Lensch, 'Die neuen Wehrvorlagen', *NZ*, 30.2 (1912), pp. 68–75; 'Eine Improvisation', *NZ*, 30.2 (1912), pp. 308–13; 359–68; 'Miliz und Abrüstung', *NZ*, 30.2 (1912), pp. 765–72; K. Radek, 'Zu unserem Kampfe gegen den Imperialismus', *NZ*, 30.2 (1912), pp. 194–9; 233–41; K. Kautsky, 'Krieg und Frieden', *NZ*, 29.2 (1911), pp. 97–107; 'Die volks- und staatswirthschaftliche Bilanz der Rüstungen', *NZ*, 29.2 (1911), pp. 421–2; 'Der erste Mai und der Kampf gegen den Militarismus', *NZ*, 30.2 (1912), pp. 97–109; 'Ökonomie und Wehrhaftigkeit', *NZ*, 30.2 (1912), pp. 261–6; 319–23; 342–50; 'Der improvisierte Bruch', *NZ*, 30.2 (1912), pp. 461–7; 513–23; 'Die neue Taktik', *NZ*, 30.2 (1912), pp. 654–64; 688–98; 723–33; 'Nochmals die Abrüstung', *NZ*, 30.2 (1912), pp. 841–54. See also U. Ratz, 'Karl Kautsky und die Abrüstungskontroverse in der deutschen Sozialdemokratie 1911–1912', *International Review of Social History*, 11 (1966), pp. 197–227; and Salvadori, *Karl Kautsky and the Socialist Revolution*, pp. 169–80.

47 Eckstein, 'Militarismus und Volkswirtschaft', p. 170.
48 The details of the Krupp scandal are now well established: H. Wohlgemuth, *Karl Liebknecht: Eine Biographie*, Berlin, 1973, p. 217; Bartel, *Die Linken in der deutschen Sozialdemokratie*, p. 96; Trotnow, *Karl Liebknecht*, p. 119. Liebknecht's collection of materials about the Krupp affair are in Karl Liebknecht NL 1/28, ZPA, Institut für die Geschichte der Arbeiterbewegung.
49 Karl Liebknecht speech to the Reichstag, 18 April 1913, *Gesammelte Reden und Schriften*, 6, pp. 263–5, and again 19 and 26 April 1913, *ibid.*, pp. 270–96.
50 Bebel, *Nicht stehendes Heer sondern Volkswehr*, p. 74; Liebknecht, *Militarism and Anti-militarism*, p. 38.
51 Liebknecht, *Gesammelte Reden und Schriften*, 6, p. 269.
52 See E. Matthias and E. Pickart, ed., *Die Reichstagsfraktion der deutschen Sozialdemokratie 1898 bis 1918*, 1, Dusseldorf, 1966, pp. 332–3; Trotnow, *Karl Liebknecht*, pp. 122–4.
53 E. Bernstein, 'The Marauders', *The Nation*, 13 (26 April 1913), pp. 141–3; R. Fletcher, 'Revisionism and Militarism: War and Peace in the pre-1914 Thought of Eduard Bernstein', *Militärgeschichtliche Mitteilungen*, 31 (1982), pp. 23–36.
54 Cain, 'J. A. Hobson, Cobdenism and the Radical Theory of Economic Imperialism'.
55 See Liebknecht's unfinished manuscript 'Die Internationale der Rüstungsindustrie', *Gesammelte Reden und Schriften*, 7, pp. 3–33, and his speech to the Reichstag, 11 May 1914, *ibid.*, pp. 141–309.
56 *Ibid.*, p. 291.
57 See chapter 4.
58 In particular, John Newbold co-operated with Liebknecht and the two were supposed to write a joint work, of which Liebknecht's unfinished manuscript was supposed to be a part. But they had difficulty in finding publishers in 1914, and after the outbreak of the war Newbold had to settle for publishing separately, though he dedicated his pamphlet to Liebknecht. In France, André Morizet wrote on the French arms industry for *L'Humanité*. See J. Newbold, *How Europe Armed for the War, 1871–1914*, London, 1916; unsigned letter from Newbold to Liebknecht, 27 May 1914, giving details of their joint work,

Karl Liebknecht NL 1/42, ZPA, Institut für die Geschichte der Arbeiter-bewegung; Liebknecht, *Gesammelte Reden und Schriften*, 7, pp. 308–9, and editors' introduction, *ibid.*, p. 10, and Trotnow, *Karl Liebknecht*, pp. 124–5.

59 See the files of the British Embassy in Berlin: PRO, FO 244/821, and the British Ambassador, Sir Edward Goschen, to Sir Edward Grey, 21 April 1913, and, following the trial of the War Ministry officials, Granville to Grey, 8 August 1913: PRO, FO, 271/1650.

60 Eckstein used one empirical study of rates of growth in military spending and national income: M. Nachimson, 'Die Belastung der deutschen Volkswirth-schaft durch den Militarismus', *NZ*, 29.1 (1911), pp. 516–21.

61 N. I. Bukharin, *The Economic Theory of the Leisure Class*, New York, 1972.

62 See Berghahn, *Militarism*, for an introductory survey.

6 THE TIDES OF PACIFISM, 1907–14

1 The Weberian case has become the standard view through the work of Roth, *The Social Democrats in Imperial Germany*, and Groh, *Negative Integration*. For a good critique from the point of view of social history, see Evans, *Rethinking German History*, pp. 192–220; on the question of 'embourge-oisement', see Geary, *European Labour Protest*; on the ideological history of the movement, see P. Gay, *The Dilemma of Democratic Socialism: Eduard Bernstein's Challenge to Marx*, New York, 1962; Steinberg, *Sozialismus und deutsche Sozialdemokratie*.

2 Schorske, *German Social Democracy*, pp. 59–62.

3 See also Nolan, *Social Democracy and Society*, pp. 175–9.

4 M. Beer, 'Der Kampf um den stillen Ozean', *NZ*, 23.2 (1905), pp. 649ff.; 'Der britisch–russische Ausgleich im Mittelasien', *NZ*, 26.1 (1907), pp. 61–7; and 'Die weltpolitische Lage', *NZ*, 26.2 (1908), pp. 592–600.

5 *Handbuch…1906*, pp. 12–13.

6 See the exchange between Eduard David and Georg Ledebour, *Protokoll Essen 1907*, pp. 259–60; for revisionist views on foreign policy generally see Fletcher, *Revisionism and Empire*, especially pp. 55–64.

7 Karl Liebknecht, cited by Mandelbaum, *Die Erörterungen innerhalb der deutschen Sozialdemokratie*, p. 22, and Groh, 'The "Unpatriotic Socialists" and the State', p. 164.

8 Bley, *Bebel und die Strategie der Kriegsverhütung, 1904–1913*.

9 Hyndman had attracted a barrage of international criticism for supporting the dreadnought programme in public.

10 See Saul, 'Der Kampf um die Jugend zwischen Volksschule und Kaserne, p. 117.

11 See D. S. Linton, '*Who Has the Youth Has the Future*': The Campaign to Save Young Workers in Imperial Germany, Cambridge, 1991.

12 See Vaillant's reply to Nieuwenhuis at the 1891 Congress: *Congrès international ouvrier socialiste tenu à Bruxelles du 16 au 23 août 1891*, p. 69. On his and Jaurès' later campaign, see Drachkovitch, *Les Socialistes allemands et français et la problème de la guerre*, and Haupt, *Socialism and the Great War*.

13 Haupt, *Socialism and the Great War*.

14 Groh, *Negative Integration*, pp. 539–43.

15 *Vorwärts*, 22 August 1911.

16 *Ibid.*, 24 August 1911.

17 *Ibid.*, 20, 22, 24, 26, 30, 31 August 1911; 1, 4 and 5 September 1911.

18 *Vorwärts*, 5 September 1911 quoted estimates of the different non-Social Democratic papers which ranged from 100,000 (*Vossische Zeitung*) to 200,000 (*Nord-deutsche Zeitung*), to 250,000 (*Berliner Tageblatt*), to 500,000.

19 F. Giovanoli, *Die Maifeierbewegung. Ihre wirtschaftlichen und soziologischen Ursprünge und Wirkungen*, Karlsruhe, 1925, pp. 93–5.

20 See the Prussian police's *Übersicht über die allgemeine Lage der sozialdemokratischen und anarchistischen Bewegung im Jahre 1911*, Polizeipräsidium Rep. 30 Berlin C 15875, pp. 17–18, Brandenburgisches Landeshauptsarchiv.

21 K. Liebknecht, *Gesammelte Reden und Schriften*, 4, pp. 451–4.

22 *Vorwärts*, 16 October 1912 and 20 October 1912. See also the Prussian police report, *Übersicht über die allgemeine Lage der sozialdemokratischen und anarchistischen Bewegung im Jahre 1912*, pp. 20–1, Polizeipräsidium Rep. 30 Berlin C 15876, Brandenburgisches Landeshauptsarchiv; Groh, *Negative Integration*, p. 357.

23 *Übersicht über die allgemeine Lage der sozialdemokratischen und anarchistischen Bewegung im Jahre 1912*, p. 21, Polizeipräsidium Rep. 30 Berlin C 15876, Brandenburgisches Landeshauptsarchiv.

24 *Vorwärts*, 21 October 1912, and see I. M. Krivoguz, *Voprosy istorii KPSS*, 5 (1962), pp. 79–96, the only study so far on the 1912 peace movement.

25 See report of the Police President of Berlin to the Minister of Interior, 18 November 1912, Rep. 30 Berlin C 15838, Bl. 238–40, Brandenburgisches Landeshauptsarchiv.

26 See *Congrès international extraordinaire Bâle 24–25 novembre 1912: Conference internationale socialiste de Stockholm 1917*, intr. G. Haupt, Geneva, 1980; Haupt, *Socialism and the Great War*, chapters 3 and 4; Braunthal, *History of the International*, pp. 342–6; Joll, *The Second International*, pp. 156–60.

27 This conclusion is also endorsed by the *Vorwärts* accounts. But the absence of middle-class *organisations* is striking, including from the Bern peace conference of 11 May 1913, which the SPD and SFIO organised to give socialist support to 'all efforts by bourgeois groups and parties' for peace and disarmament. While many non-socialists attended from France (83 of 121), 28 of the 34 Germans were Social Democrats: Haupt, *Socialism and the Great War*, p. 118.

28 R. Luxemburg, 6 June 1913, 'Unsere Aktion gegen die Militärvorlage', *Gesammelte Werke*, 3, p. 227.

29 The manifesto was issued on 1 March 1913: Haupt, *Socialism and the Great War*, pp. 102–13. A copy exists in the Prussian police files, Rep. 30 Berlin C 15804, Bl. 110, Brandenburgisches Landeshauptsarchiv.

30 Scheidemann at the Jena Congress of 1913: *Protokoll über die Verhandlungen des Parteitages der Sozialdemokratischen Partei Deutschlands. Abgehalten in Jena vom 14. bis 20. September 1913*, pp. 228–32; Haupt, *Socialism and the Great War*, p. 109.

31 See chapter 4 above and Hobson, *Psychology of Jingoism*; Liebknecht, *Militarism and Anti-Militarism*.

32 *Vorwärts*, 22 October 1911; Haupt, *Socialism and the Great War*, pp. 54 and 110.

33 *Congrès socialiste international Copenhague 28 août–3 septembre 1910*, intr. G.
     Haupt, Geneva, 1981, p. 714–15, and Ledebour, 3 April 1911, *Sten. Ber. RT*,
     pp. 6138–9. He referred explicitly to the International's adoption of dis-
     armament.

34 See the introduction above. On the small and ineffectual German Peace Society,
     see Chickering, *Imperial Germany and a World without War*.

35 See Evans, *Proletarians and Politics*, p. 178, on the latent pacifism of Social
     Democratic dockers in Hamburg in the 1890s.

36 K.-E. Moring, *Die sozialdemokratische Partei in Bremen 1890–1914*, Hanover,
     1968, p. 169; P. Lensch, 'Die neuen Wehrvorlagen', *NZ*, 30.2 (1912), pp.
     68–75; 'Eine Improvisation', *NZ*, 30.2 (1912), pp. 308–13; 359–68; 'Miliz und
     Abrüstung', *NZ*, 30.2 (1912), pp. 765–72; K. Radek, 'Kapitalistisches
     Wettrüsten, Volksherr und Sozialdemokratie', in *In den Reihen der deutschen
     Revolution 1909–1919*, Munich, 1921, pp. 208–70; U. Ratz, 'Karl Kautsky und
     die Abrüstungskontroverse in der deutschen Sozialdemokratie 1911–1912',
     pp. 197–227; Salvadori, *Karl Kautsky and the Socialist Revolution*, pp. 169–80.

37 Kautsky, 'Der Kongress von Kopenhagen', *NZ*, 28.2 (1910), pp. 775–6; cited
     by Salvadori, *Karl Kautsky and the Socialist Revolution*, pp. 170–1.

38 Calkins, *Hugo Haase*, pp. 32–3; Groh, *Negative Integration*, pp. 296–302.

39 Groh, *Negative Integration*, pp. 200–3.

40 K. Kautsky, 'Krieg und Frieden', *NZ*, 29.2 (1911), pp. 97–107.

41 J. Jaurès, *Congrès socialiste international Stuttgart 6–24 août 1907*, intr. G.
     Haupt, Geneva, 1978, pp. 464–6; M. Sembat, *Faites un roi, sinon faites la paix*,
     Paris, 1913, p. 126; his book had gone through eighteen editions by the end of
     the year.

42 Calkins, *Hugo Haase*, p. 37.

43 For examples from 1911 and 1912, see Rep. 30 Berlin C 15868, Bl. 59 and
     15804, Bl. 44, Brandenburgisches Landeshauptarchiv.

44 G. Krumeich, *Armaments and Politics in France on the Eve of the First World
     War: The Introduction of Three-Year Conscription, 1913–1914*, Leamington
     Spa, 1984, p. 235.

45 Ernst Haase, ed., *Hugo Haase: Sein Leben und Wirken*, Berlin, 1929; cited in
     Groh, 'The "Unpatriotic Socialists"', p. 168.

46 G. Plekhanov, *Congrès international ouvrier socialiste tenu à Zurich du 6 au 12
     août 1893*, p. 228. The leader of the Free Trade Unions, Carl Legien also laid
     claim to this argument in retrospect, though in August 1914 he seems to have
     been more worried about government repression if the labour movement
     opposed the war, rather than what might happen if it sought to prevent it.
     Nonetheless, the very convenience he found in the argument suggests how
     many Social Democrats were persuaded by it. See H.-J. Bieber, *Gewerkschaften
     in Krieg und Revolution: Arbeiterbewegung, Staat, Militär in Deutschland
     1914–1920*, 1, Hamburg, 1981, pp. 73–5.

47 Indeed ever since the Sino-Japanese conflict, Social Democratic specialists on
     international relations had been hoping for a war between Russia and Japan.
     H. Cunow, 'Unsere Interessen in Ostasien', *NZ*, 15.1 (1896), p. 809.

48 Speech to the Reichstag, 25 February 1905, *Sten. Ber. RT*, p. 4791.

49 K. Kautsky, 'Patriotismus, Krieg und Sozialdemokratie', *NZ*, 23.2 (1905), p.
     368. Strikingly, even in his famous debate with Bebel at the 1907 party congress,

Kautsky's image of imperialist conflict excluded Russia altogether: 'Let us think about Morocco for example. Yesterday the German government was aggressive, tomorrow the French and we can't tell whether maybe the day after it won't be the English. It changes all the time. But Morocco is never worth a single drop of proletarian blood.' *Protokoll Essen* 1907, p. 261.

50 Already by the autumn of 1905, Bebel had reached these conclusions predicting that the danger of a European war now loomed nearer than ever. Again Bebel's premonitions proved correct. The major confrontation between Austria and Russia over the Balkans in 1908 convinced other Social Democrats, including Kautsky (who had disputed Bebel's position in 1907), that this was the most dangerous issue facing the Reich. Kautsky, 'Österreich und die Mächte', *NZ*, 27.1 (1909), pp. 945–7; K. Radek, 'Die auswärtige Politik der russischen Konterrevolution', *NZ*, 29.1 (1910), p. 69. By 1911 Kautsky had retreated to Bebel's position all along the line: see Kautsky, 'Krieg und Frieden', p. 104. Not even Karl Liebknecht questioned this attitude to Russia: Trotnow, *Karl Liebknecht*, p. 113 and Liebknecht, *Militarism and Anti-Militarism*, pp. 115–19. Some centre left leaders in the party, like Georg Ledebour and Rudolf Hilferding, took a little longer to accept that Russia had recovered enough to pose a serious threat. R. Hilferding, 'Der Parteitag und die auswärtige Politik', *NZ*, 29.2 (1911), pp. 799–806 and 'Der Balkankrieg und die Grossmächte', *NZ*, 31.1 (1912), pp. 73–82; and G. Ledebour, 'Ein fadenscheiniger Rüstungsvorwand', *NZ*, 31.1 (1913), pp. 929–34.

51 At the 1907 Party Congress Lensch and Kautsky had put this view jointly: Lensch, *Protokoll Essen 1907*, p. 234. By 1911, Lensch was in a small minority. On his group during the first world war, see R. Sigel, 'Die Lensch-Cunow-Haenisch-Gruppe: Ihr Einfluss auf die Ideologie der deutschen Sozialdemokratie im ersten Weltkrieg', *Internationale wissenschaftliche Korrespondenz zur Geschichte der deutschen Arbeiterbewegung*, 11, no. 4 (1975), pp. 421–36.

52 Evans, *Proletarians and Politics*, pp. 180–2 and compare with the discussion of Social Democratic Russophobia in chapter 2 above.

53 At the Basel Congress Haase attacked the 'criminal intrigues of the tsarist government' and declared that 'an understanding between England, France and Germany would be without the slightest doubt the most powerful foundation of civilisation and human progress'. *Congrès international extraordinaire Bâle*, p. 47. Bernstein, Sembat and J. L. Hammond all made similar appeals. On Bernstein, see Fletcher, *Revisionism and Empire*, pp. 172–8; Sembat, *Faites un roi*, p. 268; on the policy of *The Nation*, see the letter by its editor J. L. Hammond to Bertrand Russell of October 1914, Russell, *Autobiography*, p. 46. For Vaillant's views, see Haupt, *Socialism and the Great War*, pp. 119–21.

54 *Congrès international extraordinaire Bâle*, p. 62.

55 Ledebour, 2 December 1912, *Sten. Ber. RT*, p. 2475; David, 3 December 1912, *Sten. Ber. RT*, pp. 2509–10. Maehl, *August Bebel*, pp. 507–8, wrongly interprets David's position as openly condoning aggression against Russia.

56 R. Luxemburg, 27 May 1913, 'Die weltpolitische Lage', *Gesammelte Werke*, 3, p. 215; 'Unsere Aktion gegen die Militärvorlage', *ibid.*, p. 227; on the Mulhouse protest, see Groh, 'The "Unpatriotic Socialists"', p. 163.

57 Haase, *Protokoll der Reichskonferenz der Sozialdemokratie Deutschlands vom 21., 22. und 23. September 1916 in Berlin*, Berlin, 1916, p. 60; David, 31 July 1914, S. Miller, ed., *Das Kriegstagebuch des Reichstagsabgeordneten Eduard David 1914–1918*, Dusseldorf, 1966, p. 3; Groh, *Negative Integration*, p. 634; Calkins, *Hugo Haase*, p. 45.

58 See chapters 4 and 5 above.

59 See Calkins, *Hugo Haase*, pp. 25–31; Schorske, *German Social Democracy*, p. 124; D. K. Buse, 'Ebert and the Coming of World War I: A Month from his Diary', *International Review of Social History*, 13 (1968), pp. 430–48.

60 Luxemburg, 'Unsre Aktion gegen die Militärvorlage', *Gesammelte Werke*, 3, p. 229.

61 For the police reports and a complete set of press cuttings, see Rep. 30, Polizeipräsidium Berlin C, 15805, Bl. 69–141, Brandenburgisches Landeshauptsarchiv.

62 E. Haase, *Hugo Haase*, p. 24 for Haase's role; *Vorwärts*, 25 July 1914, for text of the declaration.

63 Buse, 'Ebert and the Coming of World War I', p. 440 and G. Kotowski, *Friedrich Ebert: Aufstieg eines deutschen Arbeiterführers*, 1, Berlin, 1963, p. 226.

64 Miller, *Burgfrieden und Klassenkampf*, p. 40; David, *Kriegstagebuch*, p. 3.

65 There is some evidence that this was an independent initiative of Haase's, that Ebert and the SPD executive had instructed him to continue to call for the congress to be postponed indefinitely. See Schorske, *German Social Democracy*, p. 286; Miller, *Burgfrieden*, p. 39.

66 Haupt, *Socialism and the Great War*, p. 220 and appendix; K. Kautsky, *Vergangenheit und Zukunft der Internationale*, Vienna, 1920, p. 12.

67 Nolan, *Social Democracy and Society*, p. 247.

68 Groh, *Negative Integration*, pp. 637–9, reproduces the police reports, while *Vorwärts*, 29 July 1914, claimed the higher figure.

69 F. Klein, ed., *Deutschland im ersten Weltkrieg*, 1, Berlin, 1968, pp. 263–5, based on the overview provided by *Vorwärts*, 29 July 1914 and 30 July 1914. See also J. Reulecke, 'Der 1. Weltkrieg und die Arbeiterbewegung im rheinisch-westfälischen Industriegebiet', in Reulecke, ed., *Arbeiterbewegung an Rhein und Ruhr*, Wuppertal, 1974, pp. 210 ff.

70 Groh, *Negative Integration*, p. 638. Having unquestioningly accepted the lower police estimate, he suggests only a quarter of the Berlin SPD turned out: see also Rep. 30 Berlin C, 15805, Bl. 120, Brandenburgisches Landeshauptsarchiv.

71 *Vorwärts*, 28 July 1914.

72 Haupt, *Socialism and the Great War*; Groh, *Negative Integration*.

73 Heckart, *From Bassermann to Bebel*.

74 E. Zechlin, 'Bethmann Hollweg, Kriegsrisiko und SPD: 1914', in *Erster Weltkrieg: Ursachen, Entstehung, Kriegsziele*, W. Schieder, ed., Cologne, 1969. There is some doubt over the reliability of the heavily edited published extracts of Rietzler's diary.

75 For Luxemburg, see *Vorwärts*, 30 July 1914; cited J. Kuczynski, *Der Ausbruch des ersten Weltkrieges und die deutsche Sozialdemokratie: Chronik und Analyse*, Berlin, 1957, pp. 56ff. Liebknecht, 'Hat die Sozialdemokratie alles getan, um den Krieg zu verhindern?', *Gesammelte Reden und Schriften*, 8, pp. 222–4.

76 In this instance the Prussians were imitating the French 'Carnet B': indeed both governments pursued uncannily similar tactics towards their own labour movements during the July crisis. In his marginalia at the time, Wilhelm threatened to have the Social Democratic leaders arrested or shot: *Die deutschen Dokumente zum Kriegsausbruch 1914*, Foreign Ministry, ed., 2, Berlin, 1927, p. 48.

77 If the published extracts from Rietzler's diary are to be believed, he was afraid that: 'The Social Democratic demonstration for peace would be fatal... the socialists would not fight; of course there are generals who want to meddle immediately and shoot "in order to teach the Reds a lesson". For the first day of mobilisation all social democratic leaders are scheduled to be arrested' (27 July 1914). Cited K. Jarausch, *The Enigmatic Chancellor: Bethmann Hollweg and the Hubris of Imperial Germany*, New Haven, 1973, p. 168.

78 Buse, 'Ebert and the Coming of World War I', p. 442: Ebert did not return to Berlin until 4 August and so took no further part in the policy debate: *ibid.*, p. 444.

79 David, *Kriegstagebuch*, p. 3.

80 See Miller, *Burgfrieden*, pp. 46–8.

81 *Ibid.*, pp. 52–9.

82 F. Schade, *Kurt Eisner und die bayerische Sozialdemokratie*, Hanover, 1961, p. 110; Groh, *Negative Integration*, pp. 358–9.

83 Haupt, *Socialism and the Great War*, pp. 262–3.

84 K. Zetkin, 5 August 1914, NL 5/48, Bl. 18, ZPA, Institut für die Geschichte der Arbeiterbewegung. Even when Karl Liebknecht did break party discipline and vote against the war credits on 2 December 1914, both Luxemburg and Zetkin tried to dissuade him.

85 *Protokoll der Reichskonferenz 1916 in Berlin*, Berlin, 1916.

86 Bieber, *Gewerkschaften in Krieg*, p. 73.

87 Frank to Gustav Mayer, 27 August 1914, Miller, 'Zum 3. August 1914', *Archiv für Sozialgeschichte*, 4 (1964), p. 521.

88 Karl Liebknecht, n.d., NL 1/26, 85/86, ZPA, Institut für die Geschichte der Arbeiterbewegung.

Bibliography

ARCHIVES

Archiv der sozialen Demokratie (AdSD), Bonn-Bad Godesberg

Dittmann, Henke, Molkenbuhr, Noske, Quarck, Schönlank, Severing Nachlässe; Verschiedene Original Briefe und Dokumente; Fotokopien von Briefen und Dokumenten
On microfilm (originals at the IISH): Bebel, Bernstein, Motteler and Vollmar Nachlässe

International Institute of Social History (IISH), Amsterdam

Marx-Engels, Wilhelm Liebknecht, Kautsky, Guesde and Domela Nieuwenhuis Nachlässe

ZPA, Institut für die Geschichte der Arbeiterbewegung, IV, 3/2/1078, Berlin

Bebel, Bernstein, Eisner, Liebknecht, Kautsky, Zetkin Nachlässe

Brandenburgisches Landeshauptsarchiv, Potsdam

Rep. 30 Berlin C, 15804–5: Die antimilitaristische Bewegung 1911–14
Rep. 30 Berlin C, 15838: Demonstrationen jeder Art
Rep. 30 Berlin C, 15868–70: Die internationale Bewegung 1909–15
Rep. 30 Berlin C, 15874–7: Übersicht über die allgemeine Lage der sozial-demokratischen und anarchistischen Bewegung im Jahre 1910–13
Rep. 30 Berlin C, 15905: Politische Gesinnung in Militär
Rep. 30 Berlin C, 15910: Politische Massenstreik 1914–17

Public Records Office (PRO), Kew

Foreign Office Files

NEWSPAPERS AND JOURNALS

Archiv für die Geschichte des Sozialismus und der Arbeiterbewegung, Vienna
Archiv für Sozialwissenschaft und Sozialpolitik, Tübingen

Der Sozialdemokrat, Zürich and London
Die Internationale, Berlin
Die Neue Zeit, Berlin
Sozialistische Monatshefte, Berlin
Vorwärts, Berlin

PUBLISHED DOCUMENTS

Le Congrès marxiste de 1889. Le Congrès possibiliste de 1889, intr. M. Winock, Geneva, 1976
Congrès international ouvrier socialiste tenu à Bruxelles du 16 au 23 août 1891, intr. M. Winock, Geneva, 1976
Congrès international ouvrier socialiste tenu à Zurich du 6 au 12 août 1893, intr. M. Winock, Geneva, 1977
Congrès international socialiste des travailleurs et des chambres syndicales ouvriers Londres 26 juillet-2 août 1896, intr. M. Winock, Geneva, 1980
Congrès socialiste international Paris 23–27 septembre 1900, intr. M. Winock, Geneva, 1980
Congrès socialiste international Amsterdam 14–20 août 1904, intr. G. Haupt, Geneva, 1980
Congrès socialiste international Stuttgart 6–24 août 1907, intr. G. Haupt, Geneva, 1978
Congrès socialiste international Copenhague 28 août-3 septembre 1910, intr. G. Haupt, Geneva, 1981
Congrès international extraordinaire Bâle 24–25 novembre 1912: Conference internationale socialiste de Stockholm 1917, intr. G. Haupt, Geneva, 1980
Die deutschen Dokumente zum Kriegsausbruch 1914, Foreign Ministry, ed., 2, Berlin, 1927
Handbuch für sozialdemokratische Wähler. Der Reichstag 1893–98, ed. Executive of the German Social Democratic Party, Berlin, 1898
Handbuch für sozialdemokratische Wähler. Der Reichstag 1898–1903, ed. Executive of the German Social Democratic Party, Berlin, 1903
Handbuch für sozialdemokratische Wähler anlässich der Reichstagsauflösung 1906, ed. Executive of the German Social Democratic Party, Berlin, 1907
Handbuch für sozialdemokratische Wähler. Der Reichstag 1907–1911, ed. Executive of the German Social Democratic Party, Berlin, 1911
Programmatische Dokumente der deutschen Sozialdemokratie, D. Dowe and K. Klotzbach, ed. and intr., Bonn/Berlin, 1984
Protokoll des Vereinigungs-Congresses der Sozialdemokraten Deutschlands. Abgehalten zu Gotha, vom 22. bis 27. Mai 1875, Leipzig, 1875
Protokoll des Socialisten-Congresses zu Gotha vom 19. bis 23. August 1876, Berlin, 1876
zu Gotha vom 27. bis 29. Mai 1877, Hamburg, 1877
Protokoll des Kongresses der deutschen Sozialdemokraten. Abgehalten auf Schloss Wyden in der Schweiz, vom 20. bis 23. August 1880, Zurich, 1880
Protokoll über den Kongress der deutschen Sozialdemokratie in Kopenhagen. Abgehalten vom 29. März bis 2. April 1883, Zurich, 1883

Verhandlungen des Parteitages der deutschen Sozialdemokratie in St. Gallen.
Abgehalten vom 2. bis 6. Oktober 1887, Zurich, 1888

Protokoll über die Verhandlungen des Parteitages der Sozialdemokratischen Partei
Deutschlands. Abgehalten zu Halle a. S. vom 12. bis 18. Oktober 1890, Berlin,
1890

  zu Erfurt vom 14. bis 20. Oktober 1891, Berlin, 1891
  zu Berlin vom 14. bis 21. November 1892, Berlin, 1892
  zu Köln a. Rh. vom 22. bis 28. Oktober 1893, Berlin, 1893
  zu Frankfurt a. M. vom 21. bis 27. Oktober 1894, Berlin, 1894
  zu Breslau vom 6. bis 12. Oktober 1895, Berlin, 1895
  zu Gotha vom 11. bis 16. Oktober 1896, Berlin, 1896
  zu Hamburg vom 3. bis 9. Oktober 1897, Berlin, 1897
  zu Stuttgart vom 3. bis 8. Oktober 1898, Berlin, 1898
  zu Hannover vom 9. bis 14. Oktober 1899, Berlin, 1899
  zu Mainz vom 17. bis 21. September 1900, Berlin, 1900
  zu Lübeck vom 22. bis 28. September 1901, Berlin, 1901
  zu München vom 14. bis 20. September 1902 Mit einem Anhang: Bericht über die
    2. Frauenkonferenz am 13. und 14. September in München, Berlin, 1902
  zu Dresden vom 13. bis 20. September 1903, Berlin, 1903
  zu Bremen vom 18. bis 24. September 1904, Berlin, 1904
  zu Jena vom 17. bis 23. September 1905, Berlin, 1905
  zu Mannheim vom 23. bis 29. September 1906 sowie Bericht über die 4.
    Frauenkonferenz am 22. und 23. September 1906 in Mannheim, Berlin, 1906
  zu Essen vom 15. bis 21. September 1907, Berlin, 1907
  zu Nürnberg vom 13. bis 19. September 1908 sowie Bericht über die 5.
    Frauenkonferenz am 11. und 12. September 1908 in Nürnberg, Berlin, 1908
  zu Leipzig vom 12. bis 18. September 1909, Berlin, 1909
  in Magdeburg vom 18. bis 24. September 1910, Berlin, 1910
  in Jena vom 10. bis 16. September 1911 sowie Bericht über die 6. Frauenkonferenz
    am 8. und 9. September 1911 in Jena, Berlin, 1911
  in Chemnitz vom 15. bis 21. September 1912, Berlin, 1912
  in Jena vom 14. bis 20. September 1913, Berlin, 1913

Protokoll der Reichskonferenz der Sozialdemokratie Deutschlands vom 21., 22. und
23. September 1916 in Berlin, Berlin, 1916

Stenographische Berichte über die Verhandlungen des Deutschen Reichstages, Berlin,
1871–1918

ARTICLES AND BOOKS:

Abendroth, W. *Aufstieg und Krise der deutschen Sozialdemokratie*, Mainz, 1964
  'August Bebels Kampf gegen Militarismus und Krieg', in *Sozialdemokratie und*
    Sozialismus: August Bebel und die Sozialdemokratie, Abendroth, Fülberth,
    Hofschen, Ott and Stuby, eds., Cologne, 1974, pp. 29–51
Abrams, L. 'Drink and the Working Class in Late Nineteenth-Century Bochum',
  German History, 3 (1986), pp. 3–14
  Workers' Culture in Imperial Germany: Leisure and Recreation in the Rhineland
  and Westphalia, London, 1992
Adamy, K. 'Der antimilitaristische Kampf Wilhelm Liebknechts gegen den

preussisch-deutschen Militärstaat (1870/71–1890)', unpublished PhD thesis, Pädagogische Hochschule, Potsdam, 1968

Adler, F. 'Der Parteitag in Wien', *NZ*, 31.1 (1912), pp. 217–21

Adler, V. *Gegen den Krieg und die Kriegshetzer*, Vienna, 1912

Aufsätze, Reden und Briefe, 11 vols., Executive Committee of SPDÖ, ed., Vienna, 1922–9

Briefwechsel mit August Bebel und Karl Kautsky, F. Adler, ed., Vienna, 1954

Albrecht, W., *et al.* 'Frauenfrage und deutsche Sozialdemokratie vom Ende des 19. Jahrhunderts bis zum Beginn der zwanziger Jahre', *Archiv für Sozialgeschichte*, 19 (1979), pp. 459–510

Albret, H., and A. Keel *Die Majestätsbeleidigungsaffäre des 'Simplicissimus'-Verlegers Albert Langen*, Frankfurt, 1985

Alexinsky, G. 'Kann Russland einen Krieg führen?', *NZ*, 31.1 (1913), pp. 668–80

'Das ausländische Kapital im Wirtschaftsleben Russlands', *NZ*, 32.1 (1913), pp. 435–41

Allen, A. T. *Satire and Society in Wilhelmine Germany: Kladderadatsch and Simplicissimus, 1890–1914*, Lexington, Kentucky, 1984

Anderson, E. *Hammer or Anvil: The Story of the German Working Class Movement*, London, 1945

Anderson, P. *Considerations on Western Marxism*, London, 1976

'The Antinomies of Antonio Gramsci', *New Left Review*, 100 (1976), pp. 5–78

Andler, C. *Le Socialisme impérialiste dans l'Allemagne contemporaine*, Paris, 1918

Andreucci, F. 'La diffusione e la volgarizzazione del marxismo', *Storia del marxismo*, 2, Turin, 1979, pp. 6–58

'La questione coloniale e l'imperialismo', *Storia del marxismo*, 2, Turin, 1979, pp. 868–93

Angel, P. *Edouard Bernstein et l'évolution du socialisme allemand*, Paris, 1961

Arato, A. 'L'antimomia del marxismo classico: marxismo e filosofia', *Storia del marxismo*, 2, Turin, 1979, pp. 696–757

Askew, J. B. 'Der britische Imperialismus', *NZ*, 1914, Ergänzungsheft 19

Badia, G. *Rosa Luxemburg: journaliste, Polémiste, Revolutionaire*, Paris, 1975

Baker, R. 'Socialism in the Nord, 1880–1914: A Regional View of the French Socialist Movement', *International Review of Social History*, 12 (1967), pp. 357–89

Balugdgitsch, Z. 'Saloniki und die makedonische Frage', *NZ*, 16.2 (1898), pp. 368–72

'Aus der neuesten serbischen Statistik', *NZ*, 16.2 (1898), pp. 492–6

Baran, P. *The Political Economy of Growth*, Harmondsworth, 1973

and P. M. Sweezy *Monopoly Capital*, London, 1968

Baron, S. *Plekhanov: The Father of Russian Marxism*, Stanford, 1963

Barraclough, G. *The Origins of Modern Germany*, Oxford, 1946

Bartel, H. *August Bebel: Eine Biographie*, Berlin, 1963

'August Bebels Stellung zur Vaterlandsverteidigung', *Beiträge zur Geschichte der deutschen Arbeiterbewegung*, 5 (1963), pp. 846–60

'Zum Verhältnis der deutschen Sozialdemokratie zur revolutionären Bewegung Russlands in den achziger Jahren des 19. Jahrhunderts', *Marxismus und deutsche Arbeiterbewegung*, Berlin, 1970, pp. 587–98

et al. Revolutionäre Sozialdemokratie und Reichsgründung 1871, Frankfurt, 1970

Bartel, W. *Die Linken in der deutschen Sozialdemokratie im Kampfe gegen Militarismus und Krieg*, Berlin, 1958

Basso, L. *Rosa Luxemburg: A Reappraisal*, London, 1975

Bauer, O. 'Die Kolonialpolitik und die Arbeiter', *NZ*, 23.2 (1905), pp. 265–9

'Über britischen Imperialismus', *NZ*, 25.1 (1907), pp. 535–40

Die Nationalitätenfrage und die Sozialdemokratie, Vienna, 1907

'Bemerkungen zur Nationalitätenfrage', *NZ*, 26.1 (1908), pp. 792–802

'Die Akkumulation des Kapitals', *NZ*, 31.1 (1913), pp. 831–8; 862–74

Bauer, R. 'Die II. Internationale über Krieg und Frieden', *Zeitschrift für Geschichtswissenschaft*, 12.2, Berlin, 1964, pp. 768–76

Bealey, F. 'Les Travaillistes et la guerre des Boers', *Le Mouvement Social*, 45 (1963), pp. 39–70

Bebel, A. 'Deutschland, Russland und die orientalische Frage', *NZ*, 4, 1886, pp. 502–15

'Die internationale Arbeiterkongress zu Brüssel', *NZ*, 9.2 (1891), pp. 713–17

Nicht stehendes Heer sondern Volkswehr, Stuttgart, 1898

'Die Reform einer Milizarmee', *NZ*, 18.1 (1899), pp. 325–38

'Musketiere einer ostdeutscher Garnison', *NZ*, 22.2, 1904, pp. 446–7

'Marinesorgen', *NZ*, 23.1 (1904), pp. 271–4

'Ein Buch über die Revolution in Russland', *NZ*, 23.2 (1905), pp. 284–6

'Das Fazit der letzten Reichstagssession', *NZ*, 24.2 (1906), pp. 345–50

Der Sozialdemokratie im deutschen Reichstag: Die parlamentarische Tätigkeit des Deutschen Reichtages und der Landtage und die Sozialdemokratie, Berlin, 1909

August Bebels Briefwechsel mit Friedrich Engels, W. Blumenberg, ed., The Hague, 1965

August Bebels Briefwechsel mit Karl Kautsky, K. Kautsky Jr., ed., Assen, 1971

Schriften 1862–1913, 1, C. Stephan, ed., Frankfurt, 1981

Aus Meinem Leben, Berlin, 1980

Ausgewählte Reden und Schriften, 3 vols., Berlin, 1978–83

and W. Liebknecht *Gegen den Militarismus und die neuen Steuern*, Berlin, 1893

Becker, J. J. *Comment les français sont entrés dans la guerre*, Paris, 1977

Beer, M. 'Der moderne englische Imperialismus', *NZ*, 16.1 (1897), pp. 300–16

'Sozialer Imperialismus', *NZ*, 20.1 (1901), pp. 209–17

'England und seine Konkurrenten', *NZ*, 21.1 (1902), pp. 37–43

'Imperialistische Politik', *NZ*, 21.1, 1902, pp. 389–95

'Der russische-japanische Konflikt', *NZ*, 22.1 (1903), pp. 427–33

'Der Kampf um den stillen Ozean', *NZ*, 23.1 (1904), pp. 372–81; 414–23

'Der Kampf um den stillen Ozean', *NZ*, 23.2 (1905), pp. 617–24; 649–56

'Der Friede in Asien', *NZ*, 24.1 (1905), pp. 91–7

'Einige Fragen der äusseren Politik', *NZ*, 24.2 (1906), pp. 377–82

'Der britisch-russische Ausgleich im Mittelasien', *NZ*, 26.1 (1907), pp. 61–7

'Die weltpolitische Lage', *NZ*, 26.2 (1908), pp. 592–600

'Die Türkei als konstitutionelles Reich', *NZ*, 26.2 (1908), pp. 935–41

Belfort Bax, E. 'Kolonialpolitik und Chauvinismus', *NZ*, 1897 (16.1), pp. 420–7

Berger, M. *Engels, Armies and Revolution: The Revolutionary Tactics of Classical Marxism*, Hamden, Connecticut, 1977

Berghahn, V. R. *Der Tirpitz-Plan: Genesis und Verfall einer innenpolitischen Krisenstrategie unter Wilhelm II*, Dusseldorf, 1971

Germany and the Approach of War in 1914, London, 1973
Militarism: The History of an International Debate, 1861–1979, Leamington Spa, 1981
Berki, R. N. 'On Marxian Thought and the Problem of International Relations', *World Politics*, 24 (1971), pp. 80–105
Socialism, London, 1975
Berner, E. *Der männermordende Militarismus*, Vienna, 1903
Bernhardi, F. von *Germany and the Next War*, London, 1914
Bernstein, E. *The International Working Men's Congress of 1889: A Reply to 'Justice'*, London, 1889
'Nieuwenhuis über die deutsche Sozialdemokratie', *NZ*, 10.2 (1892), pp. 673–7
'Quis tulerit ...', *NZ*, 11.1 (1892), pp. 86–91
'Der Streik als politisches Kampfmittel', *NZ*, 12.1 (1894), pp. 689–95
'Das neue Kalifornien', *NZ*, 14.1 (1895), pp. 52–7
'Die Kämpfe ums Burenland', *NZ*, 14.1 (1895), pp. 484–90
'Die Transvaalwirren und ihr internationaler Rückschlag', *NZ*, 14.1 (1896), pp. 612–20
'Deutschland als Konkurrent Englands', *NZ*, 14.2 (1896), pp. 755–8
'Die deutsche Sozialdemokratie und die türkischen Wirren', *NZ*, 15.1 (1896), pp. 108–16
'Kreta', *NZ*, 15.1 (1897), pp. 687–92
'Kreta und die russische Gefahr', *NZ*, 15.2 (1897), pp. 10–20
'Der Sieg der Türken und die Sozialdemokratie', *NZ*, 15.2 (1897), pp. 260–8
'Die Briefe von Karl Marx über den Krimkrieg und die Orientfrage', *NZ*, 16.1 (1897), pp. 209–17
'Stehendes Heer und Überproduktion', *NZ*, 17.2 (1899), pp. 50–6
Die Voraussetzungen des Sozialismus und die Aufgaben der Sozialdemokratie, Stuttgart, 1899
'Sozialdemokratie und Imperialismus', *Sozialistische Monatshefte*, 1900, pp. 238–51
'The Marauders', *The Nation*, 13 (26 April 1913), pp. 141–3
'Die Internationale der Arbeiterklasse und der europäische Krieg', *Archiv für Sozialwissenschaft und Sozialpolitik*, 40, 1915, pp. 267–322
My Years of Exile: Reminiscences of a Socialist, London, 1921
Eduard Bernsteins Briefwechsel mit Friedrich Engels, H. Hirsch, ed., Assen, 1970
Cromwell and Communism, London, 1980
Best, G. *War and Society in Revolutionary Europe, 1770–1870*, New York, 1982
Bevan, E. *German Social Democracy During the War*, London, 1918
Bieber, H.-J. *Gewerkschaften in Krieg und Revolution: Arbeiterbewegung, Staat, Militär in Deutschland 1914–1920*, 1, Hamburg, 1981
Blackbourn, D. *Class, Religion and Local Politics in Wilhelmine Germany: The Centre Party in Württemberg before 1914*, London, 1980
Patricians and Populists, London, 1987
and G. Eley *Peculiarities of German History: Bourgeois Society and Politics in Nineteenth-Century Germany*, Oxford, 1984
Blänsdorf, A. 'Friedrich Ebert und die Internationale', *Archiv für Sozialgeschichte*, 9 (1969), pp. 321–428

Die Internationale und der Weltkrieg, Stuttgart, 1979

Blanning, T. C. W. 'The Death and Transfiguration of Prussia', *Historical Journal*, 29, 2 (1986), pp. 433–59

Blaug, M. *Economic Theory in Retrospect*, Cambridge, 1985

Bleiber, H. 'Die Moabit Unruhen 1910', *Zeitschrift für Geschichtswissenschaft*, 2 (1955), pp. 173–211

Bley, H. *Bebel und die Strategie der Kriegsverhütung, 1904–1913: Eine Studie über Bebels Geheimkontakte mit der britischen Regierung und Edition der Dokumente*, Göttingen, 1975

Bloemgarten, S. 'De tweede Internationale en de geboorte van de SDAP (1889–1896)', *Tijdschrift voor sociale geschiedenis*, 22 (1981), pp. 101–41

Böhm-Bawerk, E. von *Karl Marx and the Close of his System*, P. Sweezy, ed., London, 1975

Boll, F. *Frieden ohne Revolution? Friedensstategien der deutschen Sozialdemokratie vom Erfurter Programm 1891 bis zur Revolution 1918*, Bonn, 1980

Bottomore, T., and P. Goode, eds., *A Dictionary of Marxist Thought*, Oxford, 1983

Austro-Marxism, London, 1978

Botz, G., and H. Konrad 'Die Stellungnahmen Otto Bauers und anderer österreichischer Sozialdemokraten zum Imperialismus vor dem Ersten Weltkrieg', *Internationale Tagung der Historiker der Arbeiterbewegung: 'VIII. Linzer Konferenz' 1972*, Vienna, 1974, pp. 46–55

Bouvier, B. W. *Französische Revolution und deutsche Arbeiterbewegung: Die Rezeption des revolutionären Frankreich in der deutschen sozialistischen Arbeiterbewegung von den 1830er Jahren bis 1905*, Bonn, 1982

Boyd, B. A. *Rudolf Virchow: The Scientist as Citizen*, New York, 1991

Brailsford, H. N. *The War of Steel and Gold*, London, 1914

Braunthal, J. *History of the International, 1864–1914*, London, 1966

Breuilly, J. 'Liberalism and Social Democracy: A Comparison of British and German Labour Politics, c. 1850–75', *European History Quarterly*, 15 (1985), pp. 3–41

Brewer, A. *Marxist Theories of Imperialism*, London, 1980

Brüggemeier, F.-J., and J. Kocka *'Geschichte von unten – Geschichte von innen': Kontroversen um die Alltagsgeschichte*, Hagen, 1985

Brunner, O., W. Conze, and R. Koselleck, eds. *Geschichtliche Grundbegriffe*, 4, Stuttgart, 1978

Brunte, E. 'Landwirtschaft und Militarismus in Schweden', *NZ*, 19.1 (1900), pp. 396–403

Bukharin, N. *Imperialism and the Accumulation of Capital*, New York and London, 1972

Imperialism and the World Economy, London, 1972

The Economic Theory of the Leisure Class, New York, 1972

Selected Writings on the State and the Transition to Socialism, R. Day, ed. and intr., London, 1982

and E. Preobrazhensky *The ABC of Communism*, E. H. Carr, ed. and intr., Harmondsworth, 1969

Bürgi, M. 'Hintergründe und Bedeutung des Entscheidenes für einen internationalen Arbeiterkongresses in Zürich', *IISH Symposium Internationalism in the Labour Movement before 1940*, Amsterdam (*mimeo*), 1985

Buhr, V. *Der Sozialismus in der deutschen Armee: Selbst-Erlebtes*, Berlin, 1893

Buse, D. K. 'Ebert and the Coming of World War I: A Month from his Diary', *International Review of Social History*, 13 (1968), pp. 430–48

Cahm, E. 'Socialism and the Nationalist Movement in France at the Time of the Dreyfus Affair', E. Cahm and V. Fisera, eds., *Socialism and Nationalism in Contemporary Europe (1848–1945)*, 2, Nottingham, 1979, pp. 48–64

Cain, P. J. 'J. A. Hobson, Cobdenism and the Radical Theory of Economic Imperialism, 1898–1914', *Economic History Review*, 31 (1978), pp. 565–84

'Capitalism, Internationalism and Imperialism in the Thought of Richard Cobden', *British Journal of International Studies*, 5.3 (1979), pp. 229–47

Calkins, K. R. *Hugo Haase: Democrat and Revolutionary*, Durham, North Carolina, 1979

Calwer, R. 'Die Vorbereitung neuer Handelsverträge', *NZ*, 16.2 (1898), pp. 289–97; 323–9

Campanella, A. 'Garibaldi and the First Peace Congress in Geneva in 1867', *International Review of Social History*, 5 (1960), pp. 456–86

Caplan, J. 'Postmodernism, Poststructuralism and Deconstruction: Notes for Historians', *Central European History*, 3/4 (1989), pp. 260–78

Carr, E. H. *What is History?*, Harmondsworth, 1964

Carsten, F. *War against War: British and German Radical Movements in the First World War*, London, 1982

Ceadel, M. *Thinking about War and Peace*, Oxford, 1987

Chickering, R. *Imperial Germany and a World without War: The Peace Movement and German Society, 1892–1914*, Princeton, 1975

We Men Who Feel Most German: A Cultural Study of the Pan-German League, 1886–1914, London, 1984

Clausewitz, C. von *On War*, M. Howard and P. Paret, eds., Princeton, 1976

Cobban, A. *A History of Modern France, 1871–1962*, 3 vols., Harmondsworth, 1965

Cobden, R. *The Political Writings*, 2 vols., London, 1867

Speeches on Questions of Public Policy, 2 vols., J. Bright and J. E. Rogers, eds., London, 1878

Coetzee, M. S. *The Army League: Popular Nationalism in Wilhelmine Germany*, Oxford, 1990

Cohen, G. A. *Karl Marx's Theory of History: A Defence*, Oxford, 1978

Cohen, S. *Bukharin and the Bolshevik Revolution*, London, 1974

Cole, G. D. H. *The Second International, 1889–1914*, 2 vols., London, 1956

Colletti, L. *From Rousseau to Lenin*, London, 1972

Marxism and Hegel, London, 1973

'Introduction', K. Marx, *Early Writings*, Harmondsworth, 1975, pp. 7–56

Collins, H., and C. Abramsky *Karl Marx and the British Labour Movement: Years of the First International*, London, 1965

Collotti, E. 'Karl Liebknecht e il problema della rivoluzione socialista in Germania', *Annali*, Milan, 1973, pp. 326–43

Conze, W., and D. Groh *Die Arbeiterbewegung in der nationalen Bewegung*, Stuttgart, 1966

Conze, W., R. Stumpf and M. Geyer 'Militarismus', in O. Brunner, W. Conze and R. Koselleck, eds., *Geschichtliche Grundbegriffe*, 4, Stuttgart, 1978, pp. 1–47

Craig, G. *The Politics of the Prussian Army*, New York, 1964
  Germany, 1866–1945, Oxford, 1978
Cummins, I. *Marx, Engels and National Movements*, London, 1980
Cunow, H. 'Die Kolonialpolitik der Spanier auf den Philippinen und der jetzige
  Aufstand', *NZ*, 15.1 (1896), pp. 196–204; 243–50
  'Unsere Interessen in Ostasien', *NZ*, 15.1 (1896), pp. 805–11
  'Die Transvaalkrisis', *NZ*, 18.1 (1899), pp. 24–9; 47–51
  'England und Russland in Asien', *NZ*, 18.1 (1900), pp. 556–60
  'Handelsvertrags- und imperialistische Expansionspolitik', *NZ*, 18.2 (1900), pp.
  207–15; 234–42
  'Die Freihandelsbewegung vor der Ära der Bismarckschen Wirthschaftspolitik',
  NZ, 19.2 (1901), pp. 100–9
  'Bismarcks geniale Wirthschaftspolitik', *NZ*, 19.2 (1901), pp. 164–72
  'Das letzte Jahrzeht deutscher Handelspolitik', *NZ*, 19.2 (1901), pp. 364–74
  'Zollkriegs-Betrachtungen', *NZ*, 19.2 (1901), pp. 577–85
  'Amerikanische Expansionspolitik in Ostasien', *NZ*, 20.2 (1902), pp. 388–93;
  429–36
Däumig, E. 'Eine deutsche Kolonialarmee', *NZ*, 18.2 (1900), pp. 616–22; 651–5
  'Schlachtopfer des Militarismus', *NZ*, 18.2 (1900), pp. 365–71
  'Die dreijährige Dienstzeit der berittenen Truppen', *NZ*, 19.1 (1900), pp.
  196–200
David, E. *Die Sozialdemokratie im Weltkrieg*, Berlin, 1915
  Das Kriegstagebuch des Reichtagsabgeordneten Eduard David 1914–1918, S.
  Miller, ed., Dusseldorf, 1966
Dawson, W. H. *German Socialism and Ferdinand Lassalle*, London, 1888
  Germany and the Germans, 2 vols., London, 1894
  The Evolution of Modern Germany, London, 1908
  Municipal Life and Government in Germany, London, 1916
Dehio, L. *Germany and World Politics in the Twentieth Century*, London, 1965
Demeter, K. *Das deutsche Offizierkorps in Gesellschaft und Staat 1650–1945*,
  Frankfurt, 1962
Descamps *The Organisation of International Arbitration: A Memorial Addressed to
  the Powers at the Request of the Inter-Parliamentary Conference*, London,
  1896
Deutscher, I. *The Prophet Armed: Trotsky, 1879–1921*, Oxford, 1954
Dietze, A. and W., eds. *Ewiger Friede: Dokumente einer deutschen Diskussion um
  1800*, Leipzig, 1989.
Dommanget, M. *Histoire du premier mai*, Paris, 1953
Domela Nieuwenhuis, F. 'Die sozialistische Bewegung in Holland', *NZ*, 9.1
  (1890), pp. 51–7
  Die verschiedenen Strömungen in der deutschen Sozialdemokratie, Berlin, 1892
  'Bernstein und seine Kampfesweise', *NZ*, 11.1 (1892) pp. 80–5
  'La Question militaire au congrès de Zurich. Discours', *Almanach de la
  question sociale illustré pour 1894*, 4th yr., 1893, pp. 187–92
  Rede gehouden voor den Soc.-Dem. Militairenbond, Amsterdam, 1893
  Le Socialisme en danger, Brussels, 1894
  *Le Militarisme et l'attitude des anarchistes et socialistes revolutionnaires devant la
  guerre*, Paris, 1901

Van Christ tot Anarchist: Gedenkschriften, Amsterdam, 1910

Dominick III, R. 'Wilhelm Liebknecht and German Social Democracy, 1869–1900', unpublished PhD thesis, University of North Carolina at Chapel Hill, 1973

Dornemann, L. *Clara Zetkin: Ein Lebensbild*, Berlin, 1957

Dowe, D. 'The Workers' Choral Movement before the First World War', *Journal of Contemporary History*, 13, 2 (1978), pp. 269–76

Drachkovitch, M. *Les Socialistes allemands et français et la problème de la guerre, 1870–1914*, Geneva, 1953

Draper, H. *Karl Marx's Theory of Revolution*, 3 vols., New York, 1977–86

Drott, K., ed. *Sozialdemokratie und Wehrfrage Dokumente aus einem Jahrhundert Wehrdebatten*, Berlin/Hanover, 1956

Droz, J., ed. *Histoire générale du socialisme*, 2, Paris, 1974

Düwell, W. 'Zur Frage des Generalstreiks', *NZ*, 23.1 (1904), pp. 248–54

Dunn, J. M. *Rethinking Modern Political Theory*, Cambridge, 1985

Earle, E. M., ed. *Makers of Modern Strategy: Military Thought from Machiavelli to Hitler*, Princeton, 1943

Eckstein, G. 'Was bedeutet der Generalstreik?', *NZ*, 22.1 (1903), pp. 357–63
  'Die Arbeiterbewegung in modernen Japan', *NZ*, 22.1 (1904), pp. 494–501; 532–40; 577–81; 598–63; 665–73
  'Imperialismus und Rüstungsbeschränkung', *NZ*, 30.2 (1912), pp. 907–16
  'Militarismus und Volkswirtschaft', *NZ*, 31.2 (1913), pp. 116–25; 165–72

Eisner, F. *Kurt Eisner: Die Politik des libertären Sozialismus*, Frankfurt, 1979

Eisner, K. *Wilhelm Liebknecht: Sein Leben und Wirken*, Berlin, 1906

Eley, G. *Reshaping the German Right: Radical Nationalism and Political Change after Bismarck*, New Haven, 1980
  From Unification to Nazism: Reinterpreting the German Past, Boston, 1986

Elster, J. *Making Sense of Marx*, Cambridge, 1985

Engelberg, E. *Revolutionäre Politik und rote Feldpost 1878–1890*, Berlin, 1959

Engels, F. *Friedrich Engels' Briefwechsel mit Karl Kautsky*, B. Kautsky, ed., Vienna, 1955
  The Peasant War in Germany, Moscow, 1965
  and P. and L. Lafargue *Correspondance, 1868–1895*, 3 vols., E. Bottigelli, ed., Paris, 1956–9

Epkenhans, M. 'Grossindustrie und Schlachtflottenbau 1897–1914', *Militärgeschichtliche Mitteilungen*, 1 (1988), pp. 65–140

Erickson, J., and H. Mommsen 'Militarism', in C. D. Keving, ed., *Marxism, Communism and Western Society: A Comparative Encyclopaedia*, Munich, 1973, 5, pp. 436–55

Evans, R. J. *The Feminist Movement in Germany, 1894–1933*, London, 1976
  Death in Hamburg: Society and Politics in the Cholera Years, 1830–1910, Oxford, 1987
  Rethinking German History, London, 1987
  Proletarians and Politics: Socialism, Protest and the Working Class in Germany before the First World War, Hemel Hempstead, 1990
  ed. *Society and Politics in Wilhelmine Germany*, London, 1978
  The German Working Class, 1888–1933: The Politics of Everyday Life, London, 1982

Fainsod, M. *International Socialism and the World War*, Cambridge, Mass., 1935

Fassbender-Ilge, M. H. *Liberalismus, Wissenschaft, Realpolitik: Untersuchung des 'Deutschen Staats-Wörterbuchs' von J. Caspar Bluntschli und Karl Brater als Beitrag zur Liberalismusgeschichte zwischen 48er Revolution und Reichsgründung*, Frankfurt, 1981

Feldman, G. *Army, Industry and Labour in Germany, 1914–1918*, Princeton, 1966

Ferro, M. 'Les Socialistes revolutionnaires russes', *Le Mouvement social*, 45 (1963), pp. 93–100

Fetscher, I. 'Bernstein e la sfida all'ortodossia', *Storia del marxismo*, 2, Turin, 1979, pp. 237–74

Fischer, F. *Germany's War Aims in the First World War*, London, 1967
  Krieg der Illusionen, Dusseldorf, 1969
  Juli 1914: Wir sind nicht hineingeschlittert, Reinbeck, 1983

Fletcher, R. 'Revisionism and Militarism: War and Peace in the pre-1914 Thought of Eduard Bernstein', *Militärgeschichtliche Mitteilungen*, 31 (1982), pp. 23–36
  Revisionism and Empire: Socialist Imperialism in Germany 1897–1914, London, 1984
  ed. *Bernstein to Brandt: A Short History of German Social Democracy*, London, 1987

Flüchtig, N. 'Zur Frage des Generalstreiks', *NZ*, 22.1 (1903), pp. 445–8

Förster, S. *Der doppelte Militarismus: Die Heeresrüstungspolitik zwischen Status-Quo-Sicherung und Aggression, 1890–1913*, Stuttgart, 1985

Fricke, D. 'Zur Rolle des Militarismus nach Innen in Deutschland vor dem ersten Weltkrieg', *Zeitschrift für Geschichtswissenschaft*, 6, 1958, pp. 1298–1310
  'Zum Bündnis des preussisch-deutschen Militarismus mit dem Klerus gegen die Sozialistische Arbeiterbewegung am Ende des 19. Jahrhunderts', *Zeitschrift für Geschichtswissenschaft*, 8.2 (1960), pp. 1378–95
  'Die Sozialistischen Monatshefte und die imperialistische Konzeption eines Kontinentaleuropa (1905–1918)', *Zeitschrift für Geschichtswissenschaft*, 23.1 (1975), pp. 528–37

Fröhlich, P. *Rosa Luxemburg: Ideas in Action*, London, 1972

Fülberth, G. 'Il marxismo di Mehring', *Annali*, Milan, 1973, pp. 216–31

Gallie, W. *Philosophers of Peace and War*, Cambridge, 1978

Gallisot, R. 'Nazione e nazionalita nei dibattiti del movimento operaio', *Storia del marxismo*, 2, Turin, 1979, pp. 787–864

Gankin, O. H., and H. H. Fisher *The Bolsheviks and the World War: The Origins of the Third International*, Stanford, 1940

Garnier-Thenon, M. 'Jaurès et l'armée nouvelle', *Revue Socialiste*, 148 (1961), pp. 504–20

Gasman, D. *The Scientific Origins of National Socialism: Ernst Haeckel and the German Monist League*, London, 1971

Gay, P. *The Dilemma of Democratic Socialism: Eduard Bernstein's Challenge to Marx*, New York, 1962

Geary, R. J. 'Karl Kautsky and the Development of Marxism', unpublished PhD thesis, Cambridge, 1971
  'The German Labour Movement, 1848–1919', *European Studies Review*, 6, 3 (1976), pp. 297–330
  European Labour Protest, 1848–1919, London, 1981

Karl Kautsky, Manchester, 1987

Geiss, I. 'The Outbreak of the First World War and German War Aims', *Journal of Contemporary History*, 1, 3 (1966), pp. 75–91

Gemkow, H. *Friedrich Engels' Hilfe beim Sieg der deutschen Sozialdemokratie über das Sozialistengesetz*, Berlin, 1957

Gerschenkron, A. *Bread and Democracy in Germany*, Los Angeles, 1943
Economic Backwardness in Historical Perspective, Cambridge, Mass., 1962

Getzler, I. *Martov*, Melbourne, 1967
'Georgij V. Plechanov: la dannazione dell'ortodossia', *Storia del marxismo*, Turin, 1979, pp. 411–40

Geyer, D. 'Die russische Parteispaltung im Urteil der deutschen Sozialdemokratie', *International Review of Social History*, 3 (1958), pp. 195–219 and 418–44
'Arbeiterbewegung und "Kulturrevolution" in Russland', *Vierteljahrshefte für Zeitgeschichte*, 10 Jg. (1962), pp. 43–55

Giovanoli, F. *Die Maifeierbewegung: Ihre wirtschaftlichen und soziologischen Ursprünge und Wirkungen*, Karlsruhe, 1925

Giddens, A. *The Nation State and Violence*, Cambridge, 1985

Gilbert, A. *Marx's Politics*, Oxford, 1981

Gillis, J. R. *The Prussian Bureaucracy in Crisis, 1840–1860*, California, 1971

Goldbeck, E. *Kasernen-Zucht: Ein letztes Wort an Herrn Rudolf Krafft*, Berlin, 1896
Henker Drill: Schülerselbstmord, Soldatenselbstmorde, Berlin, 1908

Goldberg, H. *The Life of Jean Jaurès*, Madison, 1962

Goldstein, B. M. 'Ludwig Quidde and the Struggle for Democratic Pacifism in Germany, 1914–1930', unpublished PhD thesis, New York University, 1984

Goltz, C. von der *The Nation in Arms: A Treatise on Modern Military Systems and the Conduct of War*, London, 1906

Gottschallch, W. 'Sviluppo e crisi del capitalismo in Rudolf Hilferding', *Annali*, Milan, 1973, pp. 197–215

Gramsci, A. *Selections from the Prison Notebooks*, London, 1971

Grebing, H. *The History of the German Labour Movement: A Survey*, London, 1969

Grimm, R. 'Erfahrungen mit dem schweizerischen Milizsystem', *NZ*, 30.2 (1912), pp. 385–93; 442–9

Groh, D. 'The "Unpatriotic Socialists" and the State', *Journal of Contemporary History*, 1.4 (1966), pp. 151–77
Negative Integration und revolutionärer Attentismus: Die deutsche Sozialdemokratie am Vorabend des ersten Weltkrieges, Frankfurt, 1973

Grumbach, S. 'Der "imperialistische Sozialismus"', *NZ*, 30.2 (1913), pp. 736–41

Grünberg, C. *Die Internationale und der Weltkrieg: Materialen*, Leipzig, 1916
Die sozialistische Volkswehr an der Stelle des stehenden Kasernheeres! Praktische Ausregungen und Vorschläge für eine sofortige Unrüstung Deutschlands im Sinne des Erfurter Programms, Berlin, 1919

Grunwald, M. 'Marx über Steuerreform', *NZ*, 18.2 (1900), 568–71

Gurney, P. 'Internationalism and the British Co-operative Movement between c. 1869–1919', *IISH Symposium Internationalism in the Labour Movement before 1940*, Amsterdam (*mimeo*), 1985

Haase, E., ed. *Hugo Haase: Sein Leben und Wirken*, Berlin, 1929

Habermas, J. *Legitimationsprobleme im Spätkapitalismus*, Frankfurt, 1973

Haenisch, K. *Die deutsche Sozialdemokratie in und nach dem Weltkrieg*, Berlin, 1916

Haitsma Mulier, E. O. G. *The Myth of Venice and Dutch Republican Thought in the Seventeenth Century*, Assen, 1980

Hall, A. *Scandal, Sensation and Social Democracy: The SPD Press and Wilhelmine Germany, 1890–1914*, Cambridge, 1977

Hamerow, T. *Restoration, Revolution, Reaction: Economics and Politics in Germany, 1815–1871*, Princeton, 1958

Hansen, E. 'Workers and Socialists: Relations between the Dutch Trade-Union Movement and Social Democracy, 1894–1914', *European Studies Review*, 7 (1977), pp. 199–226

Hardie, K. 'Der Kapitalismus und der Krieg in Südafrika', *NZ*, 18.1 (1900), pp. 816–20

Harding, N. *Lenin's Political Thought*, 2 vols., London, 1977 and 1981

Haupt, G. *La Deuxième Internationale, 1889–1914: Etude critique des sources: Essai bibliographique*, The Hague, 1964

Socialism and the Great War: The Collapse of the Second International, Oxford, 1972

'Un partito guida: l'influenza della socialdemocrazia tedesca nel Sudest europeo', *L'Internazionale socialista dalla Commune a Lenin*, Turin, 1978

'D'Amsterdam à Bâle', *Le Mouvement social*, 111 (1980), pp. 7–19

Aspects of International Socialism, 1871–1914, Cambridge, 1986

ed. *Correspondance entre Lénine et Camille Huysmans, 1905–1914*, preface C. Huysmans, Paris, 1963

Le Congrès manquée: L'Internationale à la veille de la première guerre mondiale: Etudes et documents, Paris, 1965

La Deuxième internationale et l'orient, Paris, 1967

Le Bureau socialiste international: Comptes rendus, manifestes, circulaires, 1, 1900–1907, Paris/s'Gravenhage, 1969

and M. Löwy and C. Weill *Les Marxistes et la question nationale, 1848–1914*, Paris, 1974

and J. Howorth, eds. 'Edouard Vaillant, délégué au Bureau socialiste international: Correspondance avec le secretariat international (1900–1915)', *Annali*, Milan, 1976, pp. 219–305

Hauriou, A. 'Jaurès et le problème de l'armée', *Cahiers internationaux*, 106 (1959), pp. 67–71

Hayes, C. 'The History of German Socialism Reconsidered', *American Historical Review*, 23 (1917), pp. 62–101

Hayhurst, S. 'In Pursuit of Peace: Bertrand Russell's Political Ideals and the Problem of War', unpublished PhD thesis, University of Cambridge, 1990

Heckart, B. *From Bassermann to Bebel*, New Haven, 1974

Hegel, G. W. F. *The Philosophy of History*, C. Friedrich, intr., New York, 1956

The Philosophy of Right, Oxford, 1967

Heinemann, H., and T. Meyer, eds. *Bernstein und der demokratische Sozialismus*, Berlin/Bonn, 1978

Hellmann, E. 'Unsere Taktik im Kampf gegen die Rüstungsvorlage', *NZ* 31.2 (1913), pp. 393–7

Henderson, W. O. *The Life of Friedrich Engels*, 2, London, 1976
Hervé, G. *L'Antipatriotisme*, Paris, 1906
   Le Congrès de Stuttgart et l'Antipatriotisme, Paris, 1907
   L'Internationalisme, Paris, 1910
Hickey, S. H. *Workers in Imperial Germany: The Miners of the Ruhr*, Oxford, 1985
Hilden, P. *Working Women and Socialist Politics in France, 1880–1914: A Regional Study*, Oxford, 1986
Hilferding, R. 'Zur Frage des Generalstreiks', *NZ*, 22.1 (1903), pp. 134–42
   'Parlamentarismus und Massenstreik', *NZ*, 23.2 (1905), pp. 804–16
   'Der Parteitag und die auswärtige Politik', *NZ*, 29.2 (1911), pp. 799–806
   'Sozialdemokratische Steuerpolitik', *NZ*, 30.2 (1912), pp. 221–5
   'Der Balkankrieg und die Grossmächte', *NZ*, 31.1 (1912), pp. 73–82
   'Die Erneurung des Dreibundes', *NZ*, 31.1 (1912), pp. 459–66
   'Totentanz', *NZ*, 31.1 (1913), pp. 745–9
   'Taumel', *NZ*, 31.1 (1913), pp. 849–54
   'Böhm-Bawerk's Criticism of Marx', in *Karl Marx and the Close of his System*, P. Sweezy, ed., London, 1975
   Finance Capital: A Study of the Latest Phase of Capitalist Development, T. Bottomore, ed., London, 1981
Hilden, P. *Working Women and Socialist Politics in France, 1880–1914: A Regional Study*, Oxford, 1986
Hillgruber, A. *Zweierlei Untergang*, Berlin, 1986
Hinsley, F. H. *Power and the Pursuit of Peace*, Cambridge, 1963
Hintze, O. *The Historical Essays of Otto Hintze*, F. Gilbert, ed., New York, 1975
Hobsbawm, E. J. *Industry and Empire*, Harmondsworth, 1969
   'Mass-Producing Traditions: Europe, 1870–1914', in *The Invention of Tradition*, E. J. Hobsbawm and T. Ranger, eds., Cambridge, 1983, pp. 263–307
   ed., *History of Marxism*, 1, Brighton, 1982
   ed., *Storia del marxismo*, 2, Turin, 1979
Hobson, J. A. *Psychology of Jingoism*, London, 1901
   Imperialism: A Study, London, 1954
Hoffmann, H. H., ed. *Das deutsche OffizierKorps 1888–1918*, Boppard, 1980
Höhle, T. *Franz Mehring: Sein Weg zum Marxismus 1869–1891*, Berlin, 1958
Höhn, R. *Verfassungskampf und Heereseid: Der Kampf des Bürgertums um das Heer 1815–1850*, Leipzig, 1938
   Sozialismus und Heer, 3 vols., Bad Harzburg, 1959 and 1969
   Die vaterlandslosen Gesellen. Der Sozialismus im Lichte der Geheimberichte der preussischen Polizei, 1878–1914, 1 (1878–90), Cologne, 1964
Holms, J. *Sound Military Reform: Are We to Obtain it?*, London, 1872
   The British Army in 1875 With Suggestions on its Administration and Organisation, London, 1876
Horne, J. 'L'Idée de nationalisation dans les mouvements ouvriers européens jusqu'à la deuxième guerre mondiale', *Le Mouvement Social*, 134 (1986), pp. 9–36
Howard, M. *War in European History*, Oxford, 1976
Howorth, J. 'The Left in France and Germany, Internationalism and War: A Dialogue of the Deaf (1900–1914)', in *Socialism and Nationalism in Con-*

temporary Europe (1848–1945), 2, E. Cahm and V. Fisera, eds., Nottingham, 1979, pp. 81–100

Edouard Vaillant: La création de l'unité socialiste en France: La politique de l'action totale, Paris, 1982

'French Workers and German Workers: The Impossibility of Internationalism, 1900–1914', *European History Quarterly*, 15 (1985), pp. 71–97

Hull, I. V. *The Entourage of Kaiser Wilhelm II, 1888–1918*, Cambridge, 1982

Hunt, J. C. *The People's Party in Württemberg and Southern Germany, 1890–1914*, Stuttgart, 1975

Hunt, R. N. *The Political Ideas of Marx and Engels*, 2 vols., London, 1975 and 1984

Hussain, A., and K. Tribe *Marxism and the Agrarian Question*, London, 1983

Ito, N. 'Die japanische Arbeiterbewegung und der Marxismus um die Jahrhundertwende (1895–1910)', *Internationale Tagung der Historiker der Arbeiterbewegung: 'IX. Linzer Konferenz'* 1973, Vienna, 1975, pp. 122–31

Jacoby, R. 'The Politics of Crisis Theory: Toward the Critique of Automatic Marxism II', *Telos*, 23 (1975), pp. 3–52

Jaekh, G. 'Historische Rückblicke zur Frage der Reichsfinanzreform', *NZ*, 22.2 (1904), pp. 68–78

Jäger, W. *Historische Forschung und politische Kultur in Deutschland: Die Debatte 1914–1980 über den Ausbruch des ersten Weltkrieges*, Göttingen, 1984

Jansen, R. *Georg von Vollmar*, Dusseldorf, 1958

Jakubowski, F. *Ideology and Superstructure in Historical Materialism*, London, 1976

Jarausch, K. *Students, Society and Politics in Imperial Germany: The Rise of Academic Illiberalism*, Princeton, 1982

The Enigmatic Chancellor: Bethmann Hollweg and the Hubris of Imperial Germany, New Haven, 1973

Jaurès, J. *L'Organisation socialiste de la France: L'armée nouvelle*, Paris, 1911

Textes choisis, M. Reberioux, ed. and intr., Paris, 1959

Actes du colloques: Jaurès et la nation, Toulouse, 1965

Jaurès et la classe ouvrier, M. Reberioux, intr., Paris, 1981

Jemnitz, J. 'The First International and the War (1864–1866)', *Acta Historica*, 11 (1965), pp. 57–93

The Danger of War and the Second International (1911), Budapest, 1972

'Stellungnahme der internationalen Arbeiterbewegung zu den Fragen des Militarismus und Imperialismus zwischen 1907 und 1912', *Internationalen Tagung der Historiker der Arbeiterbewegung: 'VIII. Linzer Konferenz' 1972*, Vienna, 1974, pp. 31–8

John, H. *Das Reserveoffizierkorps im deutschen Kaiserreich, 1890–1914*, Frankfurt, 1981

John, M. 'Bourgeois Law and Society in Imperial Germany', *Past and Present*, 119 (1988), pp. 105–31

Politics and the Law in late Nineteenth-Century Germany: The Origins of the Civil Code, Oxford, 1989

Joll, J. *The Second International, 1889–1914*, London, 1955

Jong, A. de *Domela Nieuwenhuis*, Amsterdam, 1981

Jong, R. de *Ferdinand Domela Nieuwenhuis Archief: Inventaris*, Amsterdam, 1956

Judt, T. *Socialism in Provence, 1871–1914*, Cambridge, 1979

Julliard, J. 'La CGT devant la guerre, 1900–1914', *Le Mouvement social*, 49 (1985), pp. 47–62

Jung, W. *August Bebel: Deutscher Patriot und internationaler Sozialist*, Pfaffenweiler, 1988

Kaarsholm, P. 'Internationalism in Working Class and Socialist Opposition to Imperialism in the Period of the South African War, 1899–1902', *IISH Symposium Internationalism in the Labour Movement before 1940*, Amsterdam (*mimeo*), 1985

Kaelbe, H. *Industrialisierung und soziale Ungleicheit: Europa im 19. Jahrhundert: Eine Bilanz*, Göttingen, 1983

Kant, I. *Kant's Political Writings*, H. Reiss, ed. and intr., Cambridge, 1970

Kapp, Y. *Eleanor Marx*, 2 vols., London, 1972 and 1976

Katayama, Sen 'Japanisch-amerikanische Probleme', *NZ*, 28.2 (1910), pp. 732–42

Katzenstein, S. 'Zur neuen Militärvorlage', *NZ*, 16.2 (1898), pp. 628–30

Katznelson, I., and A. Zollberg, eds. *Working Class Formation: Nineteenth-Century Patterns in Western Europe and the United States*, Princeton, 1986

Kautsky, K. 'Auswanderung und Kolonisation', *NZ*, 1 (1883), pp. 365–70; 393–404

'Sudan', *NZ*, 2 (1884), pp. 129–35

'Tongking', *NZ*, 2 (1884), pp. 156–64

'Die chinesischen Eisenbahnen und das europäische Proletariat', *NZ*, 4 (1886), pp. 515–25; 529–49

'Die moderne Nationalität', *NZ*, 5 (1887), pp. 392–405; 442–51

'Militarismus und Überproduktion', *NZ*, 5 (1887), pp. 141–3

'Der erweiterte deutsche Militärstaat', *NZ*, 5 (1887), pp. 331–3

Karl Marx's ökonomische Lehren, Stuttgart, 1887

'Boulanger und die französischen Sozialisten', *NZ*, 6 (1888), pp. 299–308

'Die Arbeiterbewegung in Österreich', *NZ*, 8 (1890), pp. 49–56; 97–106; 154–63

'Deutsche und amerikanische Zollpolitik', *NZ*, 9.1 (1891), pp. 313–26

'Futter fürs Pulver', *NZ*, 10.2 (1892), pp. 257–60

'Militär- und Polizeistaatliches', *NZ*, 10.2 (1892), 385–8

'Der erste Mai und der Militarismus', *NZ*, 11.2 (1893), pp. 100–3

'Kapitalismus und Militarismus', *NZ*, 11.2 (1893), pp. 193–6

'Moloch in Nöthen', *NZ*, 12.1 (1893), pp. 161–4

'Finis Poloniae?', *NZ*, 14.2 (1896), pp. 484–91; 513–25

'Ältere und neuere Kolonialpolitik', *NZ*, 16.1 (1898), pp. 769–91; 801–16

'Demokratische und reaktionäre Abrüstung', *NZ*, 16.2 (1898), pp. 740–6

'Friedrich Engels und das Milizsystem', *NZ*, 17.1 (1898), pp. 335–42

'Schippel und der Militarismus', *NZ*, 17.1 (1899), pp. 618–26; 644–54; 686–91

'Siegfried der Harmlose', *NZ*, 17.1 (1899), pp. 787–91

'Der Krieg in Südafrika', *NZ*, 18.1 (1899), pp. 196–203

'Militarismus und Sozialismus in England', *NZ*, 18.1 (1900), pp. 587–97

'Schippel, Brentano und die Flottenvorlage', *NZ*, 18.1 (1900), pp. 740–51; 772–82; 804–16

'Grundzüge der Handelspolitik', *NZ*, 20.1 (1901), pp. 332–41; 364–76; 396–408; 353–7

'Was nun?', *NZ*, 21.2 (1903), pp. 390–8

'Allerhand revolutionäres', *NZ*, 22.1 (1904), pp. 588–98; 620–27; 652–7; 685–95; 732–40

'Der Kongress zu Amsterdam', *NZ*, 22.2 (1904), pp. 673–82

'Republik und Sozialdemokratie in Frankreich', *NZ*, 23.1 (1904), pp. 260–70; 300–9; 332–41; 363–71; 397–414; 436–49; 467–81

'Patriotismus, Krieg und Sozialdemokratie', *NZ*, 23.2 (1905), pp. 343–8; 364–71

'Die Folgen des japanischen Sieges und die Sozialdemokratie', *NZ*, 23.2 (1905), pp. 460–8; 492–9; 529–37

'Die Fortsetzung einer unmöglichen Diskussion', *NZ*, 23.2 (1905), pp. 681–92; 717–27

'Noch einmal die unmögliche Diskussion', *NZ*, 23.2 (1905), pp. 776–85

'Der mögliche Abschluss einer unmöglicher Diskussion', *NZ*, 23.2 (1905), pp. 795–80

'Grundsätze oder Pläne?', *NZ*, 24.2 (1906), pp. 781–8

'Mein Verrat an der russichen Revolution', *NZ*, 24.2 (1906), pp. 854–60

'Die Situation des Reiches', *NZ*, 25.1 (1906/1907), pp. 420–8; 453–61; 484–500

'Der 25. Januar', *NZ*, 25.1 (1907), pp. 488–96

'Ausländische und deutsche Parteitaktik', *NZ*, 25.1 (1907), pp. 724–31; 764–73

(Karl Emil) 'Die bürgerlichen Parteien und der Militarismus', *NZ*, 25.2 (1907), pp. 132–4

(Karl Emil) 'Anti-Militarismus', *NZ*, 25.2 (1907), pp. 241–5

(Karl Emil) 'Der internationale Kongress in Stuttgart', *NZ*, 25.2 (1907), pp. 660–7

'Der Stuttgarter Kongress', *NZ*, 25.2 (1907), pp. 724–30

'Der Essener Parteitag', *NZ*, 25.2 (1907), pp. 852–8

(Karl Emil) 'Der deutsche Imperialismus und die innere Politik', *NZ*, 26.1 (1907), pp. 148–63

Patriotismus und Sozialdemokratie, Leipzig, 1907

'Methoden der Kolonialverwaltung', *NZ*, 26.1 (1908), pp. 613–21

'Nationalität und Internationalität', *NZ* (1908), Ergänzungsheft, 1

'Österreich und Serbien', *NZ*, 27.1 (1909), pp. 860–3

'Österreich und die Mächte', *NZ*, 27.1 (1909), pp. 939–49

'Sozialistische Kolonialpolitik', *NZ*, 27.2 (1909), pp. 33–43

'Sozialdemokratische Finanzreform', *NZ*, 27.2 (1909), pp. 229–33

The Social Revolution and On the Morrow of the Social Revolution, London, 1909

The Road to Power, Chicago, 1909

'Was nun?', *NZ*, 28.2 (1910), pp. 33–40; 68–80

'Eine neue Strategie', *NZ*, 28.2 (1910), pp. 332–41; 364–74; 412–21

'Zwischen Baden und Luxemburg', *NZ*, 28.2 (1910), pp. 652–67

'Schlusswort', *NZ*, 28.2 (1910), pp. 760–5

'Der Kongress von Kopenhagen', *NZ*, 28.2 (1910), pp. 772–81

'Finanzkapital und Krisen', *NZ*, 29.1 (1911), pp. 762–72; 797–804; 838–46; 874–83

'Krieg und Frieden', *NZ*, 29.2 (1911), pp. 97–107

'Eine Richtigstellung', *NZ*, 29.2 (1911), p. 248

'Die volks- und staatswirthschaftliche Bilanz der Rüstungen', *NZ*, 29.2 (1911), pp. 421–2

'Zum Parteitag', *NZ*, 29.2 (1911), pp. 793–9

'Die Aktion der Masse', *NZ*, 30.1 (1911), pp. 43–9; 77–84; 106–17

'Der erste Mai und der Kampf gegen den Militarismus', *NZ*, 30.2 (1912), pp. 97–109

'Ökonomie und Wehrhaftigkeit', *NZ*, 30.2 (1912), pp. 261–6; 319–23; 342–50

'Der improvisierte Bruch', *NZ*, 30.2 (1912), pp. 461–7; 513–23

'Die neue Taktik', *NZ*, 30.2 (1912), pp. 654–64; 688–98; 723–33

'Nochmals die Abrüstung', *NZ*, 30.2 (1912), pp. 841–54

'Der Krieg und die Internationale', *NZ*, 31.1 (1912), pp. 185–93

'Der Baseler Kongress und die Kriegshetzer in Österreich', *NZ*, 31.1 (1912), pp. 337–46

'Der jüngste Radikalismus', *NZ*, 31.1 (1912), pp. 436–46

'Die Berner Konferenz', *NZ*, 31.2 (1913), pp. 265–9

'Krieg und Kapitalismus', *NZ*, 31.2 (1913), pp. 428–44

'Armee und Volk', *NZ*, 32.1 (1913), pp. 401–5

'Die Einigung in England und Russland', *NZ*, 32.1 (1913), pp. 465–73

'Massendemonstrationen vor Gericht', *NZ*, 32.2 (1914), pp. 652–7

'Der Imperialismus', *NZ*, 32.2 (1914), pp. 908–22

'Notiz. Friedrich Engels und der Krieg', *NZ*, 32.2 (1914), p. 964

'Die Internationale und der Burgfrieden', *NZ*, 33.1 (1914), pp. 18–19

'Die Internationalität und der Krieg', *NZ*, 33.1 (1914), pp. 225–50

Vergangenheit und Zukunft der Internationale, Vienna, 1920

The Outbreak of the World War: German Documents, collected by K. Kautsky and ed. M. Montgelas and W. Schückling, New York, 1924

Wehrfrage und Sozialdemokratie, Berlin, 1928

Sozialisten und Krieg, Prague, 1937

The Class Struggle, New York, 1971

Socialism and Colonial Policy: An Analysis, Belfast, 1975

Keck, T. 'Kant and Socialism: An Exchange of Letters between Paul Natorp and August Bebel', *Archiv für Sozialgeschichte*, 15 (1975), pp. 323–9

Kehr, E. *Economic Interest, Militarism and Foreign Policy*, G. Craig, ed., Berkeley, 1977

Kendall, W. 'Russian Emigration and British Marxist Socialism', *International Review of Social History*, 8 (1963), pp. 351–78

Kirchner, J. 'Die internationale Frauenbewegung im Kampf um Frieden und gesellschaftlichen Fortschritt zwischen den Internationalen Sozialistenkongressen von Paris und Stuttgart', *VIII Klara-Zetkin-Kolloquium der Forschungsgemeinschaft 'Geschichte des Kampfes der Arbeiterklasse um die Befreiung der Frau'*, Leipzig, 1985, pp. 52–9

Kissinger, H. A. *A World Restored: Metternich, Castlereagh and the Problems of Peace, 1812–22*, London, 1957

American Foreign Policy, New York, 1977

Kitchen, M. *The German Officer Corps, 1890–1914*, Oxford, 1968

'Friedrich Engels' Theory of War', *Military Affairs*, 41 (1977), pp. 119–23

The Political Economy of Germany, 1815–1914, London, 1978

Klaer, K.-H. *Der Zusammenbruch der Zweiten Internationale*, Frankfurt, 1981

Klein, F., ed. *Deutschland im ersten Weltkrieg*, 1, Berlin, 1968

Klein, F., A. Laschitza, B. Radlak and F. Tych 'Die Stellung der internationalen Arbeiterbewegung zu Militarismus und Imperialismus zwischen den Kongressen in Stuttgart und Basel (1907–1912)', *Internationale Tagung der Historiker der Arbeiterbewegung: 'VIII. Linzer Konferenz' 1972*, Vienna, 1974, pp. 1–16

Koch, H. W. *Der Sozialdarwinismus: Seine Genese und sein Einfluss auf das imperialistische Denken*, Munich, 1973

ed. *The Origins of the First World War*, London, 1972

Kocka, J. *Klassengesellschaft im Krieg, 1914–1918*, Göttingen, 1973

ed. *Arbeiter und Bürger im 19. Jahrhundert Varianten ihres Verhältnisses im europäischen Vergleich*, Munich, 1986

Koenker, D., W. G. Rosenberg and R. G. Suny, eds. *Party, State and Society in the Russian Civil War*, Bloomington, 1989

Kolakowski, L. *Main Currents of Marxism*, 3 vols., Oxford, 1978

Konig, E. *Von Revisionismus zum 'demokratischen Sozialismus': Zur Kritik des ökonomischen Revisionismus in Deutschland*, Berlin, 1964

Korsch, K. *Karl Marx*, New York, 1938

Marxism and Philosophy, London, 1970

Kotowski, G. *Friedrich Ebert: Aufstieg eines deutschen Arbeiterführers*, 1, Berlin, 1963

Krafft, R. *Kasernenelend: Offene Kritik der Verhältnisse unserer Unteroffiziere und Soldaten*, Stuttgart, 1895

'Gedanken zu einer Reform des Militärstrafrechts', *NZ*, 18.2 (1900), pp. 114–17

'Der Zukunftskrieg', *NZ*, 19.1 (1901), pp. 814–19

'Randglossen zu den deutschen Manövern', *NZ*, 19.2 (1901), pp. 217–21

'Wie der Moloch wächst', *NZ*, 21.2 (1903), pp. 12–15

'Zum Prozess Bilse', *NZ*, 22.1 (1903), pp. 239–42

Die Opfer der Kaserne, Berlin, 1904

'Etwas von der Kriegskunst', *NZ*, 22.2 (1904), pp. 241–6

'Aus den Tagen der dreijährigen Dienstzeit', *NZ*, 23.1 (1905), pp. 509–14

'Der ostasiatische Krieg und die Volkswehr', *NZ*, 23.2 (1905), pp. 407–11

'Der Militarismus im Deutschen Reiche', *NZ*, 25.1 (1907), pp. 515–18

'Ein Netz', *NZ*, 26.2 (1908), pp. 618–20

Kriegel, A. *Les Internationales ouvriers, 1864–1943*, Paris, 1964

'Patrie ou révolution: Le mouvement ouvrier français devant la guerre (juillet-août 1914)', *Revue d'histoire économique et sociale*, 3 (1965), pp. 363–86

Le Pain et les roses, Paris, 1968

'La IIe Internationale (1889–1914)', *Histoire général du socialisme*, 2, J. Droz, ed., Paris, 1974, pp. 555–84

and J.-J. Becker *1914: La Guerre et le mouvement ouvrier français*, Paris, 1964

Krumeich, G. *Armaments and Politics in France on the Eve of the First World War: The Introduction of Three-Year Conscription, 1913–1914*, Leamington Spa, 1984

and W. Mock 'Marcel Sembat und Rudolf Hilferding Sozialisten und Regierungsverantwortung', in *Die geteilte Utopie: Sozialisten in Frankreich und Deutschland: Biografische Vergleiche zur politischen Kultur*, M. Christadler, ed., Opladen, 1985

Kuczynski, J. *Der Ausbruch des ersten Weltkrieges und die deutsche Sozialdemokratie: Chronik und Analyse*, Berlin, 1957

Kuhnert, F. *Die heilige Vehme des Militarismus nach kriegsgerichtlichen Erkenntnissen*, Nuremberg, 1893
'Die Opfer der Kaserne', *NZ*, 22.1 (1904), pp. 773–5
Lafargue, P. 'Die sozialistische Bewegung in Frankreich von 1876–1890', *NZ*, 8 (1890), pp. 337–53
'Der boulangeristische Zusammenbruch', *NZ*, 9.1 (1890), pp. 145–9
'Der Bankerott der russischen Finanzen', *NZ*, 13.2 (1895), pp. 133–42
Lagardelle, H. 'Der Nationalismus in Frankreich', *NZ*, 20.1 (1901), pp. 21–5; 44–7
Langewiescher, D., and K. Schoenhoven 'Arbeiterbibliotheken und Arbeiterlektüre im wilhelminischen Deutschland', *Archiv für Sozialgeschichte*, 16, 1976, pp. 135–204
Langhorne, R. *The Collapse of the Concert of Europe*, London, 1981
Lawrence, J. 'Class and Gender in the Making of Urban Toryism, 1880–1914', *English Historical Review*, 428 (1993), pp. 629–52
and M. Taylor 'Poverty of Protest: Gareth Stedman Jones and the Politics of Language – A Reply', *Social History*, 18,7 (1993), pp. 1–15
Ledebour, G. 'Soldatenschutzgesetze', *NZ*, 22.1 (1903), pp. 108–13
'Die Einschränkung der Seerüstung', *NZ*, 27.2 (1909), pp. 99–106
'Die Interessenkämpfe im Südwestafrika', *NZ*, 28.2 (1910), pp. 516–22; 578–85
'Ein fadenscheiniger Rüstungsvorwand', *NZ*, 31.1 (1913), pp. 929–34
Leidigkeit, K.-H. *Wilhelm Liebknecht und August Bebel in der deutschen Arbeiterbewegung, 1862–1869*, Berlin, 1957
Lemmermann, H. *Kriegserziehung im Kaiserreich*, 2 vols., Bremen, 1984
Lenin, V. I. *Collected Works*, 47 vols. (trans. from 4th Russian ed.), Moscow, 1960–80
Lensch, P. 'Politischer Massenstreik und politische Krisis', *NZ*, 23.2 (1905), pp. 662–4
'Die neuen Wehrvorlagen', *NZ*, 30.2 (1912), pp. 68–75
'Eine Improvisation', *NZ*, 30.2 (1912), pp. 308–13; 359–68
'Miliz und Abrüstung', *NZ*, 30.2 (1912), pp. 765–72
'Schluss mit Zabern', *NZ*, 32.1 (1914), pp. 641–4
Die deutsche Sozialdemokratie und der Weltkrieg, Berlin, 1915
Lenz, J. *The Rise and Fall of the Second International*, New York, 1932
Leon, D. de *Flashlights of the Amsterdam International Socialist Congress*, New York, 1904
Leser, N. 'Austro-Marxism: A Reappraisal', *Journal of Contemporary History*, 1, no. 2 (1966), pp. 117–33
Zwischen Reformismus und Bolschewismus: Der Austromarxismus als Theorie und Praxis, Vienna, 1968
'Der Austromarxismus als Strömung des marxistischen Zentrums', *Internationale Tagung der Historiker der Arbeiterbewegung: 'VIII. Linzer Konferenz' 1972*, Vienna, 1974, pp. 56–67
Lichtheim, G. *Marxism: An Historical and Critical Study*, London, 1961
A Short History of Socialism, Glasgow, 1975
Lidtke, V. *The Outlawed Party: Social Democracy in Germany, 1878–1890*, Princeton, 1964
The Alternative Culture: Socialist Labour in Germany, 1878–1890, Princeton, 1985

Liebknecht, K. *Studien über die Bewegungsgesetze der sozialen Entwicklung*, 'Morris' (pseudonym for Rudolf Manasse) ed., Munich, 1922
Gesammelte Reden und Schriften, 9 vols., Berlin, 1958–74
Militarism and Anti-Militarism with Special Regard to the International Young Socialist Movement, Cambridge, 1973
Liebknecht, W. *Zur orientalischen Frage oder Soll Europa kosakisch werden? Ein Mahnwort an das deutsche Volk*, Leipzig, 1878
'Skizzen vom Brüsseler Kongress', *NZ*, 9.2 (1891), pp. 835–8
Briefwechsel mit Karl Marx und Friedrich Engels, G. Eckert, ed., The Hague, 1963
Briefwechsel mit deutschen Sozialdemokraten I: 1862–1878, G. Eckert, ed., Assen, 1973
Gegen Militarismus und Eroberungskrieg: Aus Schriften und Reden, Berlin, 1986
Liebman, M. *Leninism under Lenin*, London, 1975
London, J. *The Iron Heel*, London, 1974
Longuet, J. *Les Socialistes allemands contre la guerre et le militarisme*, Paris, 1913
Losche, P. 'Arbeiterbewegung und Wilhelminismus', *Geschichte in Wissenschaft und Unterrecht*, 20 (1969), pp. 519–33
Louis, P. 'Die Kolonialpolitik Frankreichs und der Sozialismus', *NZ*, 18.2 (1900), pp. 672–84
Lucas, E. *Zwei Formen von Radikalismus in der deutschen Arbeiterbewegung*, Frankfurt, 1976
Lukacs, G. *History and Class Consciousness*, London, 1971
Lusnia, M. 'Unbewaffnete Revolution?', *NZ*, 22.1 (1904), pp. 559–67
Lütkens, G. 'Das Kriegsproblem und die marxistische Theorie', *Archiv für Sozialwissenschaft und Sozialpolitik*, 49 (1922), pp. 467–517
Lützenkirchen, R. *Der sozialdemokratische Verein für den Reichstagswahlkreis Dortmund-Hörde*, Dortmund, 1970
Luxemburg, R. *Rosa Luxemburg im Kampf gegen den deutschen Militarismus: Prozessberichte und Materialen aus den Jahren 1913 bis 1915: Mit einem Anhang*, Berlin, 1960
The Accumulation of Capital, J. Robinson, intr., London, 1963
Rosa Luxemburg Speaks, M.-A. Waters, ed., New York, 1970
Gesammelte Werke, 6 vols., Berlin, 1970–5
Selected Political Writings, D. Howard, ed., New York, 1971
Einführung in die Nationalökonomie, Reinbeck bei Hamburg, 1972
The Accumulation of Capital: An Anti-Critique, New York, 1972
Gesammelte Briefe, 5 vols., Berlin, 1982–4
McLeod, H. 'Protestantism and the Working Class in Imperial Germany', *European Studies Review*, 12 (1982), pp. 323–44
Maehl, W. H. 'The Triumph of Nationalism in the German Socialist Party on the Eve of the First World War', *Journal of Modern History*, 24 (1952), pp. 292–306
'The Role of Russia in German Socialist Foreign Policy, 1914–18', *International Review of Social History*, 4 (1959), pp. 177–98
August Bebel: Shadow Emperor of the German Workers, Philadelphia, 1980
Maguire, J. M. *Marx's Theory of Politics*, Cambridge, 1978
Mai, A. 'Wehrvorlage und Volkswirtschaft', *NZ*, 31.2 (1913), pp. 307–13

Maier, C. S. *The Unmasterable Past: History, Holocaust and German National Identity*, Cambridge, Mass., 1988

Man, H. de *Zur Psychologie des Sozialismus*, Jena, 1927

Manchester, W. *The Arms of Krupp*, New York, 1973

Mandel, E. *Marxist Economic Theory*, London, 1968

Mandelbaum, K. *Die Erörterungen innerhalb der deutschen Sozialdemokratie über das Problem des Imperialismus (1895–1914)*, Schweinfurt, 1926

Mann, H. *Man of Straw (Der Untertan)*, Harmondsworth, 1984

Mann, L. 'Soldatenmisshandlungen und Sozialdemokratie', *NZ*, 32.1 (1913), pp. 949–52

Mann, M. 'Capitalism and Militarism', in *War, State and Society*, M. Shaw, ed., London, 1984

Mannheim, K. *Ideology and Utopia*, London, 1960

Marchlewski, J. (Karski) 'Das Urteil eines bürgerlichen Ideologen über den Militarismus', *NZ*, 17.2 (1899), pp. 171–4

'Völkerrecht und Militarismus', *NZ*, 17.2 (1899), pp. 197–207; 229–39

'Um die Finanzreform', *NZ*, 27.2 (1909), pp. 225–8

'Steuerprobleme', *NZ*, 28.1 (1910), pp. 783–91

'Kopenhagen', *NZ*, 28.2 (1910), pp. 900–7

Krieg, Zusammenbruch und Revolution, Leipzig/Berlin, 1911

'Das "Kulturwerk" des preussischen Polenpolitik', *NZ*, 29.2 (1911), pp. 161–8

Sozialismus oder Imperialismus, Berlin, 1960

Martin, J. 'Die neue Ära in Elsass-Lothringen', *NZ*, 29.2 (1911), pp. 325–7

'Die Rückkehr zur Diktatur in Elsass-Lothringen', *NZ*, 31.2 (1913), pp. 297–302

'Reichlandschicksale – Reichschicksale', *NZ*, 32.1 (1914), pp. 716–20

Marx, K. *A Contribution to the Critique of Political Economy* (new ed.), M. Dobb, ed., Moscow, 1970

Grundrisse: Foundations of Critique of Political Economy (Rough Draft), Harmondsworth, 1973

Capital: A Critique of Political Economy, 3 vols. (new ed.), E. Mandel, ed., Harmondsworth, 1976–81

and F. Engels *Selected Correspondence*, Moscow, 1965

Werke, 39 vols., Berlin, 1962–8

Collected Works, vols. 1–22 and 38–41, Moscow/London, 1975–86

Mason, T. 'Women in Nazi Germany', *History Workshop*, 1 (1976), pp. 74–113, and 2, pp. 5–32

'National Socialism and the German Working Class to May 1933', *New German Critique*, 1977, pp. 49–93

Massow, C. von *Reform oder Revolution?*, Berlin, 1894

Matthias, E. 'Kautsky und der Kautskyanismus: Die Funktion der Ideologie in der deutschen Sozialdemokratie vordem ersten Weltkrieg', *Marxismusstudien*, 2, 1957, pp. 151–97

and E. Pickart *Die Reichstagsfraktion der deutschen Sozialdemokratie 1898 bis 1918*, 2 vols., Dusseldorf, 1966

Mayer, A. J. 'Internal Causes and Purposes of War in Europe, 1870–1956: A Research Assignment', *Journal of Modern History*, 31, no. 3 (1969), pp. 291–303

Mayer, G. *Johann Baptist von Schweitzer und die Sozialdemokratie*, Jena, 1909

'Die Trennung der proletarischen von der bürgerlichen Demokratie in Deutschland (1863–1870)', *Archiv für die Geschichte des Sozialismus und der Arbeiterbewegung*, 2 (1912), pp. 1–67
'Der deutsche Marxismus und der Krieg', *Archiv für Sozialwissenschaft und Sozialpolitik*, 43 (1916), pp. 108–70
Friedrich Engels: Eine Biographie, 2 vols., Frankfurt, 1975
Meerfeld, J. 'Nachdenkliche Betrachtungen', *NZ*, 31.2 (1913), pp. 398–401
'Mein Schlusswort', *NZ*, 31.2 (1913), pp. 857–60
Mehring, F. 'Diplomatisches und polizistisches', *NZ*, 15.1 (1896), pp. 193–6
'Weltpolitik', *NZ*, 15.1 (1897), pp. 801–4
'Der Tanz mit Moloch', *NZ*, 16.1 (1897), pp. 321–4
'Kiao-Tschau', *NZ*, 16.1 (1898), pp. 511–16
'Das Schiffgeld', *NZ*, 18.1 (1900), pp. 545–8
'Flottenfrage und Reichstag', *NZ*, 18.1 (1900), pp. 577–80
'Die Unruhen in China', *NZ*, 18.2 (1900), pp. 352–6
'Episoden des Zollkriegs' *NZ*, 20.1 (1900), pp. 129–32
'Die Zolltariffdebate', *NZ*, 20.1 (1901), pp. 321–4
'Zur Freihandelsrede von Marx', *NZ*, 20.1 (1901), pp. 353–7
'Die russische Hegemonie', *NZ*, 22.1 (1904), pp. 481–4
'Der russisch-japanische Krieg', *NZ*, 22.1 (1904), pp. 617–20
'Die Lage Deutschlands', *NZ*, 22.2 (1904), pp. 33–6
'Maifest und Militarismus', *NZ*, 22.2 (1904), pp. 97–100
'Zwischen zwei Fronten', *NZ*, 23.1 (1904), pp. 393–7
'Imperialistisches', *NZ*, 23.2 (1905), pp. 393–6
'Friedens- und Verfassungsfragen', *NZ*, 23.2 (1905), pp. 745–8
'Kriegssachen', *NZ*, 23.2 (1905), pp. 425–8
'Die Revolution in Permanenz', *NZ*, 24.1 (1905), pp. 169–72
'Algeciras', *NZ*, 24.1 (1906), pp. 737–40
'Kolonialskandale', *NZ*, 24.2 (1906), pp. 41–5
'Das zweite Jena', *NZ*, 25.1 (1906), pp. 81–4
'Preussische Polenpolitik', 25.1 (1906), pp. 353–6
'Prätorianergesinnung', *NZ*, 25.2 (1907), pp. 177–80
'Der Prozess Liebknecht', *NZ*, 26.1 (1907), pp. 81–4
'Der Prozess Moltke-Harden', *NZ*, 26.1 (1907), pp. 145–8
'Die Finanzklemme', *NZ*, 26.1 (1907), pp. 249–52
'Molochs Methoden', *NZ*, 26.1 (1907), pp. 682–3
'Eine Friedenskundgebung', *NZ*, 26.2 (1908), pp. 897–900
'Die halbe Milliarde', *NZ*, 27.1 (1908), pp. 41–4
'Die Balkankrise', *NZ*, 27.1 (1908), pp. 73–6
'Aus Molochs Schuldbuch', *NZ*, 27.1 (1909), pp. 689–92
'Die Finanzmisere', *NZ*, 27.2 (1909), pp. 393–6
'Elsass-Lothringen', *NZ*, 29.1 (1910), pp. 385–8
'Das Marokko Abentreuer', *NZ*, 29.2 (1911), pp. 505–7
'Die Sozialdemokratie in der Armee und die Wehrvorlage', *NZ*, 31.2 (1913), pp. 259–62
Karl Marx: The Story of his Life, London, 1936
Geschichte der deutschen Sozialdemokratie, 2 vols., Berlin, 1960
Zur Kriegsgeschichte und Militärfrage, Berlin, 1967

On Historical Materialism, London, 1975
Aufsätze zur Geschichte der Arbeiterbewegung, Berlin, 1980
Meinecke, F. *Die Idee der Staatsräson*, (new ed.) Munich, 1963
Mergner, G. 'Solidarity with the "Savages": The Relationship of the German
  Social Democrats to African Resistance in the Former German Colonies
  around the Turn of the Century', *IISH Symposium Internationalism in the
  Labour Movement before 1940*, Amsterdam (*mimeo*), 1985
Meyer, R. 'Der grosse Generalstab und die nörgelden Zeitungsschreiber', *NZ*, 10.2
  (1892), pp. 260–8
Michels, R. 'Die deutsche Sozialdemokratie im internationalen Verbande', *Archiv
  für Sozialwissenschaft und Sozialpolitik*, 25 (1907), pp. 148–231
Political Parties, New York, 1959
Miller, S. 'Zum 3. August 1914', *Archiv für Sozialgeschichte*, 4 (1964), pp. 515–23
  *Burgfrieden und Klassenkampf: Die deutsche Sozialdemokratie im ersten Welt-
  krieg*, Dusseldorf, 1974
  and H. Potthoff *A History of German Social Democracy: From 1848 to the
  Present*, Leamington Spa, 1986
Mitchell, A. *Victors and Vanquished: The German Influence on Army and Church in
  France after 1870*, Chapel Hill, 1984
Moch, G. *L'Armée d'une démocratie*, Paris, 1900
  La Reforme militaire: Vive la milice!, Paris, 1900
  Histoire sommaire de l'arbitrage, Paris, 1905
Mommsen, W. J. 'Domestic Factors in German Foreign Policy before 1914',
  Central European History, 6 (1973), pp. 3–43
  'Das Kaiserreich als System umgangener Entscheidungen', in *Vom Staat des
  Ancien Regime zum modernen Staat*, H. Berding, K. Düwell *et al.*, eds.,
  Munich, 1978
  Max Weber and German Politics, 1890–1920, Chicago, 1984
  and J. Osterhammel, eds. *Max Weber and his Contemporaries*, London, 1987
Montesquieu, C. de *The Spirit of the Laws*, A. Cohler *et al.*, eds., Cambridge, 1989
Mooser, J. *Arbeiterleben in Deutschland, 1900–1970: Klassenlagen, Kultur und
  Politik*, Frankfurt, 1984
Morgan, K. *Keir Hardie: Radical and Socialist*, London, 1975
Morgan, R. *The German Social Democrats and the First International, 1864–1872*,
  Cambridge, 1965
Moring, K.-E. *Die Sozialdemokratische Partei in Bremen, 1890–1914*, Hanover,
  1968
Moses, J. A. *The Politics of Illusion*, London, 1975
Mosse, G. L. *The Nationalisation of the Masses: Political Symbolism and Mass
  Movements for the Napoleonic Wars Through the Third Reich*, New York, 1975
Müller, D. H. *Idealismus und Revolution: Zur Opposition der Jungen gegen den
  sozialdemokratischen Parteivorstand 1890 bis 1894*, Berlin, 1975
Müller, H. *Der Klassenkampf in der deutschen Sozialdemokratie: Mit einem
  polemischen Nachwort: K. Kautsky's Abenteuer in Zürich*, Zurich, 1892
Mueller, I. *De la guerre: Le Discours de la deuxième internationale, 1889–1914*,
  Geneva/Paris, 1980
Munck, R. *The Difficult Dialogue: Marxism and Nationalism*, London, 1986
Na'aman, S. *Ferdinand Lassalle: Eine neue politische Biographie*, Hanover, 1970

Nachimson, M. 'Einige Zahlen zur Charakteristik der finanziellen Lage Deutschlands', *NZ*, 27.2 (1909), pp. 355–8

'Die Belastung der deutschen Volkswirthschaft durch den Militarismus', *NZ*, 29.1 (1911), pp. 516–21

'Die Militärausgaben der europäischen Grossmächte', *NZ*, 29.2 (1911), pp. 47–51

Negt, O. 'Il marxismo e la teoria della rivoluzione nell'ultimo Engels', *Storia del marxismo*, 2, Turin, 1979, pp. 110–79

'Rosa Luxemburg e il rinnovamento del marxismo', *Storia del marxismo*, 2, Turin, 1979, pp. 318–55

Nettl, J. P. 'The German Social Democratic Party as Political Model', *Past and Present*, 30 (1965), pp. 65–95

Rosa Luxemburg, 2 vols., London, 1966

Newbold, J. *How Europe Armed for the War, 1871–1914*, London, 1916

Newton, D. *British Labour and the Struggle for Peace, 1889–1914*, Oxford, 1985

Nicolaievsky, B., and O. Maenchen-Helfen *Karl Marx: Man and Fighter*, Harmondsworth, 1976

Nipperdey, T. *Die Organisationen der deutschen Parteien vor 1918*, Dusseldorf, 1961

Nachdenken über die deutsche Geschichte, Munich, 1986

Nishikawa, M. 'The Debates on the Question of War at the Congresses of the Second International, 1907–1912', *Internationale Tagung der Historiker der Arbeiterbewegung: 'VIII. Linzer Konferenz'* 1972, Vienna, 1974, pp. 39–45

Noack, V. 'Die Militäranwärter', *NZ*, 25.2 (1907), pp. 803–9

Nolan, M. *Social Democracy and Society: Working Class Radicalism in Dusseldorf, 1890–1920*, Cambridge, 1981

Nolte, E. *Der europäische Bürgerkrieg, 1917–1945*, Frankfurt, 1987

Noske, G. 'Die Taktik der Fraktion', *NZ*, 31.2 (1913), pp. 425–8

Kolonialpolitik und Sozialdemokratie, Stuttgart, 1914

Öckel, H. *Volkswehr gegen Militarismus: Zur Militärfrage in der proletarischen Militärpolitik in Deutschland von der Mitte des 19. Jahrhunderts bis zum ersten Weltkrieg*, Berlin, 1962

Olberg, O. 'Der italienische Generalstreik', *NZ*, 23.1 (1904), pp. 18–24

'Die italienische Parteiaktion vor dem tripolitanischen Krieg', *NZ*, 30.1 (1911), pp. 33–43

'Eine Stichprobe italienischer Kolonialpolitik', *NZ*, 32.2 (1914), pp. 679–83

Owtscharenko, N. 'Zur Herausbildung der aussenpolitischen Konzeption der Sozialdemokratie im Kampf gegen die imperialistische "Weltpolitik" an der Wende vom 19. zum 20. Jahrhundert', *Marxismus und deutsche Arbeiterbewegung*, Berlin, 1970, pp. 527–86

'Zum Militärprogramm der deutschen Sozialdemokratie an der Wende vom 19. zum 20. Jahrhundert', *Jahrbuch für Geschichte*, 10 (1974), pp. 295–341

Pannekoek, A. 'Massenaktion oder Revolution', *NZ*, 30.2 (1912), pp. 541–50; 585–93; 609–16

'Marxistische Theorie und revolutionäre Taktik', *NZ*, 31.1 (1912), pp. 272–81; 365–73

'Zum Schluss', *NZ*, 31.1 (1913), pp. 611–12

'Der Streit um die Deckungsfrage', *NZ*, 31.2 (1913), pp. 769–74

'Deckungsfrage und Imperialismus', *NZ*, 32.1 (1913), pp. 110–16

Papen, F. von *Der Wahrheit eine Gasse*, Munich, 1952

Parvus (A. Helphand) 'Staatsstreich und politischer Massenstreik', *NZ*, 14.2 (1896), pp. 199–206; 261–6; 304–11; 356–64; 389–95

'Die Goldwahrung in Russland', *NZ*, 14.2 (1896), pp. 246–9

Marineforderungen, Kolonialpolitik und Arbeiterinteressen, Dresden, 1898

'Die gegenwärtige Finanzlage Russlands', *NZ*, 19.1 (1901), pp. 558–65

'Die Handelspolitik und die Doktrin', *NZ*, 19.1 (1901), pp. 580–9

'Die landwirtschaftliche Einführzölle', *NZ*, 19.1 (1901), pp. 612–19

'Die Industriezölle und der Weltmarkt', *NZ*, 19.1 (1901), pp. 708–16; 772–84

'Russland und Frankreich', *NZ*, 19.2 (1901), pp. 135–43

Die Kolonialpolitik und der Zusammenbruch, Leipzig, 1907

'Ein neues China ', *NZ*, 26.1 (1908), pp. 872–7; 923–30

'Kolonialpolitische Rundschau', *NZ*, 26.2 (1908), pp. 100–5; 193–204

'Vorgänge auf dem Balkan', *NZ*, 27.1 (1908), pp. 116–28

Paul, H.-H. *Marx, Engels und die Imperialismustheorie der II. Internationale*, Hamburg, 1978

Pavlovitch, M. 'Die Haager Konferenz', *NZ*, 26.1 (1908), pp. 544–50

'Die transiranische Eisenbahn und die englisch-russischen Beziehungen', *NZ*, 31.1 (1912), pp. 30–6

'Der Balkankrieg und die muselmännische Frage in Frankreich', *NZ*, 31.1 (1912), pp. 377–83

'Der Balkankrieg und die bürgerlichen Pazifisten', *NZ*, 31.1 (1913), pp. 574–5

'Die Putiloff-Affäre und das russisch-französische Bundnis', *NZ*, 32.1 (1914), pp. 844–50

Pelger, H., ed. *Friedrich Engels, 1820–1970: Referate, Diskussionen, Dokumente*, Hanover, 1971

Petter, W. 'Die schweizerische Miliz: Historische Bedingungen des schweizerischen Modells', *Die Wehrstruktur in der Bundesrepublik Deutschland: Analyse und Optionen*, Bonn, 1972, pp. 345–51

Pinzani, C. *Jaurès, l'Internazionale e la guerra*, Bari, 1970

Plamenatz, J. *German Marxism and Russian Communism*, London, 1954

Plekhanov, G. V. 'Die sozialpolitischen Zustände Russlands im Jahre 1890', *NZ*, 9.2 (1891), pp. 661–8; 691–5; 731–9; 765–70; 791–800; 827–34

'La Question militaire au Congres de Zürich', *L'Ere Nouvelle*, 1, no. 4 (1893), pp. 302–7

In Defence of Materialism: The Development of the Monist Theory of History, London, 1947

Pöls, W. *Sozialistenfrage und Revolutionsfurcht in ihrem Zusammenhang mit den angeblichen Staatsstreichplänen Bismarcks*, Lübeck, 1960

Popowitsch, M. 'Die Nationalitätenkämpfe und die Reformen in der Türkei', *NZ*, 22.2 (1904), pp. 617–21; 659–63

'Neue Reformaktion der Mächte in Makedonien', *NZ*, 23.1 (1905), pp. 818–22

Procacci, G. 'Studi sulla seconda Internationale e sulla socialdemocrazia tedesca', *Annali*, Milan, 1958, pp. 105–46

Przeworski, A. *Capitalism and Social Democracy*, Cambridge, 1986

Pugh, G. T. 'Economic Theory and Political Thought in German Social Democracy: An Essay on the "Rezeption" of Marx's Capital with particular

Reference to Kautsky, Parvus, Hilferding and Luxemburg', unpublished PhD thesis, University of Kent, 1983

Puhle, H.-J. *Agrarische Interessenpolitik und preussischer Konservatismus im wilhelminischen Reich*, Hanover, 1966

Quelch, H. 'Die Social Democratic Party, Hyndman und die Rüstungsfrage', *NZ*, 29.2 (1911), pp. 270–3

Quidde, L. *Caligula: Schriften über Militarismus und Pazifismus*, H.-U. Wehler, ed. and intr., Frankfurt, 1977

Radek, K. 'Zwischen Dreibund und Tripelentente', *NZ*, 27.2 (1909), pp. 913–20; 161–74

'Unterseeboote in der deutsche Marine', *NZ*, 28.1 (1910), pp. 529–34

'Die Lage in Marokko', *NZ*, 28.1 (1910), pp. 580–7

'Der Aufstand in Albanien', *NZ*, 28.2 (1910), pp. 431–29

'Die auswärtige Politik der russischen Konterrevolution', *NZ*, 29.1 (1910), pp. 68–78

'Der Baghdadbahn', *NZ*, 29.2 (1911), pp. 252–8; 293–300

'Der neue Marokkokurs Deutschlands', *NZ*, 29.2 (1911), pp. 649–59

'Die Liquidation der Marokkofrage', *NZ*, 30.1 (1911), pp. 261–9; 314–23

'Zu unserem Kampfe gegen den Imperialismus', *NZ*, 30.2 (1912), pp. 194–9; 233–41

In den Reihen der deutschen Revolution 1909–1919, Munich, 1921

Rakovsky, C. 'Der Bauerbewegung in Rumänien', *NZ*, 28.1 (1910), pp. 612–21

'Aus Bulgarien', *NZ*, 29.2 (1911), pp. 685–9

Rappoport, C. 'Der Kongress der sozialistischen Partei in Nancy', *NZ*, 25.2 (1907), pp. 817–23

'Marokko und die Kolonialpolitik Frankreichs', *NZ*, 26.1 (1908), pp. 752–9

'Der Kampf gegen den Militarismus in Frankreich', *NZ*, 31.2 (1913), pp. 47–52

'Der auserordentliche französische sozialistische Kongress', *NZ*, 32.2 (1914), pp. 772–6

Ratz, U. 'Karl Kautsky und die Abrüstungskontroverse in der deutschen Sozialdemokratie 1911–1912', *International Review of Social History*, 11 (1966), pp. 197–227

'Briefe zum Erscheinen von Karl Kautskys "Weg zur Macht"', *International Review of Social History*, 12 (1967), pp. 432–77

Georg Ledebour 1850–1947: Weg und Wirken eines sozialistischen Politikers, Berlin, 1969

Reberioux, M. 'Jean Jaurès e il marxismo', *Annali*, Milan, 1973, pp. 528–53

'Le Socialisme et la première guerre mondiale (1914–1918)', *Histoire générale du socialisme*, 2, J. Droz, ed., Paris, pp. 585–642

'Il dibattito sulla guerra', *Storia del marxismo*, 2, Turin, 1979, pp. 897–935

Renner, K. *Marxismus, Krieg und Internationale*, Stuttgart, 1917

Retallack, J. '"What is to be done?" The Red Specter, Franchise Question and the Crisis of Conservative Hegemony in Saxony, 1896–1909', *Central European History*, 23.4 (1990), pp. 271–312

Reulecke, J. 'Der 1. Weltkrieg und die Arbeiterbewegung im rheinisch-westfälischen Industriegebiet', in Reulecke, ed., *Arbeiterbewegung an Rhein und Ruhr*, Wuppertal, 1974, pp. 210 ff

Riazanov, D. ed. 'Marx, "Was soll aus der Türkei in Europa werden?"' *NZ*, 28.2 (1910), pp. 4–12

'Zur Stellungnahme von Marx und Engels während des deutsch-französischen Krieges', *NZ*, 33.2 (1915), pp. 161–71

'Die auswärtige Politik der alten Internationale und ihre Stellungsnahme zum Krieg', *NZ*, 33.2 (1915), pp. 329–34; 360–9; 438–43; 463–9; 509–19

'Vaillant und Liebknecht im Anfang des deutsch-französischen Krieges', *NZ*, 34.1 (1916), pp. 550–61

'Karl Marx und Friedrich Engels zur polnischen Frage', *Archiv für die Geschichte des Sozialismus und der Arbeiterbewegung*, 6 (1916), pp. 175–221

Karl Marx and Friedrich Engels, New York, 1973

Ricardo, D. *On the Principles of Political Economy and Taxation*, P. Sraffa, ed., Cambridge, 1951

Richard, H. *Defensive War: Extracted from a Lecture Delivered at the Hall of Commerce, Threadneedle St. London, 6th February 1845*, London, 1846

Report of the Proceedings of the Third General Peace Congress Held in Frankfurt, London, 1851

On Standing Armies and their Influence on the Industrial, Commercial and Moral Interests of Nations, London, 1868

International Arbitration, London, 1873

Ritter, G. *Staatskunst und Kriegshandwerk*, 1, Munich, 1954

Der Schlieffenplan, Munich, 1956

Robertson, J. *The Scottish Enlightenment and the Militia Issue*, Edinburgh, 1985

Röhl, J. C. G. *Germany without Bismarck: The Crisis of Government in the Second Reich, 1890–1900*, Berkeley, 1967

Roland-Holst, H. 'Der politische Streik auf dem zehnten Parteitag der niederländischen Sozialdemokratie', *NZ*, 22.2 (1904), pp. 143–6

'Der politische Massenstreik in der russischen Revolution', *NZ*, 24.2 (1906), pp. 213–23

'Zur Massenstreikdebatte', *NZ*, 24.2 (1906), pp. 684–93

Rosdolsky, R. 'Friedrich Engels und das Problem der "geschichtslosen" Völker', *Archiv für Sozialgeschichte*, 4 (1964), pp. 87–251

The Making of Marx's 'Capital', London, 1980

Rosenberg, A. *Imperial Germany*, London, 1931

Democracy and Socialism, London, 1939

Die Entstehung der Weimarer Republik, ed. K. Kersten, Frankfurt, 1961

Rosenberg, H. *Bureaucracy, Aristocracy and Autocracy*, Cambridge, Mass., 1958

Machteliten und Wirtschaftskonjunktoren, Göttingen, 1978

Roth, G. *The Social Democrats in Imperial Germany: A Study in Working Class Isolation and National Integration*, Totowa, 1963

Rothstein, T. 'Der südafrikanische Krieg und der Niedergang des englischen Liberalismus', *NZ*, 19.2 (1901), pp. 452–7

'Die S. D. P., Hyndman und die Rüstungsfrage', *NZ*, 29.2 (1911), pp. 179–86

'Die Engländer in Ägypten', *NZ* (1911), Ergänzungsheft 10

'Englands auswärtige Politik', *NZ*, 30.1 (1912), pp. 581–96

'England und die Balkankrise', *NZ*, 31.1 (1912), pp. 122–9

'Der Streit um die Baghdadbahn', *NZ*, 31.1 (1913), pp. 520–32

Rousseau, J. J. *Political Writings*, F. Watkins, ed., London, 1953

Rowthorn, R. 'Rosa Luxemburg and the Political Economy of Militarism', in R. Rowthorn, *Capitalism, Conflict and Inflation*, London, 1980

Russell, B. *German Social Democracy*, London, 1896

The Autobiography of Bertrand Russell, 3 vols., London, 1967–9

Sakasow, J. 'Die makedonische Frage', *NZ*, 21.1 (1903), pp. 5–12

'Die Spaltung in der bulgarischen sozialdemokratischen Arbeiterpartei', *NZ*, 22.1 (1904), pp. 472–5

'Der ferne Krieg und der nahe Osten', *NZ*, 22.2 (1904), pp. 518–22

'Die Balkanwirren', *NZ*, 25.1 (1906), pp. 84–7

'Die neue Balkangefahr', *NZ*, 31.2 (1913), pp. 366–71

Saldern, A. von *Vom Einwohner zum Bürger. Zur Emanzipation der städischen Unterschicht Göttingens 1890–1920*, Berlin, 1973

Salvadori, M. 'La socialdemocrazia tedesca e la rivoluzione russa del 1905. Il dibattito sullo sciopero di massa e sulle "differenze" fra Oriente e Occidente', in *Storia del marxismo*, Hobsbawm, ed., Turin, 1979, pp. 549–94

Karl Kautsky and the Socialist Revolution, 1880–1938, London, 1979

Saul, K. 'Der "Deutsche Kriegerbund". Zur innenpolitischen Funktion eines "nationalen" Verbandes im Kaiserlichen Deutschland', *Militärgeschichtliche Mitteilungen*, 1 (1969), pp. 95–159

'Der Kampf um die Jugend zwischen Volksschule und Kaserne. Ein Beitrag zur "Jugendpflege" im Wilhelminischen Reich, 1890–1914', *Militärgeschichtliche Mitteilungen*, 1 (1971), pp. 97–143

Staat, Industrie und Arbeiterbewegung. Zur Innen- und Sozialpolitik des Wilhelminischen Deutschlands, 1903–1914, Dusseldorf, 1974

Schade, F. *Kurt Eisner und die bayerische Sozialdemokratie*, Hanover, 1961

Scharlau, W. 'Parvus und Trockij, 1904–1914: Ein Beitrag zur Theorie der permanenten Revolution', *Jahrbücher für Geschichte Osteuropas*, 10 (1962), pp. 349–80

and Zeman, Z. *The Merchant of Revolution: The Life of Alexander Israel Helphand (Parvus), 1867–1924*, London, 1965

Schippel, M. 'Die Parteien und die Militärfrage', *NZ*, 11.2 (1893), pp. 207–10

'Die Finanzen des Reiches', *NZ*, 11.2 (1893), pp. 270–4

'War Friedrich Engels milzgläubich?' *Sozialistische Monatshefte*, 2, 1898, pp. 495–8

'Friedrich Engels und das Milizsystem', *NZ*, 17.1 (1899), pp. 580–8; 613–17

'Siehe da: das stehende Milizheer', *NZ*, 17.1 (1899), pp. 780–6

'Balkanwirren und Demokratie einst und heute', *Sozialistische Monatshefte*, 21, 1908

Schmitt, C. *The Concept of the Political*, New Brunswick, 1976

Schneider, M. 'Religion and Labour Organization: The Christian Trade Unions in the Wilhelmine Empire', *European Studies Review*, 12 (1982), pp. 345–69

Schoenbaum, D. *Zabern 1913: Consensus Politics in Imperial Germany*, London, 1982

Schorske, C. *German Social Democracy, 1905–1917: The Development of the Great Schism*, Cambridge, Mass., 1955

Schröder, H.-C. *Sozialismus und Imperialismus: Die Auseinandersetzungen der deutschen Sozialdemokratie mit dem Imperialismusproblem und der 'Weltpolitik' vor 1914*, Hanover, 1968

Gustav Noske und die Kolonialpolitik des deutschen Kaiserreichs, Bonn, 1979

Schröder, W. *Das persönliche Regiment: Reden und sonstige öffentliche Äusserungen Wilhelms II*, Munich, 1907

Handbuch der sozialdemokratischen Parteitage von 1863 bis 1909, Munich, 1910

Schulz, G. 'Die deutsche Sozialdemokratie und die Idee des internationalen Ausgleichs', *Das Zeitalter der Gesellschaft Aufsätze zur politischen Sozialgeschichte der Neuzeit*, Munich, 1969, pp. 173–98

Schulz, H. 'Zur Kritik des Militarismus', *NZ*, 17.2 (1899), pp. 613–19; 653–58

'Nochmals Italiens Wehrkraft', *NZ*, 30.2 (1912), pp. 553–6

'Der Militarismus in der Sackgasse', *NZ*, 31.2 (1913), pp. 65–74

'Nach den Schlachten', *NZ*, 31.2 (1913), pp. 513–17

Schumacher, H., and F. Tych *Julian Marchlewski-Karski: Eine Biographie*, Berlin, 1966

Schumpeter, J. *Aufsätze zur Soziologie*, Tubingen, 1953

Schwarzmantel, J. 'Nationalism and the French Working Class Movement, 1905–1914', *Socialism and Nationalism in Contemporary Europe (1848–1945)*, 2, Nottingham, 1979, pp. 65–80

Schwoerer, L. *No Standing Armies! The Antiarmy Ideology in Seventeenth-Century England*, Baltimore, 1974

Seidel, J. 'Die Haltung der deutschen Sozialdemokratie zur Herausbildung und Gründung der Französischen Arbeiterpartei (Parti Ouvrier) 1876/77 bis 1880', *Marxismus und deutsche Arbeiterbewegung*, Berlin, 1970, pp. 599–648

Sembat, M. *Faites un roi, sinon faites la paix*, Paris, 1913

Semmel, B., ed. *Marxism and the Science of War*, Oxford, 1981

Sen, G. *The Military Origins of Industrialisation and International Trade Rivalry*, New York, 1983

Senghaas, D. *Rüstung und Militarismus*, Frankfurt, 1972

Service, R. 'The Bolsheviks on Political Campaign in 1917: A Case Study of the War Question', CREES Seminar, London (mimeo), 1988

Sève, A. *Peace and War*, London, c.1898

Shaw, M. *Dialectics of War*, London, 1988

Sheehan, J. J. *German Liberalism in the Nineteenth Century*, Chicago, 1978

Shklar, J. N. *Men and Citizens: A Study of Rousseau's Social Theory*, Cambridge, 1969

Sievers, U. 'Klara Zetkins Kampf gegen den Militarismus in Deutschland in den Jahren vor der Jahrhundertwende bis 1907', *VIII. Klara-Zetkin-Kolloquium der Forschungsgemeinschaft 'Geschichte des Kampfes der Arbeiterklasse um die Befreiung der Frau'*, Leipzig, 1985, pp. 60–4

Sigel, R. 'Die Lensch-Cunow-Haenisch-Gruppe: Ihr Einfluss auf die Ideologie der deutschen Sozialdemokratie im ersten Weltkrieg', *Internationale wissenschaftliche Korrespondenz zur Geschichte der deutschen Arbeiterbewegung*, 11, no. 4 (1975), pp. 421–36

Skinner, Q. R. D. *The Foundations of Modern Political Thought*, 2 vols., Cambridge

Solle, Z. 'Die Sozialdemokratie in der Habsburger Monarchie und die tschechische Frage', *Archiv für Sozialgeschichte*, 6/7 (1966/1967), pp. 315–90

Spencer, H. *Principles of Sociology*, 1, London, 1885

Stedman Jones, G. 'Engels and the End of Classical German Philosophy', *New Left Review*, 79 (1973), pp. 17–36

Languages of Class, London, 1983

'Marx e il tentative di una teoria dello Stato moderno', *Problemi della Transizione*, 14 (1984), pp. 28–45

Steinberg, H.-J. 'Die Stellung der zweiten Internationale zu Krieg und Frieden', in *Studien zu Jakobinismus und Sozialismus*, H. Pelger, ed., Berlin, 1974, pp. 251–71

'Die Stellung der internationalen Arbeiterbewegung zu Militarismus und Imperialismus zwischen den Kongressen in Stuttgart und Basel (1907–1912)', *Internationale Tagung der Historiker der Arbeiterbewegung: 'VIII. Linzer Konferenz' 1972*, Vienna, 1974, pp. 17–30

'Workers' Libraries in Germany before 1914', *History Workshop*, 1 (1976), pp. 166–84

Sozialismus und deutsche Sozialdemokratie: Zur Ideologie der Partei vor dem 1. Weltkrieg, Bonn, 1979

Die deutsche sozialistische Arbeiterbewegung bis 1914: Eine bibliographische Einführung, Frankfurt, 1979

Steiner, H. 'Über die Massenkämpfe in Österreich 1907–1912', *Internationale Tagung der Historiker der Arbeiterbewegung: 'VIII. Linzer Konferenz' 1972*, Vienna, 1974, pp. 68–76

Stenkewtiz, K. *Gegen Bajonett und Dividende*, Berlin, 1960

Sticklov, G. 'La Conquête de l'armée', *NZ*, 32.1 (1913), pp. 335–6

Strandmann, H. P. von 'Staatsstreichpläne, Alldeutsche und Bethmann Hollweg', in *Die Erforderlichkeit des Unmöglichen: Deutschland am Vorabend des ersten Weltkrieges*, Frankfurt, H. P. von Strandmann and I. Geiss, eds., Frankfurt, 1965, pp. 7–45

Ströbel, H. 'Die Psychologie des Militarismus', *NZ*, 15.2 (1897), pp. 642–51

'Die Lehren des Transvaalkrieges', *NZ*, 19.2 (1901), pp. 390–9

'Zur Reichsfinanzreform', *NZ*, 26.2 (1908), pp. 860–6

'Die deutschen Flottenrüstungen', *NZ*, 28.2 (1910), pp. 819–27

'Die neue Wehrvorlage', *NZ*, 1913 (31.2), pp. 33–7

Stürmer, M. 'Staatsstreichgedanken im Bismarckreich', *Historische Zeitschrift*, 209 (1969), pp. 566–615

Das ruhelose Reich: Deutschland, 1866–1918, Berlin, 1983

Südekum, A. 'Reichsfinanzen und Finanzreform', *NZ*, 21.1 (1903), pp. 498–504

Suval, S. *Electoral Politics in Wilhelmine Germany*, Chapel Hill, 1985

Sweezy, P. M. *The Theory of Capitalist Development*, New York, 1970

Talmon, J. *The Origins of Totalitarian Democracy*, London, 1961

Taylor, A. J. P. *The Course of German History*, London, 1945

The Struggle for the Mastery of Europe, Oxford, 1954

The Trouble Makers: Dissent over Foreign Policy, 1792–1939, London, 1969

Taylor, C. *Hegel*, Cambridge, 1975

Tegel, S. 'Reformist Social Democrats, the Mass Strike and Prussian Suffrage, 1913', *European Studies Review*, 15 (1985), pp. 307–43

Tenfelde, K. *Sozialgeschichte der Bergarbeiterschaft an der Ruhr im 19. Jahrhundert*, Bonn, 1977

'Mining Festivals in the Nineteenth Century', *Journal of Contemporary History*, 13 (1978), pp. 377–412

Thomas, R. H. *Nietzsche in German Politics and Society, 1890–1918*, Manchester, 1983

Thompson, E. P. *The Making of the English Working Class*, New York, 1963
The Poverty of Theory, London, 1980

Thüringer, F. 'Zur Kolonisationsfrage', *NZ*, 2 (1884), pp. 26–30

Tobin, E. 'War and the Working Class: The Case of Düsseldorf, 1914–1918', *Central European History*, 18 (1985), pp. 257–98

Trotnow, H. *Karl Liebknecht, 1871–1919: A Political Biography*, Hamden, Connecticut, 1984

Trotsky, L. D. 'Nationalpsychologie oder Klassenstandpunkt', *NZ*, 27.1 (1908), pp. 76–84
The Bolsheviki and World Peace, [*Der Krieg und die Internationale*, pub. 1914], New York, 1918

Troyanovsky, A. 'Die Vergrösserung der russischen Armee', *NZ*, 32.2 (1914), pp. 9–15

Tuch, G. *Der erweiterte deutsche Militärstaat in seiner sozialen Bedeutung*, Leipzig, 1886

Tutzovitch, D. 'Die erste sozialdemokratische Balkankonferenz', *NZ*, 28.1 (1910), pp. 845–50

Ullrich, V. *Kriegsalltag: Hamburg im ersten Weltkrieg*, Cologne, 1982

Vandervelde, E. 'Die Belgier und der Kongostaat', *NZ*, 23.2 (1905), pp. 4–13
'Die Sozialdemokratie und das Kolonialproblem', *NZ*, 27.1 (1909), pp. 732–9; 828–37

Veblen, T. *Imperial Germany and the Industrial Revolution*, London, 1915

Victor, M. 'Die Stellung der deutschen Sozialdemokratie zu den Fragen der auswärtigen Politik (1869–1914)', *Archiv für Sozialwissenschaft und Sozialpolitik*, 60 (1928), pp. 147–79

Vlachos, G. *La Pensée politique de Kant*, Paris, 1962

Vliegen, W. H. 'Ein Schritt zur Volkswehr in Holland', *NZ*, 18.1 (1900), pp. 852–5
'Der Generalstreik als politisches Kampfmittel', *NZ*, 22.1 (1903), pp. 193–9

Voigt, W. *Wie ich Hauptmann von Köpenick wurde: Mein Lebensbild*, Leipzig and Berlin, 1909

Volkmann, E. O. *Der Marxismus und das deutsche Heer im Weltkriege*, Berlin, 1925

Vollmar, G. von *Sozialdemokratie und Vaterland*, Munich, 1906
Reden und Schriften zur Reformpolitik, Bonn-Bad Godesberg, 1977

Vorländer, K. *Kant und Marx*, Leipzig, 1911

Wada, H. 'Marx, Marxism and the Agrarian Question: II Marx and Revolutionary Russia', *History Workshop*, 12 (1981), pp. 129–50

Wallach, J. *Die Kriegslehre von Friedrich Engels*, Frankfurt, 1968

Walling, W. *Socialists and the War*, New York, 1915

Walter, M. 'Der russische Imperialismus und Deutschlands China-Abenteuer', *NZ*, 19.2 (1901), pp. 197–202; 228–38

Warandian, M. 'Die russische Politik in Armenien', *NZ*, 22.1 (1903), pp. 396–402

Weber, E. *Peasants into Frenchmen: The Modernisation of Rural France, 1870–1914*, London, 1979

Weber, M. *From Max Weber: Essays in Sociology*, H. H. Gerth and C. Wright Mills, ed. and intr., London, 1948

Wehler, H.-U. *Sozialdemokratie und Nationalstaat*, Würzburg, 1962
'Industrial Growth and Early German Imperialism', in *Studies in the Theory of Imperialism*, R. Owen and B. Suttcliffe, eds., London, 1972, pp. 71–92
The German Empire, 1871–1918, Leamington Spa, 1985
Weill, G. 'Elsass-Lothringen und das Reich', *NZ*, 19.2 (1901), pp. 641–8; 694–8
Weindling, P. *Health, Race and German Politics between National Unification and Nazism, 1870–1945*, Cambridge, 1989
Wendel, H. 'Die albanische Frage', *NZ*, 29.2 (1911), pp. 540–6
'Der türkisch-italienische Krieg', *NZ*, 30.1 (1911), pp. 65–72
'Der Balkankrieg', *NZ*, 31.1 (1912), pp. 41–5
'Um Albanien', *NZ*, 31.2 (1913), pp. 1–5
'Mars und Merkur', *NZ*, 31.2 (1913), pp. 153–6
'Zwischen Krieg und Krieg', *NZ*, 31.2 (1913), pp. 185–9
'Mazedonischer Salat', *NZ*, 32.1 (1914), pp. 713–16
'Die Waffen nieder!', *NZ*, 32.2 (1914), pp. 601–4
'Tu Felix Austria!', *NZ*, 32.2 (1914), pp. 649–52
'Europa im Feuergefahr!', *NZ*, 32.2 (1914), pp. 793–6
Wendtland, E. 'Zur Reform des Militärstrafgesetzbuchs', *NZ*, 14.2 (1896), pp. 745–9
Wette, W. *Kriegstheorien deutscher Sozialisten*, Stuttgart, 1971
'Liberale und sozialistische Milizvorstellungen im 19. Jahrhundert', *Die Wehrstruktur in der Bundesrepublik Deutschland: Analyse und Optionen*, Bonn, 1974, pp. 338–44
'Sozialismus und Heer Eine Auseinandersetzung mit R. Höhn', *Archiv für Sozialgeschichte*, 14 (1974), pp. 610–22
Gustav Noske: Eine politische Biographie, Dusseldorf, 1988
Whitfield, H. *War and Peace: Their Axioms and their Fallacies and the International Means of Securing Peace and Plenty in the Future*, London, 1855
Wiedner, H. 'Soldatenmisshandlungen im wilhelminischen Reich (1890–1914)', *Archiv für Sozialgeschichte*, 22 (1982), pp. 159–99
Willey, T. *Back to Kant: The Revival of Kantianism in German Social and Historical Thought, 1860–1914*, Detroit, 1978
Wistrich, R. 'The SPD and Antisemitism in the 1890's', *European Studies Review*, 7 (1977), pp. 177–97
Witt, P. *Die Finanzpolitik des deutschen Reiches von 1903 bis 1913*, Lübeck, 1970
Winter, J. M., and J. L. Robert, eds. *Paris, London Berlin: Capital Cities at War, 1914–1919* (forthcoming)
Wittwer, W. *Streit um die Schicksalfragen: Die deutsche Sozialdemokratie zu Krieg und Vaterlandsverteidigung, 1907–1914*, Berlin, 1967
'Zur Vorgeschichte des internationalen Sozialistenkongresses 1893 in Zürich', *Marxismus und deutsche Arbeiterbewegung*, Berlin, 1970, pp. 649–68
Wohlgemuth, H. *Burgkrieg, nicht Burgfriede! Der Kampf Karl Liebknechts, Rosa Luxemburgs und ihrer Anhänger um die Rettung der deutschen Nation in den Jahren 1914–1916*, Berlin, 1963
Karl Liebknecht: Eine Biographie, Berlin, 1973
Wolfe, B. D. 'French Socialism, German Theory and the Flaw in the Foundation of the Socialist Internationals', in *Essays in Russian and Soviet History*, J. S. Curtiss, ed., Leiden, 1963, pp. 177–97

Wolter, H. 'Marxismus und Opportunismus in der Auseinandersetzung um die aussenpolitische Konzeption der deutschen Sozialdemokratie, 1890/1891', *Marxismus und deutsche Arbeiterbewegung*, Berlin, 1970, pp. 485–526

Zechlin, E. *Staatsstreichpläne Bismarcks und Wilhelms II, 1890–1894*, Stuttgart, 1929

'Bethmann Hollweg, Kriegsrisiko und SPD: 1914', in *Erster Weltkrieg: Ursachen, Entstehung, Kriegsziele*, W. Schieder, ed., Cologne, 1969

Zetkin, C. *Ausgewählte Reden und Schriften*, 3 vols., Berlin, 1957–60

Zetkin, O. 'Die barfüssige Bande. Ein Beitrag zur Kenntniss der Lage der arbeitenden Klassen in Russland', *NZ*, 3 (1885), pp. 156–64; 202–9

Zettelbaum, M. 'Internationalität und Ethik', *NZ*, 20.2 (1902), pp. 101–5

ZK der SED, ed. *Geschichte der deutschen Arbeiterbewegung*, 8 vols., Berlin, 1966

Zuckmayer, C. *Der Hauptmann von Köpenick: Ein deutsches Märchen in drei Akten*, H. F. Garten, ed., London, 1960

Index

Page numbers in **bold** refer to illustrations.

DATE DUE